TEAMWORK

20 Steps to Success

Volume I of The Parker Team Series

"Successful teamwork requires doing lots of 'unspectacular little things,' such as having a clear purpose, building effective relationships, honoring your commitments, and an obsessive concern for communicating information."

- Glenn Parker

GLENN PARKER

HRD Press, Inc. • Amherst • Massachusetts

Copyright © 2009, Glenn Parker

Published by: HRD Press, Inc.
                  22 Amherst Road
                  Amherst, MA 01002
                  1-800-822-2801
                  413-253-3488
                  413-253-3490 (fax)
                  www.hrdpress.com

ISBN 978-1-59996-171-2

Editorial Services: Robert W. Carkhuff
Production Services: Jean S. Miller
Cover Design: Eileen Klockars

START WITH TEAM GOALS.

Where does a team begin...and end? It all begins with a goal. Call it a vision, a mission, a purpose, a charter, as long as the team has a clear sense of where it's going.

Goals provide the overall direction for the team, and are often sketched out by senior management. It is then up to the team to translate those goals into specific performance objectives, such as "Reduce the December reject rate by 25 percent" or "Increase the customer satisfaction rating for 2008 by 10 percent" or "Reduce the waiting time for patients in the emergency room to 10 minutes by June 30, 2008."

When it comes time to measure the team's success, we return to our goals again. If the team's goal is to produce such-and-such new product with such and such specifications by the third quarter of this year, how will you know the results? Did the team meet its timetable? Include all the required specifications? Stay within the budget? Objectives become the scoreboard, because they tell us how we're doing. So, first and foremost, a team has to begin with a good, solid goal.

> A team goal is a clear, specific statement of the desired outcome. All team goals should be S.M.A.R.T.

Team Objectives

are S.M.A.R.T.

SPECIFIC: The outcome or end result is very clear to everyone.

MEASURABLE: You can tell if you have achieved your goal because you can count it or see it.

ATTAINABLE: While achieving the outcome may be a challenge, it is possible with current team resources.

RELEVANT: The objective is in line with the direction provided by senior management, and supports the strategy of the business.

TIME-BOUND: All goals must be achieved within a particular time period such as by the end of the third quarter or by a specific date such as June 30.

☑ Quick Team Check:

✓ Are all your team goals SMART?

✓ Does your team have a set of clear objectives to reach the goal?

> "If you don't know where you're going, any road will take you there."
>
> *– Chinese Proverb*

SELECT THE RIGHT PEOPLE.

Most team problems and even most downright team failures can be eliminated if some thought is given to who should be on the team. Most of the time, we just accept the hand we've been dealt. A team leader will usually be told, "We want you to solve this problem by this date, and here are the people we want you to work with." Little or no thought is given to the people selected for the team, other than that they might have the skills and expertise needed to solve the problem. However, skills and expertise are not the only factors to be considered—in fact, studies of successful and unsuccessful teams clearly show that teams don't fail because they lack technical expertise—they usually fail because of such people problems as conflict among team members, poor leadership, lack of involvement and commitment by team members, and ineffective meetings.

Senior management sponsors and team leaders who are responsible for selection should look for people who have sufficient technical skills, but more importantly, they should also:

❖ Be willing and able to share their expertise with others.

❖ Feel comfortable with and enjoy working with others in groups.

❖ Communicate ideas, information, and opinions clearly and easily.

❖ Remain open to new ideas, different points of view, and feedback from others.

❖ Complete all work assignments on time (show that they're dependable).

❖ Support and work to implement all team decisions.

❖ Raise questions and concerns about the team's goals, methods, and problems.

❖ Pitch in and help other team members.

It Takes Time But It's Worth It

A large pharmaceutical company started a major initiative to reduce so-called "cycle time"—the time it takes to get a product produced and delivered to the customer. It took a team approach, and set-up teams that included representatives from operations, quality control, materials management, marketing, logistics, and purchasing. It was felt that the people closest to the key stages of the "cycle" would have the most knowledge about ways to reduce the time from raw materials to the final product.

Senior management sponsors wanted the teams to be composed of technical whizzes who were team players. As a result, they talked with department heads and made it clear that they were not interested in just warm bodies to fill slots on the team—they wanted **team players!** Later, when they assessed the program, team selection was identified as one of the key success factors. And while senior leaders admitted that it took some extra time to get the right people, they believed that it was well worth it, because the teams succeeded in dramatically reducing cycle time and significantly increasing that all-important cash flow.

"Our objective ought to be to have a good army, rather than a large one."

– George Washington

6

DEFINE EVERYONE'S ROLE.

Once the team's goals are set, it will be time to define the roles of everyone on the team. Careful role clarification can eliminate or at least minimize conflicts down the road. While everyone has a defined role as a member of the team, all teams have certain common functions that need to be filled. Assignments to these roles do not need to be permanent; in fact, many successful teams rotate these roles from time to time.

TEAM LEADER: Elected or appointed, the team leader ensures that the work gets done by coordinating task assignments, providing resources, managing outside contacts, as well as being a contributing team member.

TEAM FACILITATOR: The team facilitator can be the team leader or an outside expert. He or she manages the discussion and guides the decision-making process of the team by getting everyone involved, keeping things on track, resolving conflicts, summarizing ideas, and identifying what needs to be decided.

TEAM RECORDER: Sometimes called a scribe, the recorder records the team's decisions, action items, and other information in notes or formal minutes. This information is used to summarize the meeting, and serves as a permanent record and reminder to all members of team actions and decisions.

TEAM SPONSOR/CHAMPION: The sponsor is generally a manager who charters the team, provides the initial goals, authorizes resources, removes barriers, monitors team progress, and supports the team throughout its work.

TEAM COACH: As the name implies, this person is the team's mentor, advisor, and trainer who works with the leader and team members, but does not direct the team.

Role Clarification

Some organizations do not have the luxury of having each of these roles filled by a different person. The team leader often wears the facilitator's hat, but the facilitator might also have to be the scribe and the sponsor might have to serve as the team's coach.

We haven't forgotten the members of the team. Each individual has a role that is based on what they're expected to contribute to the team.

What is expected of individual team members? Mature teams that get derailed find this exercise a good way to get back on track and prevent problems down the road:

EXPECTATIONS EXERCISE

Ask each team member to answer these questions. Then set aside some time to discuss everyone's answers.

❶ What do you think you are expected to contribute to this team?

❷ What do you think other team members do not understand about your role?

❸ What type of help do you need from other team members in order to carry out your role successfully?

> "The world is not interested in how many storms you encountered, but whether you brought in the ship."
>
> *– Anonymous*

EMPOWER THE TEAM.

What is often forgotten in much of the discussion about the amount of authority a team should be given is the importance of *speed* and *empowerment*. Speed is a competitive advantage: The more a team is empowered to act, the quicker that a customer request will be filled, the sooner that new idea will get to the market, and the faster that product will come off the line. That translates into customer satisfaction, market share, cash flow, sales, and profits.

Empowerment typically refers to the authority given to a team or individual to make decisions about certain defined aspects of their work without *checking* with anyone. Some managers are not comfortable delegating important decisions, and some team members lack the confidence to take on more responsibility. Therefore, it's important that the sponsor and the team discuss the authority the team is being given as it relates to the work. Here are some questions for discussion:

❶ What kinds of decisions is the team empowered to make on its own?

❷ What kinds of decisions will be made jointly by the team and the sponsor?

❸ What kinds of decisions will be made by the sponsor or other manager, with input from the team?

❹ What kinds of decisions will be made solely by the sponsor or other manager?

Do whatever it takes.

A considerable amount of time and effort goes into selecting the right people for a project team, but the success of the team will depend on many things, including the motivation and commitment of each individual member. Empowering the team is key to keeping it motivated and challenged. One mid-size publishing company on the West Coast found a successful road to team empowerment that made managers and team members all feel comfortable. Each project team developing new products, enhancing existing products, or preparing new business strategies was required to produce a detailed project plan. The plan included specific objectives, a detailed time table, and a budget.

Each team's plan was reviewed with the team's sponsor and revised regularly so it conformed to overall corporate guidelines. However, once the plan was approved, the team was empowered to "do whatever it takes to accomplish the plan." The sponsor's role was to provide all the necessary support. For this organization, empowerment gave teams the freedom to act, as long as it was within the context of an approved plan.

> "Managers fear losing control, but employees very seldom 'push the button.' Knowing that they could is what counts. It makes them feel respected, trusted, and appreciated."
>
> — *Frank Navran*

OPEN YOUR TALENT BANK.

Teams need talent. They need skills, knowledge, and what is now referred to as "emotional intelligence" to get the job done. You can't have a high-performing team with low-talent team members.

Most teams have the talent—in fact they have more talent than they realize. Teams are like individuals—they rarely work up to their potential and rarely use all or even most of their expertise.

We like to put people in boxes and keep them there. It's easier to pigeonhole a person in one slot than to think that they might have a variety of talents. If you're an accountant, you're a "bean counter" and thus can't possibly know anything about customer service, right? And if you're from human resources, you're one of those "touchy-feely" types who have never run a real business. If you're an engineer, you have to "go by the book," so there's no way you have the flexibility to consider a new and daring product idea. And on and on...you get the idea.

The really effective teams open a talent bank that brings out the past experiences, underutilized skills, and specialized knowledge of team members.

> "You miss 100 percent of the shots you never take."
>
> — *Wayne Gretsky*

Inventory Your Team Talent

Try this exercise to inventory the talent on your team: Have team members "interview" each other and record what they say in response to these questions:

1. Talk about your *past work experiences*—the types of jobs, projects, and companies you've had some experience with.

2. Tell me about your *past team experiences*—the types of teams you've been on, team roles you've played, as well as the successful and unsuccessful team experiences you've had.

3. Describe your *operational* skills—the things you can do, equipment you can operate, and systems you can use.

4. Describe your *specialized knowledge*—the information you have and education you've completed.

5. Tell me about the interpersonal skills you possess and can use (emotional intelligence).

Share this information with the other team members and the sponsor. It can then be used to develop the team plan and make work assignments.

> "I have no special talent. I am only passionately curious."
>
> *– Albert Einstein*

APPRECIATE STYLE DIFFERENCES.

Most of us like to be around people just like ourselves. We look for people who "fit in"—people who are "our kind of folks." When we form teams, we think it will be smoother and therefore better if everyone on the team is the same kind of person. We tend not to want people who make waves, approach problems from a different angle, or think outside of the box.

Good teams have some diversity—diversity in technical skills, yes, but most importantly diversity in ways of thinking, values, priorities, and approaches—in a word, *style*. Style is the way you go about solving a problem, making a decision, communicating an idea, or resolving a conflict. **Role** is what you do, **style** is how you do it.

Diversity prevents teams from lapsing into ***groupthink.***

What is ***groupthink?*** Groupthink can be defined as a pattern of thought in which people conform to group values and ethics through self-deception. This first-person account of an actual team meeting shows what can happen when the pressure is on not to rock the boat:

> *"At one point during the meeting, the president asked: 'How's morale around here?' The first person to respond was the vice-president, who was sitting to the left of the president. He said that on a scale of 1 to 10, he would rate morale an 8. The remainder of the vice-presidents responded with a 7 or 8. When my turn came, I wanted to tell the truth and say 3 or 4, but I didn't have the courage."*

Different Team Player Styles

CONTRIBUTOR: A person who focuses on the immediate task of the team, believes that information is critical, sets high performance standards, and can be depended on to deliver work assignments on time.

COLLABORATOR: A goal-directed member who sees the overall goal of the team as paramount. They are willing to pitch in and help others in order to reach the goal and support the strategy of the organization.

COMMUNICATOR: The team member who helps with team process by facilitating, building a consensus, and creating a supportive work environment.

CHALLENGER: The person who questions the goals, methods, and actions of the team and pushes the team to take reasonable risks.

Successful teams have a mix of all four styles.[*]

> "I don't know the key to success, but the key to failure is trying to please everyone."
>
> — *Bill Cosby*

---

[*] For more on team player styles, see Glenn Parker, *Team Players and Teamwork,* 2nd ed., Wiley, 2008.

Ground Rules

Goals set down what the team wants to accomplish, and the ground rules or norms establish how the team members want to work together. Some teams call norms the "rules of the road" or the "behavioral contract" for team members.

Norms or rules evolve over time into shared understandings about what's okay and what's not okay to do. In most cases, they're not written down, but everyone understands that this is how things are done. Norms that simply develop over time are not always desirable. We have all been involved in groups where it's just understood that the meetings start late—people even joke about it.

Effective teams develop a set of positive ground rules that all members can support. This is worth emulating because members are more likely to adhere to rules that they have had a hand in creating.

Norms help a team in two ways:

1. Norms eliminate confusion by making clear to members what is expected of them and what they can expect from their teammates.

2. Norms serve as a basis for feedback when an individual's behavior becomes a problem. ("Carla, your interruptions make it difficult for other members to express their opinions or provide the information we need.")

ESTABLISH GROUND RULES.

Here are some examples of norms presented in the form of a team member agreement.

As a member of this team:

❶ I will not interrupt a teammate when he or she is expressing an idea, suggestion, or opinion.

❷ I will show up on time for all meetings.

❸ I will stay focused and help the team stay focused on the topic and time.

❹ I will be brief and to the point.

❺ I will respond promptly to all requests within 24 hours of receipt.

❻ I will be accountable, and will honor all my commitments.

❼ I will support a team decision, even if I initially did not agree with it.

"If you obey all the rules, you miss all the fun."

– Katherine Hepburn

What's Your

TCQ?

One signal that your team is effective is that you enjoy being around the people. You actually want to come to team meetings. You look forward to all associations and contacts with other team members. Do you know what that feeling is like? Is it true for your current team?

You know the feeling because you have had the opposite feeling so many times. When you are part of a poorly functioning team, your reaction to receiving the meeting notice is usually something like "ugh." You dread the team get-togethers and find yourself looking for excuses to avoid meetings and other contacts with team members.

A team with a positive climate bypasses formalities such as rigid voting rules and raising hands before speaking. Humor seems to be an integral part of successful teams. Members talk about team meetings as "enjoyable" and "fun" and even "a lot of laughs." When the environment is relaxed and informal, team members feel free to engage in good-natured kidding, social banter about events unrelated to work, and anecdotes regarding recent company events.

Why is an informal climate so important? Research tells us that people do their best thinking, most-creative idea-generation, best decision making, and most effective problem solving when they are relaxed.

> "If you tell the truth, you don't have to remember anything."
>
> – *Mark Twain*

A RELAXED CLIMATE.

What is your Team Culture Quotient (TCQ)?

Please review the list of automobiles below. Then select one car that best describes the culture of your team today. Please be prepared to explain your answer and, if possible, to provide examples.

_____ 1. *Mercedes Benz*—a well engineered (and well oiled) machine

_____ 2. *Cadillac*—a conservative, safe machine

_____ 3. *Mustang*—a lively, fun machine

_____ 4. *Range Rover*—a tough, resilient, all-road machine

_____ 5. *Porche 911*—a fast-paced, exciting machine

Project Planning Guide

All teams, but especially project teams, should have a plan for how the work will be completed. This work plan is where you commit yourself to a series of steps or activities that will ensure that the team's performance objectives get translated into **ACTION.** The work plan is where the rubber meets the road.

The work plan also spells out what each team member is supposed to do and when each step is supposed to get done. That's important, because as Duke Ellington once said, "Without a deadline, baby, I wouldn't do nothing."

A good work plan includes these elements:

❖ A clear statement of the goal.

❖ A set of specific objectives.

❖ A series of steps for reaching the objective.

❖ A deadline for each step.

❖ The proper sequencing of the steps.

❖ Names of team members responsible for each step.

❖ The costs involved in the project.

PREPARE A WORK PLAN.

Goal: _____

_____

Objective: _____

Action steps:	Responsibility assigned to:	Target date	Completion date
1.			
2.			
3.			

Objective: _____

Action steps:	Responsibility assigned to:	Target date	Completion date
1.			
2.			
3.			

> "It is important to distinguish between efficiency—doing things right—and effectiveness—doing the right things."
>
> *— Peter Drucker*

Project Reviews

Enough talking and planning—let's get some real work done! We have our goal, our objectives, a plan, and our operating guidelines. Now it's time to produce some work, develop that new product, come up with those new procedures, help our customers, or whatever else we have been chartered to do.

Team members need to take responsibility for accomplishing the objectives by delivering on the action items in the work plan. During this phase, team members should:

- ❖ Deliver on their commitments.

- ❖ Ask for help when they need it.

- ❖ Offer to help their teammates when they need it.

- ❖ Follow up with their teammates by returning calls immediately, providing requested information, offering suggestions, and responding in other ways.

- ❖ Communicate regularly with their teammates about the status of tasks and other project-related issues.

- ❖ Bring concerns and questions about the work to the team as soon as possible.

- ❖ Show up on time to team meetings, and be prepared to deal with the agenda items.

GET THE WORK DONE.

A good way to check how well a project is going is to conduct periodic progress reviews. Schedule a meeting with the sponsor, certain stakeholders, the team leader, and team members responsible for specific tasks in the project plan to go over what has been done.

Here is the sequence of tasks for a basic project review:

❶ Compare the tasks completed with the list of objectives spelled out in the project plan.

❷ If there are differences between what was done and what is in the plan, determine the cause for the discrepancy and analyze the impact.

❸ Decide on a course of action to correct the problems.

❹ Make revisions to the project plan based on the corrections.

"Small problems are difficult to see, but easy to fix. However, when you let these problems develop, they are easy to see but difficult to fix."

– Niccolo Macchiavelli

Hold   EFFECTIVE MEETINGS.

Did you ever think about the real cost of a team meeting? Multiply the average hourly wage of attendees by the number of people attending the meeting. Then multiply that by the length of the meeting in hours. For example, when a team of ten members with an average wage of $20 per hour meets for 2 hours, the total cost is $400 (10 x $20 x 2).

Estimate the cost of your last meeting. And by the way, that cost does not include the cost of production time that was lost because people had to attend the meeting. Was the value of the meeting equal to its cost?

How do you ensure that the value of your meeting exceeds the cost? The key to a successful team meeting is not what happens during the meeting, but what happens *prior* to the meeting. It's all in the planning.

The principal planning tool is the *agenda*—the "roadmap" for the meeting. Agendas should be prepared before the meeting and distributed to all team members several days prior to the meeting.

Here are a few general guidelines for an effective agenda:

❶ Begin with the most-important or most-complex issue.

❷ Include an approximation of the time that will be devoted to discussion of each item.

❸ Indicate what action the team will be expected to take on the item.

❹ Use clear descriptions of each agenda item.

❺ Specify the person responsible for the presentation or discussion of each agenda item.

Meeting Notice

Meeting: AAA Project Status Meeting

Meeting date: April 30, 2009

Starting time: 2:00 p.m. **Ending time:** 3:15 p.m.

Location: Conference Room A

Pre-Work: Read First Quarter Report; read Customer Survey Executive Summary; review March meeting minutes.

AGENDA

Topic	Action	Responsibility	Time
Status of Budget: Plan vs. Actual	Decision on overruns	J. Kaplan	30 min.
Creation of new work district	Decision	V. Ku	20 min.
Feedback from customers	Identify problems	S. Edwards	15 min.
Presentation at ACM conference	Decision on who will prepare	A. Carlin	10 min.

"The ideal meeting is one with me as the chair and two other members in bed with the flu."

– Lord Milverton

24

BUILD EXTERNAL NETWORKS.

No team is an island. You cannot go it alone. No matter how clear your goals, how detailed your plan, how relaxed your climate, and how effective your meetings, unless you have the support of others outside of the team, you will fail! What do you need from these "outsiders?"

INFORMATION. Teams need accurate and current information, such as customer and market data, production and safety records, and quality and problem-identification reports.

RESOURCES. Teams need all kinds of stuff: people who can provide advice and assistance;, people who can do statistical and laboratory research; people who can make prototypes; and people who can prepare test samples.

SUPPORT. Teams also need people who will provide easy, no-hassle, timely help without constant battles.

BUDGET. Yes, good old-fashioned money goes a long way when a team needs new equipment, must travel to a customer site, or add a team member.

Successful teams spend as much time managing the externals as they do on their internal team development. They work closely with their customers to stay in touch with their needs. They network with department heads to get the resources needed to complete the team's project tasks. They communicate with senior management to ensure that their support will continue to be there, and they involve their suppliers as partners in the process.

> "A decision is responsible when the group that makes it has to answer for it to those who are directly or indirectly affected by it."
> – Charles Frankel

Good Will

Ambassadors

The Block Project Team was responsible for designing an enhancement to one of the company's most successful products. The project manager began by inviting the senior management sponsor to attend the first meeting to explain the importance of the project and to outline her expectations for the team. Throughout the life of the project, the manager kept the sponsor fully informed of the team's progress.

During the course of the project, the leader and the members regularly communicated with the key department heads in the organization. They were also invited to major project review meetings. Three key people from manufacturing were asked to be adjunct members of the team since they had to evaluate the production issues of the new product. People from engineering were involved in the creation of a prototype.

In addition, there was a bi-weekly status meeting with the key stakeholders from purchasing, engineering, production planning, operations, and marketing. Notes from this meeting were circulated to others in the organization.

Toward the end of the development cycle, external activity increased even more as the product moved toward release. Representatives from sales and training were brought into the mix. In the end, the product was released ahead of schedule to the delight of everyone in the organization. Everyone was invited to the team's product launch party; the largest number of people ever to attend such an event.

RESOLVE CONFLICTS SUCCESSFULLY.

CONFLICT! We don't even like the word. It sounds like something negative or unpleasant.

Headlines such as "Middle-East Conflict" and "Labor-Management Conflict" have influenced our feelings in a negative way. Conflict is portrayed as war, and therefore, something to be avoided. In terms of effective teamwork, *nothing could be further from the truth.*

There will always be conflicts between team members and teams. In fact, disagreement is a natural consequence of a dynamic, active organization. Effective teams create a climate in which people feel free to express their opinions, even when those opinions are at odds with the views of other team members.

Problems generally arise because of the manner in which an opinion is expressed. Attacking another team member, belittling an opposing idea, using a hostile tone of voice, or making an aggressive hand gesture can lead to destructive conflict.

The goal is to resolve these conflicts by looking at the advantages, disadvantages, data, dollars, and alternative solutions of each opposing point of view, and then making a decision that is in the best interests of the customer, the team, and the organization.

Take a look at the five approaches on the next page. How does your team resolve conflicts?

How Do You

Resolve Conflicts?

Five Methods:

DENIAL: "Problem? There's no problem."

SMOOTHING OVER: "Yeah, but it's no big deal."

POWER: "It's my way or the highway."

COMPROMISE: "Let's split the difference."

PROBLEM-SOLVING: "Let's figure out what's best for everyone."

"A certain amount of opposition is of great help to a person. Kites rise against, not with the wind."

— John Neal

CREATE A CLIMATE OF TRUST.

As author and team expert Fran Rees said, "Trust is the cornerstone in a successful team." However, it's not easy to develop a climate of trust. Trust is not something you can order to take place, wish to occur or give as a gift. It develops over time as team members come to believe in and depend upon these teammates.

You gain trust and become trusted by others by being *trustworthy*. As you are "tested" by your teammates, you have an opportunity to prove yourself. And how do you do this?

❖ Do you promise more than you can deliver?

❖ Do you deliver on your commitments?

❖ Do you ask for more than you actually need?

❖ Do you "sugar-coat" problems or tell half-truths?

❖ Do you stand with your team when stuff hits the fan?

❖ Do you pitch in during times of stress?

❖ Do you freely share your knowledge and expertise?

❖ Do you share the limelight with your teammates?

❖ Do you complain to outsiders about the team?

> "The opinions which we hold of one another... are in no sense permanent... but are as eternally fluid as the sea itself."
> – Marcel Proust

Are You

Trustworthy?

Are you trustworthy? A study by the DDI Center for Applied Behavioral Research identified the top five Trust-Building Behaviors. Read each statement and take a moment to think about how our teammates see you. Use the scale to respond to each statement. Place the number of your answer in the space next to each statement.

❶ = Strongly disagree   ❹ = Agree
❷ = Disagree   ❺ = Strongly agree
❸ = Neither disagree nor agree

_____ 1. I communicate with my teammates openly and honestly, without distorting any information.

_____ 2. I show confidence in my teammates' abilities by treating them as skilled, competent associates.

_____ 3. I listen to and value what they say, even though I may not always agree.

_____ 4. I keep my promises and commitments to my teammates.

_____ 5. I make sure my actions are consistent with my words. In other words, I practice what I preach.

_____ **TOTAL SCORE**

Interpreting Your Results

20-25   Supreme Court Candidate

12-19   Go to Trust College for post-grad training

5-11   Go directly to jail

COMMUNICATE
COMMUNICATE

It's hard to communicate too much. In fact, most teams do not communicate enough, yet good communication is directly linked to trust. There are two parts to team communication:

❶ Interpersonal communication. How open, trusting, and effective is the communication between and among team members? Do members freely share ideas, information, disagreements, and problems with each other?

❷ Communication of information. Is there a free-flow of information to and from the team? Do members get all the information they need to do their job in a timely manner, and do they keep others informed about their work?

Want to get better at team communication? Use these questions to facilitate a discussion at a team meeting:

- ❖ What information do we need from upper management? Where and when should we get it?

- ❖ What information should we send up to management? How and how often should it be sent?

- ❖ What other groups depend on us for information? How and when should we provide this information?

- ❖ What information should we communicate to each other? How and when should we send it?

31

Quick Communications Quiz

Directions: Indicate which of the following statements best represents your views regarding communication. Answer True (T) or False (F).

_____ ❶ Technical information is more likely to be understood if you tell your teammate to listen carefully.

_____ ❷ Key concepts are more easily understood and remembered if you use repetition to reinforce them.

_____ ❸ You can determine whether or not a teammate understands what you have said by asking him or her to summarize what they think you said.

_____ ❹ Listening is more effective when you anticipate what your teammate is going to say.

_____ ❺ When you are dealing with a long-winded person, it is okay to periodically and politely interrupt him or her in order to paraphrase what you think they have said.

Answers: 1) F 2) T 3) T 4) F 5) T

"Is this the party to whom I am speaking?"

_– Lily Tomlin as Ernestine
the telephone operator_

GET EVERYONE COMMITTED.

We all want to be involved with people who care about and pledge to work with us to accomplish our goal. We want commitment from our spouse, significant other, children, employees, and of course, our teammates. *How do you get commitment?* You don't get commitment by ordering it, or praying for it—the road to commitment is through **INVOLVEMENT.** You get committed team members by involving them in as many things as possible.

❖ When members are **involved in team decisions,** they will support those decisions and work hard to implement them.

❖ When members are **involved in setting team goals,** they will do whatever it takes to see that they are accomplished.

❖ When members are **involved in defining their role** on the team, they will be motivated to do their work with skill and efficiency.

❖ When members are **involved in creating the team's operating guidelines,** they will be more inclined to live by them.

❖ When members are **involved in developing the work plan,** they will do the work to complete the plan.

Here is a true story that tells you how some people get off on the wrong foot. As you read the story, think about what's wrong and what you would have done differently.

A Commitment Story

How *Not* to Get Commitment

A senior-management steering committee for a major corporation set up an employee team to look at the process the company uses to respond to customer requests. The team consisted of employees involved in various components of the customer service function. The senior managers studied the process, and decided that the average time to handle a request could be reduced from 72 hours to 24 hours by eliminating certain steps. At the first team meeting, the steering committee presented its findings and asked the team to come up with a plan to reduce the turnaround time on requests. The team responded by saying, "What do you need us for? It looks like you've done it all yourself."

What's the problem here? Why is the team unhappy? How do you think it should have been handled by the senior managers, assuming that they wanted the team members to be committed to the goal?

"The beauty of strong lasting commitment is often best understood by a person incapable of it."

– *Murray Kempton*

MAKE DECISIONS BY CONSENSUS.

There are many ways for a team to make a decision. All of them work under certain conditions.

❖ The *team leader* can decide for the team with or without the input of team members.

❖ The decision can be made by a *majority vote* of the members.

❖ The team can reach a *unanimous* decision that everyone agrees to without reservation.

❖ The team can arrive at a *consensus* decision, where there is general agreement on a course of action that everyone can support ("We can all live with this.")

When one person makes the decision (such as the team leader or manager) it is usually fast and efficient. A majority vote is not quite as fast, but it tends to be efficient because there is little debate and the decision is made by a show of hands. However, when there is little involvement, commitment to the decision is usually lacking. When a vote is taken, there might be unhappy losers who try to derail or delay implementation of the decision.

Unanimous decisions win the support of team members, but the process can be difficult and time consuming, especially if team members stick to their guns. Consensus has its place, but it is not always appropriate, so use it carefully. The consensus technique is appropriate when:

❖ There is no clear answer to the problem.

❖ There is no single expert in the group.

❖ Commitment to the decision is essential.

❖ Sufficient time is available to discuss the issue.

Do We Have

A Consensus?

After your team has spent time thoroughly discussing the pros and cons of a particular issue, ask each team member how they feel about the proposal that's on the table by selecting one of these five options:

❶   I can say an unqualified "yes" to the decision.

❷   I find the decision acceptable.

❸   I can live with the decision, but I'm not especially enthusiastic about it.

❹   I do not fully agree with the decision, but I do not choose to block it.

❺   I do not agree with the decision, and I feel that we should explore other options.

If no one selects #5 and all the responses are either 1, 2, 3, or 4, you have a consensus and are ready to move on.

"Don't find fault, find a remedy."

– Henry Ford

REWARD TEAM RESULTS.

Reward and recognition programs are important motivators for teams, but we still need to reward individuals who make contributions to team results.

Payments under reward and recognition programs can be in the form of either cash or non-cash awards. Non-cash awards are typically merchandise or services that team members select from a catalogue of items. Some experts feel that non-cash awards are more motivational, because each time the person uses the briefcase, clock, or lawnmower, it is a reminder of the event.

Reward programs are payments to teams based on a *pre-announced formula.* The team knows in advance that if we do *this,* we will get *that.* For example, one arrangement created for a systems-design team was that if the team met the requirements by a certain date and stayed within the budget, each team member would receive a bonus of $150. The promise of a payment motivated the team to meet the requirements.

Recognition programs acknowledge outstanding performance by teams or team members *after the fact.* After the team has done some good work, the manager decides to recognize their efforts by providing each team member with some sort of acknowledgment.

Teams can create their own awards ceremonies that make achievement recognition fun, such as the "Academy Awards" event held by one corporate team. Planners made up specific awards, such as:

BEST SUPPORTING ACTOR: To the team member who was most supportive of the team process.

CAPTAIN COURAGEOUS AWARD: To the individual who consistently challenged the system—and lived to tell about it.

THE "DOMINOS DELIVERS" AWARD: To the team member who could be depended on to deliver work and anything else the team asked for on time, every time.

U.S. AIR "ON TIME EVERY TIME" AWARD: To the team member who always showed up on time and was prepared for every team meeting.

THE BMA: THE BEST MANAGER AWARD: To the manager who was most supportive of the team's work.

> "Recognition plans can add the fun, excitement, and satisfaction a company needs in these times of competitive market stress. They make everything work a bit better."
>
> *– Jerry McAdams*

ASSESS TEAM PERFORMANCE

Periodically, the team should stop to examine how well it is doing and what might be interfering with its effectiveness. (Even if it turns out you are doing well, it's good to know that.)

Teams should take an annual physical or check-up that examines the vital signs. Research tells us that being concerned about progress is a sign of a healthy team, as well as a healthy person.

This self-assessment can be formal or informal. Informal check ups can be as simple as the team leader asking, "How are we doing?" A solid group discussion based on this and other simple questions is an effective exercise. Some good questions to ask are:

- ❖ What are our strengths?

- ❖ What are we doing well?

- ❖ What things should we *stop* doing because they are reducing our effectiveness?

- ❖ What should we *begin* doing because they will increase our effectiveness?

- ❖ How can we improve our team?

A formal assessment does not have to be a long, drawn-out, complicated process. It can be based on a brief written survey, such as the Quick Team Check that follows, which all team members complete anonymously. The completed surveys can then be given to a neutral person to summarize and present to the team.

> "You can observe a lot just by watching."
>
> *– Yogi Berra*

A Quick Team Check

Directions: Please review each of the team success factors. Then indicate the extent to which you agree that the statement is true about your team by circling one number from the scale:

❶ = Strongly disagree ❹ = Agree somewhat
❷ = Disagree somewhat ❺ = Strongly agree
❸ = Neither disagree nor agree

Circle one number

We have clear goals.	1	2	3	4	5
The climate is relaxed.	1	2	3	4	5
Team member roles are clear.	1	2	3	4	5
Everyone participates.	1	2	3	4	5
We have sufficient resources.	1	2	3	4	5
Communication flows freely.	1	2	3	4	5
Management supports the team.	1	2	3	4	5
Meetings are useful.	1	2	3	4	5
Conflicts are resolved smoothly.	1	2	3	4	5
External relationships are effective.	1	2	3	4	5

TOTAL SCORE: _____

Interpreting Your Results

37–50 **High Performance** = The internal dynamics of the team are positive, and should be continued.

23–36 **Average Performance** = The team is doing well, but improvements are needed. Identify the areas where your scores were low, and develop a plan to address those issues.

10–22 **Below Average Performance** = The team needs to take a hard look at the results, and then develop a plan for change.

40

CELEBRATE TEAM ACCOMPLISHMENTS.

It is very important that the team take the time and effort to reach around and pat itself on the back. If you wait for others to recognize your work, you may wait a very long time. Too often, people are quick to criticize, but slow to praise.

So, when you've accomplished a goal, improved your processes, installed a new system, produced a new product, or put a new service into effect, celebrate the event. Congratulate yourselves, throw your own party, give out gifts to your team members, or simply bring in pizzas for everyone.

Many teams work only behind the scenes. They're not on the front lines, they don't have contact with customers, and they don't have that all important "visibility" that wins kudos from others. They keep the ship afloat by making sure the bills are paid, payroll checks get out, information systems are "up," product gets out the door, and the building is clean and secure. No one ever calls to say, "Thanks for getting my expense check out on time." It's just expected.

This is why it's so important for teams to plan their own celebrations when milestones are reached or goals are achieved. Don't wait to be recognized, plan your own celebration.

> "Don't worry when you are not recognized, but strive to be worthy of recognition."
>
> – Abraham Lincoln

41

No Cost/Low Cost

Celebrations

❖ Bring pizzas for lunch.

❖ Plan a multi-ethnic lunch or dinner where the food reflects the membership diversity of the team.

❖ Schedule an outing to a local winery, a fun restaurant, a sports bar, or a game place.

❖ Plan a picnic or barbecue with lots of sports, games, and activities.

❖ Order t-shirts, sweatshirts, or hats with the team name or logo.

❖ Hold an upscale breakfast in the company cafeteria where team accomplishments are talked about and celebrated.

❖ Give a good-quality photograph of the team to each member.

"The advantage of doing one's praising to oneself is that one can lay it on so thick and exactly in the right places."

– Samuel Butler

A Guide TO GETTING THE MOST FROM THIS BOOK.

❶ **Read the book.** Give a copy to every member and ask them to decide which step is most important for their team at this time.

❷ **Start with a team assessment.** Ask each team member to complete the Quick Team Check (page 40) and give a photo-copy of their completed survey to a neutral person who has agreed to summarize the results.

❸ **Present the assessment results.** At the next team meeting, present the summary of the Quick Team Check survey. Facili-tate a discussion of the results by identifying the strengths of the team and the areas that need improvement. Develop plans for improvement.

❹ **Facilitate an informal assessment.** At a team meeting, ask team members to complete the Quick Team Check. Then facilitate an open discussion of strengths, weaknesses, and ways to increase team effectiveness.

❺ **Take one step at a time.** Devote 15 to 30 minutes at every team meeting to a discussion of one of the 20 steps.

❻ **Use the book as a pre-work assignment.** Get people thinking about teamwork topics prior to attending a team building workshop. The workshop leader can begin the session with a discussion of these topics.

❼ **Use the book as a follow-up assignment.** The book can be given out at the end of a workshop along with an assignment to read the entire book or the parts that were not covered in the workshop.

Glenn Parker

Author

As a consultant for more than 30 years, Glenn Parker has helped create high-performance teams at hundreds of organizations including Novartis Pharmaceuticals, Merck & Company, Philips-Van Heusen, Telcordia Technologies, BOC Gases, and the U.S. Coast Guard. He is an internationally-recognized workshop facilitator, organizational consultant, and conference speaker n the area of teamwork and team meetings.

Glenn is the author of some 16 books including several best-sellers such as *Team Payers and Teamwork, Rewarding Teams: Lessons from the Trenches,* and *Cross Functional Teams: Working with Allies, Enemies and Other Strangers;* widely used instruments such as the *Parker Team Player Survey* and manuals for practitioners such as *50 Activities for Team Building, 25 Instruments for Team Building,* and *Team Workout: 50 Interactive Activities.*

His seminal work in team player styles was featured in the best-selling CRM video, *Team Building II: What Makes a Good Team Player?* Glenn is one of only 75 management thinkers recognize in the book, *The Guru Guide.* His latest book, *Meeting Excellence: 33 Tools to Lead Meetings that Get Results,* has been widely quoted and referenced in articles in the *New York Times, Forbes, CIO Magazine,* and others.

Glenn is the father of three grown children and currently lives in the Princeton, New Jersey area with his wife, Judy. In his spare time, he is an active volunteer with the American Cancer Society where he helped create **Run for Dad,** a Father's Day event designed to raise awareness about prostate cancer which regularly draws thousands of participants.

Betty Crocker

Fresh from the Freezer

Houghton Mifflin Harcourt
Boston • New York • 2016

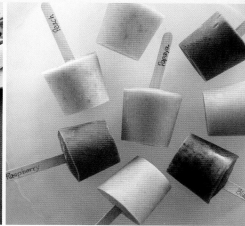

Hello Friends,

We get it—lives are busy and time is short. Just when there's no time for making a home-cooked meal, you know you're going to get that dreaded question...what's for dinner? Prepare yourselves for days like these with meals or ingredients you've prepped and thrown in the freezer, making homemade possible—even on your busiest days. This book is filled with recipes for delicious make-ahead meals and great tips that make it simple to do.

From breakfast to dinner (and not forgetting dessert) you'll find yummy recipes that will excite taste buds and satisfy like no frozen boxed pizza can do. Quick Freezer Ideas, page 216, will not only help you make meals in advance, but also to take advantage of sales at the grocery store and freeze foods so they won't go to waste. And check out the feature on Slow-Cooker-Ready Freezer Bags, page 92. We'll show how to make meals you prep and freeze—all ready to dump in your slow cooker, turn it on...and go!

Host a Freezer Meal Party, page 134, gives you everything you'll need to throw one of these popular get-togethers. Who wouldn't love to be at a party where you get to chat, nibble and sip wine...all while preparing meals that everyone can take home to put in their freezers? We'll also show you how to turn it into a party with a purpose—making meals that can help out those in need in your community!

So dive in, get started and stock your freezer. Homemade meals will be at your fingertips whenever you're hungry and short on time.

Look for these helpful icons:

[**QUICK PREP**] (15 minutes or less)

[**SLOW COOKER**]

Let's get chopping!

Betty Crocker

contents

Make-It-Easy Freezer Meals   6

• • •

1   Breakfast & Brunch   10

2   Beef & Pork   54

3   Chicken & Turkey   108

4   Fish & Seafood   162

5   Meatless   192

6   Desserts   244

• • •

Metric Conversion Guide   296

Index   297

Make-It-Easy Freezer Meals

Making meals ahead doesn't mean you need to be uber-organized or in the kitchen all day. Consider this book your one-stop cheat sheet—giving you all the tips and tricks you'll need to easily make meals in advance. Just think how good it will feel to have delicious meals on-hand—ready to pull out and cook or reheat with little effort. Never be caught by the "what's for dinner?" question again!

Top Tips for Freezing

Freshness Counts

You get out what you put in. Freezing can be tough on foods—it won't improve the quality—so start by using ingredients at their freshest: vegetables and herbs at their peak ripeness and fresh meat and poultry with good color and no odor. Set your freezer to 0°F or lower so that foods come through the freezing/thawing process successfully.

Freeze Only Once As Is

To get the best from your meals once they've been frozen and avoid potential food-safety issues, always follow this rule: Ingredients can be frozen only once in their current condition: once raw (uncooked) and once cooked.

Example: You've thawed ground beef to use for a recipe but then realize you don't have time to make the recipe. Do not refreeze the uncooked ground beef; but you can brown, cool and then freeze it now because it's cooked. When you're ready to make your recipe, you're now one step ahead! Thaw the ground beef and continue as directed.

Dress for Success

Package your meals in wraps that can take the arctic blast of your freezer—freezer plastic wrap, foil or containers specifically designed for freezer use.

Prevent freezer burn by removing as much air from packages as possible.

Freeze food in realistically sized portions. If the recipe you cooked made eight servings and you are a family of three, consider packaging the recipe for the freezer into smaller sizes, so you will use just what you need and save the remaining portion for another meal.

Help foods freeze quickly to retain better quality: allow space between them while freezing, and freeze in shallow containers instead of upright, deeper ones.

Freeze purchased frozen foods in their original packaging.

Label All Packages

You might be tempted to skip this step, thinking that you'll know what the food is when you go to use it. But given time (out of sight, out of mind) and frosty containers, there's a good chance that when you pull it from the freezer, you won't know what the mystery package is!

Always label packages with the date and name of the recipe. If using a freezer bag, write any further directions for completing the recipe (such as bake temp and time) right on the bag so you don't have to pull out the recipe again when you're ready to make the dish.

First In, First Out

Use up what you first put in the freezer before using more recently frozen foods. That way, you can keep on top of what's in there and nothing gets wasted due to being stored too long. If you have a chest-style freezer and hate to dig, keep a list near it that shows what you put in and when. Cross it off the list when you take it out.

How to Freeze and Thaw

Not all foods are great freezer candidates. Know which foods are freezer-worthy and which are not.

FREEZER-FRIENDLY FOODS

These foods get good marks for their freeze-ability. To freeze a dish that's a combination of ingredients, freeze it for the length of time given for the ingredient that can be frozen for the least amount of time. Use the chart below to know how long you can freeze at 0°F or below.

Food	Freeze Time
Bacon, cured	1 month
Bananas, raw, whole	2 to 3 months
Berries	10 to 12 months
Cakes	2 to 3 months
Cheese *Hard cheese or unopened shredded*	2 months
Cheesecakes	4 to 5 months
Fish *Uncooked* *Cooked and Breaded* *Uncooked Shellfish* *Cooked Shellfish*	3 to 6 months 2 to 3 months 3 to 4 months 1 to 2 months
Ginger, fresh, whole, unpeeled	6 months
Herbs, fresh* *basil, chives, dill, lemon balm, lemongrass, mint, oregano, sage, savory, thyme*	3 months

Food	Freeze Time
Hot Dogs	1 to 2 months
Meat *Chops, uncooked* *Ground, uncooked* *Ground, cooked* *Roasts and steaks, uncooked* *Roasts and steaks, cooked*	4 to 6 months 3 to 4 months 4 months 6 to 12 months 2 to 3 months
Pancakes and Waffles	2 to 3 months
Pasta, cooked in sauce	1 to 2 months
Pies and Pastry *Dough or Unbaked Pie Shells* *Baked Pie Shells* *Unbaked and Baked Fruit Pies* *Baked Pecan and Pumpkin Pies*	2 months 4 months 4 months 4 months
Rice, cooked	1 month
Soups, Stews, Stocks and Chili	2 to 3 months

*See Quick Freezer Ideas (page 216) for directions on freezing herbs.

UNFRIENDLY FREEZER FOODS

These ingredients don't fare well through the freeze/thaw process because the food becomes mushy, separates or is watery, so you wouldn't want to eat it. Avoid freezing these foods:

Cream or custard fillings

Dairy products — except for butter and cheese

Eggs — fresh, whole or hard-boiled

Icings made from egg whites

Fruits and veggies (high moisture) — such as celery, lettuce, watermelon

Jam

Potatoes, Idaho or russet, raw

Mayonnaise

Meringue

RULES OF THE THAW

If you cook from your freezer on a regular basis, consider moving tomorrow night's meal from the freezer to the fridge while cleaning up from tonight's meal. It's best to thaw frozen food in the refrigerator, never on the counter or it can set you up for food-safety issues. Allow 12 to 24 hours for meals to thaw completely. Bake foods 5 to 10 minutes longer than directed in the recipe to account for the cold ingredients. Some foods, like soup or chili, will thicken during storage. If this is the case, simply add a little broth, water, milk or half-and-half until the soup reaches the desired consistency.

IF IN DOUBT, THROW IT OUT

Freezing doesn't kill bacteria, and improper thawing can cause bacteria to grow. So if you are unsure how long something has been frozen or question whether something was thawed and not used soon enough, don't take any chances and discard it.

chapter one

Breakfast & Brunch

Chocolate-Cherry Bread

1 loaf (12 slices) | Prep Time: 15 Minutes | Start to Finish: 2 Hours 40 Minutes

* * *

2	cups all-purpose flour
1½	teaspoons baking powder
½	teaspoon baking soda
¼	teaspoon salt
¾	cup sugar
½	cup butter, softened
2	eggs
1	teaspoon almond extract
1	teaspoon vanilla
1	container (8 oz) sour cream
½	cup chopped dried cherries
½	cup bittersweet or dark chocolate chips

1 Heat oven to 350°F. Grease 9x5-inch loaf pan with shortening; lightly flour. In medium bowl, mix flour, baking powder, baking soda and salt; set aside.

2 In large bowl, beat sugar and butter with electric mixer on medium speed until light and fluffy, about 2 minutes. Beat in eggs until well mixed. Beat in almond extract and vanilla. Alternately add flour mixture and sour cream, beating on low speed just until blended after each addition. Stir in cherries and chocolate chips. Spread batter in pan.

3 Bake 1 hour 10 minutes to 1 hour 15 minutes or until toothpick inserted in center comes out clean. Cool 10 minutes; remove from pan to cooling rack. Cool completely, about 1 hour. Wrap tightly and store at room temperature up to 4 days, or refrigerate.

4 Freeze tightly wrapped up to 3 months. Thaw at room temperature.

1 Slice: Calories 310; Total Fat 15g (Saturated Fat 9g, Trans Fat 0g); Cholesterol 60mg; Sodium 260mg; Total Carbohydrate 39g (Dietary Fiber 1g); Protein 4g **Exchanges:** 1½ Starch, 1 Other Carbohydrate, 3 Fat **Carbohydrate Choices:** 2½

Fresh Idea Gifting alert—this bread makes a perfect present for the holidays, new neighbors, or just about any occasion. You'll probably want to double the recipe, especially because it freezes beautifully!

Monkey Bread

16 servings | Prep Time: 35 Minutes | Start to Finish: 3 Hours 25 Minutes

• • •

3½ to 4 cups all-purpose flour
⅓ cup sugar
1 teaspoon salt
1 package regular active
   or fast-acting dry yeast
   (2¼ teaspoons)
1 cup water
⅓ cup butter, softened
1 egg
¾ cup sugar
½ cup finely chopped nuts
1 teaspoon ground cinnamon
½ cup butter, melted

1 In large bowl, stir 2 cups of the flour, ⅓ cup sugar, the salt and yeast with wooden spoon until well mixed. In 1-quart saucepan, heat water and ⅓ cup butter over medium-low heat, stirring frequently, until very warm and an instant-read thermometer reads 120°F to 130°F. Add water mixture and egg to flour mixture. Beat with whisk or electric mixer on low speed 1 minute, stopping frequently to scrape batter from side and bottom of bowl with rubber spatula, until smooth. Beat on medium speed 1 minute, stopping frequently to scrape bowl. With wooden spoon, stir in enough of the remaining flour, 1 cup at a time, until dough is soft, leaves side of bowl and is easy to handle (dough may be slightly sticky).

2 Place dough on lightly floured surface. Knead about 10 minutes, sprinkling surface with more flour if dough starts to stick, until dough is smooth and springy.

3 Spray large bowl with cooking spray. Place dough in bowl, turning dough to grease all sides. Cover bowl loosely with plastic wrap; let rise in warm place 1 hour to 1 hour 30 minutes or until dough has doubled in size. Dough is ready if indentation remains when touched.

4 Spray 10-inch angel food (tube) cake pan or 12-cup fluted tube cake pan with baking spray with flour. (If angel food cake pan has removable bottom, line pan with foil before spraying to help prevent the sugar mixture from dripping in the oven during baking.) In small bowl, mix ¾ cup sugar, the nuts and cinnamon.

5 Gently push fist into dough to deflate. Shape dough into about 25 (1½-inch) balls. Dip each ball into melted butter, then into sugar mixture. Place single layer of balls in pan so they just touch. Top with another layer of balls. Cover pan loosely with plastic wrap; let rise in warm place about 40 minutes or until dough has doubled in size.

6 Move oven rack to low position so top of pan will be in center of oven. Heat oven to 375°F. Uncover bread. Bake 35 to 40 minutes or until golden brown. (If bread browns too quickly, cover loosely with foil.) Run metal spatula or knife around edge of pan to loosen bread. Place heatproof serving plate upside down on pan; holding plate and pan with pot holders, turn plate and pan over together. Let stand 1 minute so butter-sugar mixture can drizzle over bread; remove pan. Serve bread warm, pulling it apart using 2 forks or your fingers.

7 To freeze, cool completely. Wrap tightly (the whole loaf, or divide into halves or quarters). Freeze up to 3 months. Thaw at room temperature.

1 Serving: Calories 270; Total Fat 13g (Saturated Fat 6g, Trans Fat 0g); Cholesterol 40mg; Sodium 220mg; Total Carbohydrate 35g (Dietary Fiber 1g); Protein 4g **Exchanges:** 1 Starch, 1½ Other Carbohydrate, 2½ Fat **Carbohydrate Choices:** 2

Five-Grain Buttermilk-Cranberry Bread

1 loaf (12 slices) | Prep Time: 15 Minutes | Start to Finish: 1 Hour 25 Minutes

• • •

1 cup 5-grain rolled whole-grain cereal or old-fashioned oats

3 cups white whole wheat flour

⅓ cup packed brown sugar

1 teaspoon baking soda

1 teaspoon cream of tartar

¾ teaspoon salt

¼ cup cold butter, cut into small pieces

½ cup sweetened dried cranberries, cherries or raisins

1 egg

1½ cups buttermilk

1 Heat oven to 375°F. Grease large cookie sheet with shortening or cooking spray. Reserve 1 tablespoon of the cereal.

2 In large bowl, mix remaining cereal, the flour, brown sugar, baking soda, cream of tartar and salt. Cut in butter, using pastry blender or fork, until mixture looks like coarse crumbs. Stir in cranberries.

3 In small bowl, beat egg and buttermilk with whisk until well blended. Reserve 1 tablespoon buttermilk mixture. Add remaining buttermilk mixture to dry ingredients, stirring just until mixture is moistened (dough will be soft). On floured surface, knead dough 5 or 6 times.

4 On cookie sheet, shape dough into 7-inch round. Using sharp knife, cut large X shape, ¼ inch deep, into top of dough. Brush top of dough with reserved buttermilk mixture; sprinkle with reserved cereal.

5 Bake 35 to 40 minutes or until top is golden brown. Cool 30 minutes. Using serrated knife, cut into slices or wedges to serve.

6 To freeze, cool completely. Wrap tightly. Freeze up to 3 months. Thaw at room temperature.

1 Slice: Calories 230; Total Fat 6g (Saturated Fat 3g, Trans Fat 0g); Cholesterol 30mg; Sodium 320mg; Total Carbohydrate 38g (Dietary Fiber 4g); Protein 6g **Exchanges:** 2 Starch, ½ Other Carbohydrate, 1 Fat **Carbohydrate Choices:** 2½

In a Flash **This cranberry bread is a star during the holidays. With it tucked away in the freezer, you have a jump start on Thanksgiving — or any other time you crave delicious bread.**

The Ultimate Pancakes

7 servings (3 pancakes each) | **Prep Time: 30 Minutes** | **Start to Finish: 30 Minutes**

* * *

- 2 cups Original Bisquick™ mix
- 3 tablespoons sugar
- 2 teaspoons baking powder
- 1 cup milk
- 2 tablespoons vegetable oil
- 2 eggs
- 1 teaspoon vanilla, if desired

1 Brush griddle or skillet with vegetable oil, or spray with cooking spray. Heat griddle to 350°F, or heat skillet over medium heat.

2 In medium bowl, stir all ingredients with whisk or fork until blended.

3 For each pancake, pour slightly less than ¼ cup batter onto hot griddle. Cook 2 to 3 minutes or until edges are dry. Turn; cook other side until golden brown.

4 To freeze, cool completely. Place pancakes in resealable freezer plastic bag; seal bag. Freeze up to 3 months.

5 To reheat, place 3 pancakes on microwavable plate. Microwave uncovered on High 1 minute or until hot.

1 Serving: Calories 230; Total Fat 10g (Saturated Fat 3g, Trans Fat 1.5g); Cholesterol 65mg; Sodium 590mg; Total Carbohydrate 30g (Dietary Fiber 1g); Protein 5g **Exchanges:** 1½ Starch, ½ Other Carbohydrate, 2 Fat **Carbohydrate Choices:** 2

Upside-Down Banana-Walnut French Toast

10 servings | Prep Time: 15 Minutes | Start to Finish: 2 Hours 10 Minutes

• • •

1½ cups packed brown sugar

½ cup butter, melted

¼ cup light corn syrup

½ cup chopped walnuts

3 medium bananas, sliced

1 loaf (about 1 lb)
  sliced unfrosted firm
  cinnamon bread

6 eggs

1½ cups milk

1 teaspoon vanilla

Powdered sugar, if desired

1 Spray 13x9-inch (3-quart) glass baking dish with cooking spray. In large bowl, stir brown sugar, butter, corn syrup and walnuts until smooth. Gently stir in bananas. Spoon mixture into baking dish.

2 Reserve ends of bread loaf for another use; they do not soak up egg mixture very well. Arrange 2 layers of bread on banana mixture, tearing bread to fit if needed.

3 In medium bowl, beat eggs, milk and vanilla with whisk until well blended. Pour over bread.

4 Cover; refrigerate at least 1 hour but no longer than 24 hours. Or to freeze, wrap dish tightly. Freeze up to 3 months. Thaw 12 to 24 hours in refrigerator until completely thawed.

5 Heat oven to 325°F. Uncover or unwrap baking dish. Bake 45 to 55 minutes or until knife inserted in center comes out clean. Serve portions upside down, spooning sauce from bottom of dish over each serving. Sprinkle with powdered sugar.

1 Serving: Calories 490; Total Fat 19g (Saturated Fat 7g, Trans Fat 1g); Cholesterol 155mg; Sodium 380mg; Total Carbohydrate 72g (Dietary Fiber 2g); Protein 10g **Exchanges:** 3 Starch, 2 Other Carbohydrate, 3½ Fat **Carbohydrate Choices:** 5

In a Flash This brunch recipe does double duty — you can either freeze it and serve whenever you like, or prepare it the night before for a stress-free brunch.

Apricot-Stuffed French Toast

6 servings (2 slices each) | Prep Time: 20 Minutes | Start to Finish: 1 Hour 15 Minutes

* * *

1 loaf (8 oz) or ½ loaf
(1-lb size) day-old
French bread

3 oz (from 8-oz package)
cream cheese, softened

3 tablespoons
apricot preserves

¼ teaspoon grated lemon peel

3 eggs

¾ cup half-and-half or milk

2 tablespoons granulated sugar

1 teaspoon vanilla

⅛ teaspoon salt

⅛ teaspoon ground nutmeg,
if desired

2 tablespoons butter, softened

Powdered sugar, if desired

1
Spray 13x9-inch pan with cooking spray. Cut bread crosswise into 12 (1-inch) slices. Cut horizontal slit in side of each bread slice, cutting to but not through other side.

2
In medium bowl, beat cream cheese, preserves and lemon peel with electric mixer on medium speed about 1 minute or until well mixed. Spread about 2 teaspoons cream cheese mixture inside slit in each bread slice. Place stuffed bread slices in pan.

3
In medium bowl, beat eggs, half-and-half, granulated sugar, vanilla, salt and nutmeg with fork or whisk until well mixed. Pour egg mixture over bread slices; turn slices carefully to coat.

4
Cover; refrigerate at least 30 minutes but no longer than 24 hours. Or to freeze, wrap pan tightly. Freeze up to 3 months. Thaw in refrigerator overnight.

5
Heat oven to 425°F. Uncover or unwrap pan. Bake 20 to 25 minutes or until golden brown. Top with butter and sprinkle with powered sugar.

1 Serving: Calories 310; Total Fat 16g (Saturated Fat 8g, Trans Fat 1g); Cholesterol 145mg; Sodium 380mg; Total Carbohydrate 32g (Dietary Fiber 1g); Protein 9g **Exchanges:** 1 Starch, 1 Other Carbohydrate, 1 High-Fat Meat, 1½ Fat **Carbohydrate Choices:** 2

Caramel Sticky Rolls

15 rolls | Prep Time: 40 Minutes | Start to Finish: 3 Hours 20 Minutes

• • •

ROLLS

3½	to 4 cups all-purpose or bread flour
⅓	cup granulated sugar
1	teaspoon salt
2	packages regular active or fast-acting dry yeast (4½ teaspoons)
1	cup very warm milk (120°F to 130°F)
¼	cup butter, softened
1	egg

CARAMEL TOPPING

1	cup packed brown sugar
½	cup butter, softened
¼	cup light corn syrup
1	cup pecan halves, if desired

FILLING

½	cup chopped pecans or raisins, if desired
¼	cup granulated sugar or packed brown sugar
1	teaspoon ground cinnamon
2	tablespoons butter, softened

1 In large bowl, mix 2 cups of the flour, ⅓ cup granulated sugar, the salt and yeast. Add warm milk, ¼ cup butter and the egg. Beat with electric mixer on low speed 1 minute, scraping bowl frequently. Beat on medium speed 1 minute, scraping bowl frequently. Stir in enough remaining flour, ½ cup at a time, to make dough easy to handle.

2 Place dough on lightly floured surface. Knead about 5 minutes or until dough is smooth and springy. Grease large bowl with shortening. Place dough in bowl, turning dough to grease all sides. Cover bowl loosely with plastic wrap and let rise in warm place about 1 hour 30 minutes or until dough has doubled in size. Dough is ready if indentation remains when touched.

3 In 2-quart saucepan, heat brown sugar and ½ cup butter to boiling, stirring constantly; remove from heat. Stir in corn syrup. Pour into 13x9-inch pan. Sprinkle with pecan halves.

4 In small bowl, mix all filling ingredients except 2 tablespoons butter; set aside.

5 Gently push fist into dough to deflate. On lightly floured surface, flatten dough with hands or rolling pin into 15x10-inch rectangle. Spread with 2 tablespoons butter; sprinkle with filling. Roll rectangle up tightly, beginning at 15-inch side. Pinch edge of dough into roll to seal. With fingers, shape until even. With dental floss or serrated knife, cut roll into 15 (1-inch) slices.

6 Place slices slightly apart in pan. Cover loosely with plastic wrap and let rise in warm place about 30 minutes or until dough has doubled in size.

7 Heat oven to 350°F. Uncover rolls. Bake 30 to 35 minutes or until golden brown. Let stand 2 to 3 minutes. Run metal spatula or knife around edge of pan to loosen rolls. Place heatproof serving plate

In a Flash **Want to do some time shifting in the baking process? You can. After placing the slices in the pan, cover tightly with plastic wrap or foil; refrigerate 4 to 24 hours. About 2 hours before baking, remove from the refrigerator; remove the plastic wrap or foil and cover loosely with plastic wrap. Let rise in a warm place until the dough has doubled in size. If some rising has occurred in the refrigerator, rising time may be less than 2 hours. Bake as directed.**

upside down on pan; holding plate and pan with pot holders, turn plate and pan over together. Let stand 1 minute so caramel can drizzle over rolls; remove pan. Serve warm.

8 To freeze, cool completely. Wrap tightly. Freeze up to 3 months. Thaw at room temperature.

1 Roll: Calories 320; Total Fat 12g (Saturated Fat 6g, Trans Fat 0.5g); Cholesterol 45mg; Sodium 250mg; Total Carbohydrate 50g (Dietary Fiber 1g); Protein 4g **Exchanges:** 1 Starch, 2½ Other Carbohydrate, 2 Fat **Carbohydrate Choices:** 3

Cinnamon Rolls Omit caramel topping and pecan halves. Grease bottom and sides of 13x9-inch pan with shortening or cooking spray. Place dough slices slightly apart in pan. Let rise and bake as directed in Steps 6 and 7—except do not turn pan upside down. Remove rolls from pan to cooling rack. Cool 10 minutes. Drizzle rolls with vanilla glaze, if desired.

Frozen Blueberry Breakfast Bars

10 bars | Prep Time: 10 Minutes | Start to Finish: 3 Hours 35 Minutes

• • •

2½ cups oats and honey granola

¼ cup butter, melted

3 containers (5.3 oz each) Greek blueberry yogurt

¼ cup fresh blueberries

2 tablespoons oats and honey granola, coarsely crushed

1 Heat oven to 350°F. In large bowl, mix 2½ cups granola and the melted butter. Firmly press in bottom of ungreased 8-inch square pan. Bake 10 minutes. Cool 10 minutes on cooling rack. Freeze about 5 minutes or until cold.

2 Spoon yogurt over crust; gently spread to cover. Sprinkle with blueberries and crushed granola. Freeze about 3 hours or until firm.

3 Remove from freezer 10 minutes before cutting. Cut into 5 rows by 2 rows. Wrap tightly. Store in freezer up to 2 weeks.

1 Bar: Calories 180; Total Fat 7g (Saturated Fat 3g, Trans Fat 0g); Cholesterol 15mg; Sodium 100mg; Total Carbohydrate 24g (Dietary Fiber 1g); Protein 5g **Exchanges:** 1½ Starch, 1 Fat **Carbohydrate Choices:** 1½

Fresh Idea Ice cream for breakfast! Not really, but with these nutritious, frosty bars in your freezer, breakfast is sure to be fun, as well as fast.

Apple Crisp Refrigerator Oatmeal

1 serving | Prep Time: 5 Minutes | Start to Finish: 8 Hours 5 Minutes

• • •

OATMEAL

- ¼ cup old-fashioned oats
- 1 container (6 oz) apple crisp low-fat yogurt
- 1 teaspoon chia seed, if desired

TOPPINGS, IF DESIRED

- ¼ cup chopped Granny Smith apple
- ⅛ teaspoon ground cinnamon
- 2 tablespoons chopped walnuts

1 In half-pint canning jar (or other resealable container), place oats. Top with yogurt and chia seed; carefully stir to mix thoroughly. Cover; refrigerate about 8 hours.

2 Sprinkle with toppings before serving.

1 Serving: Calories 240; Total Fat 3g (Saturated Fat 1g, Trans Fat 0g); Cholesterol 10mg; Sodium 90mg; Total Carbohydrate 47g (Dietary Fiber 2g); Protein 7g **Exchanges:** 1½ Starch, 1½ Other Carbohydrate, ½ Fat **Carbohydrate Choices:** 3

Fresh Idea Check out chia seed. It is an unprocessed whole grain with a mild nutty flavor. It helps to thicken dishes, like the oatmeal here. Chia seed's thickening power is also great in smoothies.

Make-It-Your-Own Oatmeal

1 serving | Prep Time: 5 Minutes | Start to Finish: 8 Hours 5 Minutes

• • • •

OATMEAL

- 1 container (5.3 oz) 100-calorie fat-free Greek yogurt (any flavor)
- ¼ cup old-fashioned or quick-cooking oats
- 1 teaspoon chia seed

STIR-INS (SEE BELOW)

1 In container with tight-fitting cover, mix yogurt, oats and chia seed. Add desired stir-ins.

2 Cover; refrigerate at least 8 hours but no longer than 3 days.

1 Serving: Calories 190; Total Fat 2g (Saturated Fat 0g, Trans Fat 0g); Cholesterol 0mg; Sodium 45mg; Total Carbohydrate 29g (Dietary Fiber 3g); Protein 13g **Exchanges:** ½ Starch, 1 Other Carbohydrate, ½ Skim Milk, 1 Very Lean Meat **Carbohydrate Choices:** 2

Almond Oatmeal: Stir in ¼ cup toasted almonds. Calories 330 (Calories from Fat 120); Total Fat 13g (Saturated Fat 1g, Trans Fat 0g); Cholesterol 0mg; Sodium 55mg; Potassium 240mg; Total Carbohydrate 31g (Dietary Fiber 6g); Protein 21g

Banana Oatmeal: Stir in ¼ cup banana slices. Calories 220 (Calories from Fat 20); Total Fat 2g (Saturated Fat 0g, Trans Fat 0g); Cholesterol 0mg; Sodium 55mg; Potassium 210mg; Total Carbohydrate 34g (Dietary Fiber 4g); Protein 16g

Blackberry Oatmeal: Stir in ¼ cup blackberries. Calories 200 (Calories from Fat 20); Total Fat 2.5g (Saturated Fat 0g, Trans Fat 0g); Cholesterol 0mg; Sodium 55mg; Potassium 135mg; Total Carbohydrate 29g (Dietary Fiber 5g); Protein 16g

Blueberry Oatmeal: Stir in ¼ cup blueberries. Calories 210 (Calories from Fat 20); Total Fat 2g (Saturated Fat 0g, Trans Fat 0g); Cholesterol 0mg; Sodium 55mg; Potassium 105mg; Total Carbohydrate 31g (Dietary Fiber 4g); Protein 16g

Honey Oatmeal: Stir in 1 tablespoon honey or 2 tablespoons comb honey.* Calories 260 (Calories from Fat 20); Total Fat 2g (Saturated Fat 0g, Trans Fat 0g); Cholesterol 0mg; Sodium 60mg; Potassium 90mg; Total Carbohydrate 43g (Dietary Fiber 3g); Protein 16g

Pomegranate Oatmeal: Stir in ¼ cup pomegranate seeds. Calories 230 (Calories from Fat 25); Total Fat 2.5g (Saturated Fat 0g, Trans Fat 0g); Cholesterol 0mg; Sodium 60mg; Potassium 180mg; Total Carbohydrate 34g (Dietary Fiber 4g); Protein 16g

*Those with bee sting allergies should consult their physician before consuming comb honey.

Cheesy Sausage and Egg Bake

12 servings | Prep Time: 25 Minutes | Start to Finish: 1 Hour

- - -

1   **lb bulk pork sausage**

1½   **cups sliced fresh mushrooms (4 oz)**

8   **medium green onions, sliced (½ cup)**

2   **medium tomatoes, chopped (1½ cups)**

2   **cups shredded mozzarella cheese (8 oz)**

1¼   **cups Original Bisquick mix**

1½   **teaspoons salt**

1½   **teaspoons chopped fresh or ½ teaspoon dried oregano leaves**

½   **teaspoon pepper**

1   **cup milk**

12   **eggs**

1 Spray 13x9-inch (3-quart) glass baking dish with cooking spray. In 10-inch skillet, cook sausage over medium-high heat 5 to 7 minutes, stirring occasionally, until no longer pink; drain.

2 In baking dish, layer sausage, mushrooms, onions, tomatoes and cheese.

3 In large bowl, stir remaining ingredients with whisk or fork until blended. Pour over ingredients in baking dish.

4 Cover baking dish tightly. Refrigerate up to 24 hours.

5 Heat oven to 350°F. Uncover baking dish. Bake 30 to 35 minutes or until golden brown and set.

1 Serving: Calories 260; Total Fat 16g (Saturated Fat 6g, Trans Fat 0.5g); Cholesterol 240mg; Sodium 750mg; Total Carbohydrate 12g (Dietary Fiber 0g); Protein 17g **Exchanges:** 1 Starch, 2 High-Fat Meat **Carbohydrate Choices:** 1

Spinach-Pesto Egg Bakes

4 servings | Prep Time: 15 Minutes | Start to Finish: 50 Minutes

• • •

¼ cup pine nuts

1 cup frozen cut leaf spinach (from 14-oz bag), thawed, squeezed to drain

1 cup cottage cheese

1 cup shredded Monterey Jack cheese (4 oz)

¼ cup basil pesto

4 eggs, beaten

¼ cup milk

1 medium tomato, chopped

¼ cup shredded Parmesan cheese (1 oz)

Fresh basil leaves, if desired

1 Heat oven to 375°F. Lightly spray 4 (10-oz) custard cups or ramekins with cooking spray. Place cups on cookie sheet with sides.

2 Sprinkle pine nuts in ungreased 8-inch skillet. Cook over medium heat 5 to 7 minutes, stirring frequently until nuts begin to brown, then stirring constantly until light brown.

3 In medium bowl, mix spinach, cottage cheese, Monterey Jack cheese, pesto and toasted nuts. Stir in eggs and milk until well blended. Divide spinach mixture evenly among cups.

4 Bake 25 to 30 minutes or until set. Cool 2 minutes before serving.

5 To freeze, cool completely. Wrap tightly. Freeze up to 3 months. Thaw in refrigerator overnight. Unwrap; microwave 1 egg bake on High about 1 minute or until hot. Top with tomato and Parmesan cheese; garnish with basil.

1 Serving: Calories 420; Total Fat 32g (Saturated Fat 12g, Trans Fat 0g); Cholesterol 255mg; Sodium 680mg; Total Carbohydrate 8g (Dietary Fiber 2g); Protein 25g **Exchanges:** ½ Starch, ½ Vegetable, 2½ Medium-Fat Meat, ½ High-Fat Meat, 3 Fat **Carbohydrate Choices:** ½

Fresh Idea **Change up the cheese here—try Cheddar, Swiss or mozzarella. They are all sold shredded, making these individual breakfast bakes even easier.**

Impossibly Easy
Mini Breakfast Sausage Pies

6 servings (2 mini pies each) | Prep Time: 15 Minutes | Start to Finish: 1 Hour 5 Minutes

• • •

SAUSAGE MIXTURE

- ¾ lb bulk pork breakfast sausage
- 1 medium onion, chopped (½ cup)
- 1 can (4 oz) mushrooms pieces and stems, drained
- ½ teaspoon salt
- 3 tablespoons chopped fresh sage leaves
- 1 cup shredded Cheddar cheese (4 oz)

BAKING MIXTURE

- ½ cup Original Bisquick mix
- ½ cup milk
- 2 eggs

1 Heat oven to 375°F. Spray 12 regular-size muffin cups with cooking spray.

2 In 10-inch skillet, cook sausage and onion over medium-high heat 5 to 7 minutes, stirring occasionally, until sausage is no longer pink; drain. Cool 5 minutes; stir in mushrooms, salt, sage and cheese.

3 In medium bowl, stir baking mixture ingredients with whisk or fork until blended. Spoon slightly less than 1 tablespoon baking mixture into each muffin cup. Top each with about ¼ cup sausage mixture and 1 tablespoon baking mixture.

4 Bake about 30 minutes or until toothpick inserted in center comes out clean and tops are golden brown. Cool 5 minutes. With thin knife, loosen sides of pies from pan; remove from pan and place top sides up on cooling rack. Cool 10 minutes longer before serving.

5 To freeze, cool completely. Wrap tightly. Freeze up to 3 months. Thaw in refrigerator overnight. Unwrap; microwave 1 pie on High about 1 minute or until hot.

1 Serving: Calories 250; Total Fat 17g (Saturated Fat 8g, Trans Fat 0.5g); Cholesterol 105mg; Sodium 920mg; Total Carbohydrate 10g (Dietary Fiber 1g); Protein 14g **Exchanges:** ½ Starch, ½ Vegetable, 1½ High-Fat Meat, 1 Fat **Carbohydrate Choices:** ½

Ham and Swiss Breakfast Hand Pies

4 pies | Prep Time: 25 Minutes | Start to Finish: 45 Minutes

• • •

1 box refrigerated pie crusts, softened as directed on box

3 oz thinly sliced deli ham, chopped (¾ cup)

4 teaspoons chopped fresh chives or green onion tops

1 cup shredded Swiss cheese (4 oz)

1 Heat oven to 425°F. Unroll 1 pie crust on lightly floured surface. Fold sides of crust toward center; lightly press crust together to form rectangle, brushing off excess flour. Fold bottom and top of crust toward center to create smaller rectangle; lightly press together. Rotate rectangle a quarter turn so center seam is facing vertically in front of you. Roll crust to 16x6-inch rectangle, straightening ends as you roll. Cut crosswise to form 4 (6x4-inch) pieces. Repeat with second pie crust for a total of 8 pieces.

2 Place 4 of the pie crust pieces on ungreased cookie sheet. Top evenly with ham, leaving ½-inch border around edges; sprinkle with chives and cheese. Moisten crust edges with water. Place 4 remaining pie crust pieces over filling; press edges with fork to seal. Using fork, gently poke 3 holes in top of each pie.

3 Bake 20 minutes or until golden brown. Serve warm.

4 To freeze, cool completely. Wrap tightly. Freeze up to 3 months. Thaw in refrigerator overnight. Unwrap pies; place on cookie sheet. Reheat at 325°F 10 to 15 minutes or until hot.

1 Pie: Calories 560; Total Fat 33g (Saturated Fat 15g, Trans Fat 0g); Cholesterol 50mg; Sodium 830mg; Total Carbohydrate 50g (Dietary Fiber 0g); Protein 15g **Exchanges:** 1½ Starch, 2 Other Carbohydrate, ½ Lean Meat, 1 High-Fat Meat, 4½ Fat **Carbohydrate Choices:** 3

Fresh Idea Enjoy your veggies—add 1 to 2 tablespoons chopped fresh spinach to each pie, or change up the meat from ham to cooked Italian sausage or bacon. You can customize each pie so everyone gets exactly what they want.

Sausage-Wrapped Stuffed Chiles

10 servings (2 chiles each) | Prep Time: 45 Minutes | Start to Finish: 3 Hours 15 Minutes

• • • •

20 canned whole jalapeño chiles

3 cups shredded sharp Cheddar cheese (12 oz)

2 cups shredded Monterey Jack cheese (8 oz)

1 lb bulk mild pork sausage

2 cups Original Bisquick mix

2 eggs

1 package (6 oz) seasoned coating mix for pork

1 Serving: Calories 490; Total Fat 30g (Saturated Fat 15g, Trans Fat 1g); Cholesterol 110mg; Sodium 1900mg; Total Carbohydrate 31g (Dietary Fiber 1g); Protein 23g **Exchanges:** ½ Starch, 1½ Other Carbohydrate, 3 High-Fat Meat, 1 Fat **Carbohydrate Choices:** 2

1 Cut lengthwise slit in one side of each chile, leaving other side intact; remove seeds. Stuff each chile with about 2 teaspoons Cheddar cheese. Pinch edges to close; set aside.

2 In large bowl, mix remaining Cheddar cheese, the Monterey Jack cheese, sausage and Bisquick mix. Shape about 2 rounded tablespoonfuls of sausage mixture into ¼-inch-thick patties. Place 1 stuffed chile in center of each patty; wrap mixture around chile. Dip into eggs; roll in coating mix.

3 Wrap tightly. Refrigerate up to 2 hours or freeze up to 1 month.

4 Heat oven to 375°F. Spray 15x10x1-inch pan with cooking spray. Unwrap stuffed chiles; place in pan. Bake 30 to 35 minutes or until golden.

Egg and Sausage Breakfast Ring

8 servings | Prep Time: 25 Minutes | Start to Finish: 55 Minutes

½   lb bulk pork sausage

⅓   cup sliced green onions

⅓   cup chopped red bell pepper

5   eggs

¼   teaspoon salt

⅛   teaspoon pepper

3   oz (from 8-oz package) cream cheese, cut into cubes

2   cans refrigerated crescent dough sheet

½   cup shredded Cheddar–Monterey Jack cheese blend (2 oz)

1   egg, beaten

1   teaspoon sesame seed

1   Heat oven to 375°F. Spray large cookie sheet with cooking spray. In 10-inch nonstick skillet, cook sausage and onions over medium-high heat 5 to 8 minutes, stirring occasionally, until sausage is no longer pink; drain. Stir in bell pepper; cook until tender. Remove from skillet to bowl; set aside.

2   In small bowl, beat 5 eggs, the salt and pepper. Add egg mixture to skillet. Cook over medium heat, stirring occasionally from outside edge to center, until eggs are set but still moist. Stir in sausage mixture and cream cheese.

3   Unroll both cans of dough. Place dough on cookie sheet, long sides overlapping, to form 14x13-inch rectangle; firmly press edges to seal. Spoon egg mixture down center to within ½ inch of edges. Sprinkle with shredded cheese. Starting at longest side, roll up; press edges to seal. Shape into a round; pinch ends to seal. Cut 6 (2-inch) slits around top of dough.

4   Brush dough with beaten egg; sprinkle with sesame seed. Bake 25 to 30 minutes or until deep golden brown.

5   To freeze, cool completely. Wrap tightly. Freeze up to 3 months. Thaw in refrigerator overnight. Unwrap ring; place on cookie sheet. Reheat at 325°F 15 to 20 minutes or until hot.

1 Serving: Calories 480; Total Fat 31g (Saturated Fat 13g, Trans Fat 0g); Cholesterol 250mg; Sodium 1000mg; Total Carbohydrate 34g (Dietary Fiber 0g); Protein 17g **Exchanges:** 2 Starch, ½ Other Carbohydrate, 1½ High-Fat Meat, 3 Fat **Carbohydrate Choices:** 2

Smoked Sausage Spinach Pie

8 servings | Prep Time: 30 Minutes | Start to Finish: 1 Hour 55 Minutes

• • •

1 refrigerated pie crust, softened as directed on box

1 teaspoon vegetable oil

1 medium onion, chopped (½ cup)

1 cup chopped smoked sausage (6 oz)

1 box (9 oz) frozen chopped spinach, thawed, squeezed to drain

1 container (8 oz) sour cream

2 cups finely shredded Cheddar cheese (8 oz)

4 eggs

½ cup whipping cream

1 Heat oven to 375°F. Unroll pie crust; stretch and press firmly against bottom and side of 9-inch or 9½-inch glass deep-dish pie plate to fit; flute edge as desired. Prick bottom and side of crust several times with fork. Bake 10 minutes; cool.

2 Meanwhile, in 10-inch nonstick skillet, heat oil over medium heat. Cook onion in oil 2 to 3 minutes, stirring occasionally, until tender. Reduce heat to low. Stir in sausage and spinach; toss to combine. Transfer mixture to large bowl. Stir in sour cream and cheese.

3 In small bowl, beat eggs and whipping cream with fork or whisk until well blended. Gently fold egg mixture into spinach mixture until blended. Pour filling into crust-lined pie plate.

4 Place pie plate on cookie sheet in freezer. When completely frozen, wrap tightly. Freeze up to 2 months.

5 Heat oven to 375°F. Unwrap quiche. Cover crust edge with pie crust shield ring or 2- to 3-inch strip of foil. Bake 1 hour to 1 hour 10 minutes or until knife inserted in center comes out clean and crust is deep golden brown. Let stand 15 minutes before cutting.

1 Serving: Calories 440; Total Fat 34g (Saturated Fat 17g, Trans Fat 0.5g); Cholesterol 170mg; Sodium 480mg; Total Carbohydrate 15g (Dietary Fiber 1g); Protein 16g **Exchanges:** 1 Starch, ½ Medium-Fat Meat, 1½ High-Fat Meat, 4 Fat **Carbohydrate Choices:** 1

Bacon and Hash Brown Egg Bake

12 servings | Prep Time: 30 Minutes | Start to Finish: 9 Hours 40 Minutes

• • •

1   lb bacon, cut into
    1-inch pieces

1   medium red bell pepper,
    chopped (¾ cup)

1   medium onion, chopped
    (½ cup)

1   package (8 oz) sliced fresh
    mushrooms (about 3 cups)

2   tablespoons Dijon mustard

½   teaspoon salt

½   teaspoon pepper

¾   cup milk

12 eggs

1   bag (32 oz) frozen hash
    brown potatoes, thawed

2   cups shredded Cheddar
    cheese (8 oz)

1 In 12-inch skillet, cook bacon until crisp. Using slotted spoon, remove bacon from skillet to small bowl. Cover; refrigerate. Drain skillet, reserving 1 tablespoon drippings in skillet. Cook bell pepper, onion and mushrooms in drippings over medium heat 4 minutes, stirring occasionally. Stir in mustard, salt and pepper; set aside.

2 In large bowl, beat milk and eggs with whisk; set aside.

3 Spray 13x9-inch (3-quart) glass baking dish with cooking spray. Spread half of the potatoes in baking dish. Spread onion mixture over top. Sprinkle with 1 cup of the cheese. Spread remaining potatoes over top. Pour egg mixture on top. Cover; refrigerate 8 hours or overnight.

4 Heat oven to 325°F. Uncover baking dish. Bake 50 to 60 minutes or until thermometer inserted in center reads 160°F. Sprinkle with remaining 1 cup cheese and the bacon. Bake 3 to 5 minutes longer or until knife inserted in center comes out clean, top is puffed and cheese is melted. Let stand 5 minutes before serving. Cut into squares.

1 Serving: Calories 410; Total Fat 24g (Saturated Fat 12g, Trans Fat 0g); Cholesterol 265mg; Sodium 740mg; Total Carbohydrate 25g (Dietary Fiber 3g); Protein 22g **Exchanges:** 1½ Starch, 2½ High-Fat Meat, 1 Fat **Carbohydrate Choices:** 1½

Fresh Idea Enjoy every bit of this gooey, cheesy casserole by using the cheese you like best. Monterey Jack, Colby or Swiss can all be substituted for the Cheddar cheese.

Chicken Fajita Strata

12 servings | Prep Time: 30 Minutes | Start to Finish: 4 Hours

• • •

2	tablespoons vegetable oil
2	teaspoons chili powder
1	teaspoon ground cumin
½	teaspoon salt
1	clove garlic, finely chopped
1	lb boneless skinless chicken breasts, cut into thin strips
1	medium onion, cut into thin wedges
1	medium green bell pepper, cut into strips
1	to 2 medium jalapeño chiles, seeded, finely chopped
12	soft yellow corn tortillas (6 inch), cut into 1-inch strips
½	cup shredded reduced-fat Cheddar cheese (2 oz)
1	cup reduced-fat sour cream
3	tablespoons chopped fresh cilantro
¼	teaspoon ground red pepper (cayenne)
1	carton (8 oz) fat-free egg product (1 cup)
¾	cup fat-free (skim) milk
1	can (10¾ oz) condensed 98% fat-free cream of chicken soup with 45% less sodium
1	medium tomato, chopped (¾ cup)

1   In small bowl, stir together oil, chili powder, cumin, salt and garlic. Place chicken in resealable food-storage plastic bag; add chili powder mixture. Seal bag; shake to coat chicken with spices. Refrigerate 30 minutes.

2   Heat 10-inch nonstick skillet over medium-high heat. Add chicken; cook 5 to 7 minutes, stirring frequently, until no longer pink in center. Remove chicken from skillet to plate. In same skillet, cook onion, bell pepper and chiles over medium-high heat 5 to 7 minutes, stirring frequently, until crisp-tender.

3   Spray 13x9-inch (3-quart) glass baking dish with cooking spray. Arrange half of the tortilla strips in baking dish. Top with chicken, half of the vegetable mixture and ¼ cup of the cheese. Repeat layers with remaining tortilla strips, vegetables and ¼ cup cheese.

4   In medium bowl, mix sour cream, 2 tablespoons of the cilantro, the red pepper, egg product, milk and soup with whisk. Pour over chicken mixture. Cover baking dish tightly. Refrigerate 2 hours or overnight.

5   Heat oven to 350°F. Uncover baking dish. Bake 48 to 52 minutes or until egg mixture is set. Sprinkle with tomato and remaining 1 tablespoon cilantro. Let stand 5 minutes before serving. Cut into squares.

1 Serving: Calories 210; Total Fat 9g (Saturated Fat 3g, Trans Fat 0g); Cholesterol 35mg; Sodium 380mg; Total Carbohydrate 17g (Dietary Fiber 2g); Protein 15g **Exchanges:** 1 Starch, ½ Vegetable, 1½ Very Lean Meat, 1½ Fat **Carbohydrate Choices:** 1

SIMPLE MAKE-AHEAD YOGURT TREATS

Make-Ahead Frozen Yogurt Mini Bites

Here's a simple idea for breakfasts on the go!
Place a mini paper cupcake liner in each mini muffin cup.
Layer 1 tablespoon crushed ready-to-eat cereal such as
granola in the bottom of each cup. Add enough yogurt
to each cup to fill about ¾ full. Press 2 or 3 berries (or
a tablespoon of chopped fruit) lightly into the yogurt
in each cup. Cover muffin pan lightly with plastic wrap;
freeze until yogurt is firm, about 1 hour. Store the bites in
a resealable freezer plastic bag to grab whenever you're
breakfasting on the run.

Mix-and-Match Frozen Yogurt Bark

Create your own customizable Yogurt Bark — it's a super-
simple snack that comes together in no time. It's a fun
little idea to do with your kids or when you're feeling
inventive. You can keep bite-size pieces handy in the
freezer for a quick melt-in-your mouth treat anytime.

Line cookie sheet with parchment paper. Spread 4 single-
serve containers Greek yogurt (any flavor) on parchment,
about ¼ to ½ inch thick. Sprinkle with 1 cup of any
desired combination of mix-ins (see below). Press lightly
into yogurt. Freeze uncovered 1 to 2 hours or until yogurt
is firm. Break into bite-size pieces. Eat immediately or
store tightly covered in freezer.

MIX-INS

Ready-to-eat cereal

Granola

Flaked coconut

Canned fruit, drained and chopped, such as maraschino
    cherries, mandarin orange segments, pineapple tidbits

Dehydrated fruit slices, such as strawberries or mango

Mini chocolate bunny crackers

Chocolate chips

Cacao nibs

Chopped nuts

Fruity Green Smoothies

2 servings (1 cup each) | Prep Time: 10 Minutes | Start to Finish: 10 Minutes

• • •

½ cup unsweetened unflavored almond milk

3 cups packed fresh baby spinach leaves

2 tablespoons fresh lemon juice

1 tablespoon honey

1 medium ripe banana, chopped, frozen

½ cup small ice cubes

1 In blender, place all ingredients. Cover; blend on high speed until smooth, scraping down side 2 or 3 times.

2 Serve immediately, or pour into ice cube tray. Freeze about 3 hours or until firm. Remove cubes from tray and place in resealable freezer plastic bag; seal bag. Freeze up to 3 months.

3 To serve, place cubes in beverage glass to soften. Or, place cubes in blender to reblend.

1 Serving: Calories 130; Total Fat 1g (Saturated Fat 0g, Trans Fat 0g); Cholesterol 0mg; Sodium 75mg; Total Carbohydrate 27g (Dietary Fiber 3g); Protein 2g **Exchanges:** ½ Fruit, 1 Other Carbohydrate, 1 Vegetable **Carbohydrate Choices:** 2

Fresh Idea Not a fan of almond milk? Try coconut, hemp, rice or soy milk — the choice is yours.

Skinny Tropical Smoothies

2 servings (1½ cups each) | Prep Time: 10 Minutes | Start to Finish: 10 Minutes

● ● ●

½   medium ripe papaya, peeled, seeded and chopped (¾ cup)*

½   cup frozen whole strawberries (from 10-oz bag)

½   cup fat-free (skim) milk

½   cup fat-free plain yogurt

2   tablespoons honey

3   large ice cubes

Sliced papaya or fresh strawberries, if desired

Fresh mint sprigs, if desired

1 In blender, place chopped papaya, frozen strawberries, milk, yogurt, honey and ice cubes. Cover; blend on high speed until smooth.

2 Serve immediately, garnished with sliced papaya and mint, or pour into ice cube tray. Freeze about 3 hours or until firm. Remove cubes from tray and place in resealable freezer plastic bag; seal bag. Freeze up to 3 months.

3 To serve, place cubes in beverage glass to soften. Or, place cubes in blender to reblend.

*Choose papayas that are partially yellow and feel slightly soft when pressed. The skin should be smooth and free from bruises. A firm papaya can be ripened at room temperature for 3 to 5 days until mostly yellow to yellowish orange in color. Store a ripe papaya in a paper or plastic bag in the refrigerator up to 1 week.

1 Serving: Calories 140; Total Fat 0.5g (Saturated Fat 0g, Trans Fat 0g); Cholesterol 0mg; Sodium 80mg; Total Carbohydrate 29g (Dietary Fiber 2g); Protein 6g **Exchanges:** ½ Fruit, 1 Other Carbohydrate, ½ Skim Milk **Carbohydrate Choices:** 2

Fresh Idea **This smoothie recipe is versatile. You can substitute ripe mango for the papaya and other frozen fruit in place of the strawberries —your pick.**

chapter two

Beef & Pork

Make-Ahead Ground Beef

8 cups | Prep Time: 20 Minutes | Start to Finish: 1 Hour 25 Minutes

- - -

3 **lb lean (at least 80%) ground beef**

1 **cup chopped onions (2 medium)**

2 **cloves garlic, finely chopped**

1½ **teaspoons salt**

¼ **teaspoon pepper**

1 In 5-quart Dutch oven or stockpot, cook beef, onions and garlic over medium-high heat about 10 minutes, stirring occasionally, until beef is thoroughly cooked; drain.

2 Reduce heat to medium. Stir in salt and pepper. Cook 5 minutes, stirring frequently. Cool 5 minutes.

3 Line 15x10x1-inch pan with foil. Spoon beef onto foil, breaking apart as necessary. Freeze about 1 hour, stirring once, until firm.

4 Place 2 cups beef mixture in each of 4 freezer containers or resealable freezer plastic bags; seal tightly. Freeze up to 3 months.

½ **Cup:** Calories 150; Total Fat 10g (Saturated Fat 3.5g, Trans Fat 0g); Cholesterol 50mg; Sodium 260mg; Total Carbohydrate 1g (Dietary Fiber 0g); Protein 15g **Exchanges:** 2 Medium-Fat Meat **Carbohydrate Choices:** 0

Fresh Idea For Italian-flavored ground beef mix, add ½ teaspoon Italian seasoning to each 2-cup portion of the mix and stir to combine.

Sassy Sloppy Joes

6 sandwiches | Prep Time: 20 Minutes | Start to Finish: 20 Minutes

• • •

Freezer Short-cut

2 cups frozen Make-Ahead Ground Beef (recipe on page 57), thawed

⅓ cup chopped celery

⅓ cup chopped green bell pepper

⅓ cup ketchup

¼ cup water

1 tablespoon Worcestershire sauce

½ teaspoon salt

⅛ teaspoon red pepper sauce

6 burger buns, split, toasted if desired

1 In 10-inch skillet or 2-quart saucepan, stir together all ingredients except buns. Heat to boiling; reduce heat to low.

2 Cover; cook 10 to 15 minutes, stirring occasionally, until vegetables are tender. Spoon mixture into buns.

1 Sandwich: Calories 240; Total Fat 8g (Saturated Fat 3g, Trans Fat 0.5g); Cholesterol 35mg; Sodium 740mg; Total Carbohydrate 27g (Dietary Fiber 1g); Protein 14g **Exchanges:** 2 Starch, 1 Medium-Fat Meat, ½ Fat **Carbohydrate Choices:** 2

Fresh Idea Great by themselves, sloppy Joes are also fun topped with cheese, pickle slices or sliced olives.

Make-Ahead Mexican Ground Beef

8 cups | Prep Time: 15 Minutes | Start to Finish: 1 Hour 20 Minutes

• • •

3   **lb lean (at least 80%) ground beef**

2   **packages (1 oz each) taco seasoning mix**

1   In 5-quart Dutch oven or stockpot, cook beef over medium-high heat about 10 minutes, stirring occasionally, until thoroughly cooked; drain.

2   Reduce heat to medium. Stir in taco seasoning mix. Cook 3 to 5 minutes, stirring frequently, until flavors are blended. Cool 5 minutes.

3   Line 15x10x1-inch pan with foil. Spoon beef onto foil, breaking apart as necessary. Freeze about 1 hour, stirring once, until firm.

4   Place 2 cups beef mixture in each of 4 freezer containers or resealable freezer plastic bags; seal tightly. Freeze up to 3 months.

½ **Cup:** Calories 160; Total Fat 10g (Saturated Fat 3.5g, Trans Fat 0.5g); Cholesterol 55mg; Sodium 290mg; Total Carbohydrate 2g (Dietary Fiber 0g); Protein 15g **Exchanges:** 2 Medium-Fat Meat **Carbohydrate Choices:** 0

In a Flash You'll want to keep this tasty beef mix stashed in the freezer — it's an easy start for delicious dishes.

Tamale Pies

6 pies | Prep Time: 30 Minutes | Start to Finish: 2 Hours 30 Minutes

· · ·

6   disposable foil pot pie pans
    (5x1⅝ inch)

Freezer Short-cut

2   cups frozen Make-Ahead
    Mexican Ground Beef (recipe
    on page 61)

1   can (15 oz) black beans or
    pinto beans, drained, rinsed

1   can (14.5 oz) diced tomatoes,
    undrained

1   can (8 oz) tomato sauce

1   can (4.5 oz) chopped
    green chiles

1   cup yellow cornmeal

4   cups water

1   teaspoon salt

¾   cup shredded Cheddar
    cheese (3 oz)

1   Spray foil pans with cooking spray. In large bowl, mix frozen beef, beans, tomatoes, tomato sauce and chiles. Divide mixture evenly among foil pans, about ¾ cup each; set aside.

2   In small bowl, mix cornmeal and ¾ cup of the water. In 2-quart saucepan, heat remaining 3¼ cups water and the salt to boiling. Add cornmeal mixture, stirring constantly. Cook over medium heat 4 to 5 minutes, stirring constantly, until mixture thickens and boils; reduce heat.

3   Cover; simmer about 10 minutes, stirring occasionally, until very thick. Remove from heat; stir until smooth. Spoon and spread about ⅔ cup cornmeal mixture over each pie, sealing to edges.

4   Cover loosely with foil; freeze about 1 hour. Place in freezer container or resealable freezer plastic bags; seal tightly. Freeze up to 3 months. Do not thaw before baking.

5   Heat oven to 350°F. Place desired number of frozen pot pies on cookie sheet. Bake uncovered 40 to 50 minutes or until filling is hot and bubbly. Sprinkle each with 2 tablespoons cheese; bake 3 to 5 minutes longer or until cheese is melted.

1 Pie: Calories 330; Total Fat 12g (Saturated Fat 5g, Trans Fat 0.5g); Cholesterol 50mg; Sodium 1300mg; Total Carbohydrate 37g (Dietary Fiber 4g); Protein 19g **Exchanges:** 2 Starch, 1 Vegetable, ½ Very Lean Meat, 1 Medium-Fat Meat, 1 Fat **Carbohydrate Choices:** 2½

Tamale Casserole
Instead of making individual pies, spray 8-inch square (2-quart) glass baking dish with cooking spray. Spoon meat mixture into baking dish; spoon and spread cornmeal mixture over top. Cover tightly. Freeze up to 3 months. Heat oven to 350°F. Uncover baking dish. Bake 1 hour 30 minutes to 1 hour 40 minutes or until center is hot and edges are bubbly. Sprinkle with cheese; bake 3 to 5 minutes longer or until cheese is melted. Cool 5 minutes before serving.

Beef Enchiladas

8 enchiladas | Prep Time: 20 Minutes | Start to Finish: 1 Hour

. . .

1 lb ground beef

1 can (10 oz) mild
   enchilada sauce

1 jar (16 oz) black bean or
   corn salsa

2 cups shredded Mexican
   cheese blend (8 oz)

8 flour tortillas (8 inch)

1 Spray 2 (8-inch) disposable foil cake pans with cooking spray. In 10-inch nonstick skillet, cook beef over medium-high heat 5 to 7 minutes, stirring occasionally, until thoroughly cooked; drain.

2 In medium bowl, stir together beef, ¼ cup of the enchilada sauce, the salsa and 1 cup of the cheese. Spoon beef mixture down center of each tortilla; roll up. Place 4 enchiladas, seam sides down, in each pan. Top with remaining enchilada sauce and remaining 1 cup cheese.

3 Spray 2 sheets of foil with cooking spray; cover pans with foil, sprayed side down. Seal tightly. Freeze up to 3 months. Thaw in refrigerator overnight.

4 Heat oven to 350°F. Place foil-covered pan(s) on cookie sheet. Bake 35 to 40 minutes or until hot and bubbly and thermometer inserted in center reads 165°F.

1 Enchilada: Calories 400; Total Fat 20g (Saturated Fat 9g, Trans Fat 1.5g); Cholesterol 60mg; Sodium 720mg; Total Carbohydrate 32g (Dietary Fiber 2g); Protein 21g
Exchanges: 2 Other Carbohydrate, ½ Vegetable, 2 Medium-Fat Meat, 1 High-Fat Meat, ½ Fat
Carbohydrate Choices: 2

Fresh Idea Shredded lettuce, guacamole, salsa and sour cream all make great garnishes for these easy enchiladas.

Serving a Crowd? Prepare as directed, except place all the enchiladas in a freezer-safe 13x9 dish. Use only one sheet of sprayed foil to cover dish. Thaw overnight before baking.

In a Flash Forgot to take the enchiladas out of the freezer? No problem! You can bake them without thawing. Bake 1 hour, then remove the foil and bake 10 to 15 minutes longer.

Slow-Cooker Taco Ground Beef

16 tacos | Prep Time: 15 Minutes | Start to Finish: 8 Hours 15 Minutes

• • •

3 lb lean (80%) ground beef

1 bag (12 oz) frozen chopped onions, thawed

1 can (16 oz) refried beans

1 jar (16 oz) chunky-style salsa

1 package (1 oz) taco seasoning mix

16 taco shells, heated as directed on package

4 cups shredded Mexican cheese blend (16 oz)

1 Spray 5-quart slow cooker with cooking spray. Break up beef; place on bottom and press up side of slow cooker.

2 In large bowl, mix onions, beans, salsa and taco seasoning mix; place in center of slow cooker over beef. Cover; cook on Low heat setting 8 hours.

3 Drain beef mixture through strainer set over large bowl. Press with spatula or wooden spoon to break up any large chunks of beef.

4 Divide into 4 portions. Place in freezer containers or resealable freezer plastic bags; seal tightly. Freeze up to 3 months. Thaw in refrigerator overnight.

5 Transfer 1 portion beef mixture to microwavable bowl; microwave on High 2 to 3 minutes or until steaming. Spoon into 4 of the taco shells; top with 1 cup of the cheese and desired taco toppings.

1 Taco: Calories 350; Total Fat 20g (Saturated Fat 10g, Trans Fat 0.5g); Cholesterol 80mg; Sodium 590mg; Total Carbohydrate 17g (Dietary Fiber 2g); Protein 24g **Exchanges:** 1 Starch, 2 Lean Meat, 1 High-Fat Meat, 1 Fat **Carbohydrate Choices:** 1

Fresh Idea You can use 3 cups chopped fresh onions instead of the frozen onions.

In a Flash Welcome to the world's easiest taco night! In less than 5 minutes you can have your favorite tacos on the table. Take that take out!

Easy Taco Melts

8 sandwiches | Prep Time: 15 Minutes | Start to Finish: 30 Minutes

· · ·

Freezer Short-cut

2 cups frozen Make-Ahead Mexican Ground Beef (recipe on page 61), thawed

⅔ cup water

1½ cups chunky-style salsa

1 can (16.3 oz) large refrigerated flaky biscuits

1 cup shredded Monterey Jack cheese or Mexican cheese blend (4 oz)

1 cup sour cream, if desired

1 Heat oven to 375°F. Spray cookie sheet with cooking spray.

2 In 2-quart saucepan, stir together beef, water and ½ cup of the salsa. Cook over medium heat, stirring occasionally, until thickened and hot.

3 Separate dough into 8 biscuits; press each into 6-inch round. Spoon beef mixture onto center of each round; sprinkle evenly with cheese. Fold dough in half over filling; press to seal. Place on cookie sheet.

4 Bake 9 to 14 minutes or until golden brown. Serve with sour cream and remaining 1 cup salsa.

1 Sandwich: Calories 370; Total Fat 20g (Saturated Fat 8g, Trans Fat 3.5g); Cholesterol 50mg; Sodium 1470mg; Total Carbohydrate 32g (Dietary Fiber 0g); Protein 17g
Exchanges: 2 Starch, 1½ Medium-Fat Meat, 2 Fat **Carbohydrate Choices:** 2

Meat Loaf

6 servings | Prep Time: 20 Minutes | Start to Finish: 1 Hour 40 Minutes

• • •

1½ lb lean (at least 80%) ground beef

1 cup milk

1 tablespoon Worcestershire sauce

1 teaspoon chopped fresh or ¼ teaspoon dried sage leaves

½ teaspoon salt

½ teaspoon ground mustard

¼ teaspoon pepper

1 clove garlic, finely chopped, or ⅛ teaspoon garlic powder

1 egg

3 slices bread, torn into small pieces*

1 small onion, finely chopped (⅓ cup)

½ cup ketchup, chili sauce or barbecue sauce

1 In large bowl, mix all ingredients except ketchup. Spread mixture in ungreased 8x4- or 9x5-inch loaf pan. Spread ketchup over top.

2 Cover pan tightly. Freeze up to 3 months. Thaw in refrigerator overnight.

3 Heat oven to 350°F. Uncover pan. Insert ovenproof meat thermometer so tip is in center of meat loaf.

4 Bake 1 hour to 1 hour 15 minutes or until beef is no longer pink in center and thermometer reads 160°F; drain. Let stand 5 minutes; remove from pan.

*½ cup dry bread crumbs or ¾ cup quick-cooking oats can be substituted for the bread.

1 Serving: Calories 290; Total Fat 15g (Saturated Fat 6g, Trans Fat 1g); Cholesterol 110mg; Sodium 610mg; Total Carbohydrate 15g (Dietary Fiber 0g); Protein 24g **Exchanges:** ½ Starch, ½ Other Carbohydrate, 3 Medium-Fat Meat **Carbohydrate Choices:** 1

Horseradish Meat Loaf
Omit sage. Stir 1 to 2 tablespoons cream-style prepared horseradish into beef mixture.

Mexican Meat Loaf
Omit sage. Substitute ⅔ cup milk and ⅓ cup salsa for the 1 cup milk. Stir ½ cup shredded Colby–Monterey Jack cheese blend (2 ounces) and 1 can (4.5 ounces) chopped green chiles, drained, into beef mixture. Substitute ⅔ cup salsa for the ketchup.

Mini Meat Loaves
Spray 12 regular-size muffin cups with cooking spray. Divide beef mixture evenly among cups (cups will be very full). Brush tops with about ¼ cup ketchup. Place muffin pan on cookie sheet. Bake about 30 minutes or until loaves are no longer pink in center and thermometer reads 160°F when inserted in center of loaves in middle of muffin pan (outer loaves will be done sooner). Immediately remove from cups.

Meatball Provolone Burgers with Garlic-Parmesan Aioli

4 burgers | Prep Time: 30 Minutes | Start to Finish: 30 Minutes

• • •

BURGERS

- 1 lb lean (at least 80%) ground beef
- ½ cup Italian panko crispy bread crumbs
- ¼ cup milk
- ½ teaspoon salt
- ¼ teaspoon pepper
- 1 small onion, finely chopped (⅓ cup)
- 1 small green bell pepper, cut into rings
- 1 small red bell pepper, cut into rings
- 2 tablespoons olive oil
- 4 slices provolone cheese
- 4 ciabatta buns, split

GARLIC-PARMESAN AIOLI

- ⅓ cup mayonnaise
- 2 tablespoons grated Parmesan cheese
- 2 cloves garlic, finely chopped

1 Burger: Calories 670; Total Fat 38g (Saturated Fat 12g, Trans Fat 1.5g); Cholesterol 100mg; Sodium 1310mg; Total Carbohydrate 46g (Dietary Fiber 2g); Protein 36g **Exchanges:** 2 Starch, ½ Other Carbohydrate, 1 Vegetable, 3 Medium-Fat Meat, 1 High-Fat Meat, 3 Fat **Carbohydrate Choices:** 3

1. In medium bowl, mix beef, bread crumbs, milk, salt, pepper and onion. Shape mixture into 4 patties, about ½ inch thick.

2. Wrap patties tightly. Freeze up to 3 months. Thaw in refrigerator overnight.

3. Heat gas or charcoal grill. In small bowl, mix all aioli ingredients. Cover; refrigerate until serving time.

4. Place patties on grill over medium heat. Cover grill; cook 10 to 12 minutes, turning once, until meat thermometer inserted in center of patties reads 160°F. Toss green and red bell pepper rings with oil to coat. Add bell pepper rings to side of grill for last 8 to 10 minutes of cooking, turning once, until crisp-tender. During last 2 minutes of cooking, top each patty with cheese. Cook until cheese is melted.

5. Spread about 1 tablespoon aioli on cut sides of buns. Place burgers on bun bottoms; top with peppers. Cover with bun tops.

Cheeseburger Lasagna

8 servings | Prep Time: 35 Minutes | Start to Finish: 2 Hours 5 Minutes

• • •

1½	**lb lean (at least 80%) ground beef**
3	**tablespoons dried minced onion**
1	**can (15 oz) tomato sauce**
1½	**cups water**
½	**cup ketchup**
1	**tablespoon yellow mustard**
1	**egg**
1	**container (15 oz) ricotta cheese**
2	**cups shredded American-Cheddar cheese blend (8 oz)**
12	**uncooked lasagna noodles**
1	**cup shredded Cheddar cheese (4 oz)**
1	**cup shredded lettuce**
1	**medium tomato, sliced**
½	**cup dill pickle slices**

1 Heat oven to 350°F. Spray 13x9-inch (3-quart) glass baking dish with cooking spray.

2 In 12-inch nonstick skillet, cook beef and dried minced onion over medium-high heat 5 to 7 minutes, stirring occasionally, until beef is thoroughly cooked; drain. Stir in tomato sauce, water, ketchup and mustard; heat to boiling; reduce heat. Simmer 5 minutes, stirring occasionally.

3 Meanwhile, in medium bowl, beat egg with fork or whisk. Stir in ricotta cheese and 2 cups of the cheese blend.

4 Spread 1 cup beef mixture in bottom of baking dish. Top with 4 uncooked noodles. Spread half of the ricotta mixture over noodles; top with 1½ cups beef mixture. Repeat layers once with 4 noodles, remaining ricotta mixture and 1½ cups beef mixture. Top with remaining 4 noodles, beef mixture and 1 cup Cheddar cheese.

5 Cover; bake 45 minutes. Uncover; bake 25 to 35 minutes longer or until bubbly. Cover; let stand 5 to 10 minutes before cutting. Top with lettuce, tomato and pickles. Serve with additional ketchup, if desired.

6 To freeze, cool completely. Cover baking dish tightly. Freeze up to 3 months. Thaw 12 to 24 hours in refrigerator until completely thawed. Reheat lasagna covered at 350°F for 30 minutes or until thoroughly heated.

1 Serving: Calories 590; Total Fat 32g (Saturated Fat 17g, Trans Fat 1g); Cholesterol 135mg; Sodium 1050mg; Total Carbohydrate 38g (Dietary Fiber 3g); Protein 39g **Exchanges:** 2 Starch, ½ Other Carbohydrate, 5 Medium-Fat Meat, 1 Fat **Carbohydrate Choices:** 2½

In a Flash Want a do-ahead rather than a freezer recipe? Make the recipe as directed through Step 4. Cover; refrigerate 8 hours or overnight, then bake as directed.

Pan-Fried Spicy Korean Beef

4 servings | Prep Time: 20 Minutes | Start to Finish: 20 Minutes

• • •

MARINADE

2 tablespoons vegetable oil

1 tablespoon finely chopped gingerroot

3 cloves garlic, finely chopped

2 tablespoons rice vinegar or cider vinegar

2 tablespoons gochujang (Korean chile pepper paste)*

2 tablespoons packed brown sugar

¼ cup regular or reduced-sodium soy sauce

MEAT

1 lb boneless beef top sirloin steak, about 1 inch thick, cut into 1-inch pieces

Hot cooked rice or noodles, if desired

Fresh Idea Instead of serving this bold, tasty beef over rice or noodles, use it for a fun twist on tacos or wraps.

1 In 1-gallon resealable freezer plastic bag, place all marinade ingredients; seal bag and knead to combine. Add beef; seal bag. Turn bag to coat beef with marinade.

2 Lay bag flat in freezer. Freeze up to 3 months. Thaw 12 to 24 hours in refrigerator until completely thawed.

3 Heat 12-inch skillet over medium-high heat. Add beef and marinade. Cook 6 to 8 minutes, stirring frequently, until beef is of desired doneness and marinade is slightly reduced. (Reduce heat to medium if necessary to prevent sticking.) Serve over rice or noodles.

*Gochujang is a spicy Korean condiment. This dark red paste is usually made from red chiles, glutinous rice, fermented soybeans, salt and sometimes a sweetener such as sugar. It is traditionally used in various dishes such as bibimbap, tteokbokki, or also in salads, stews, soups and marinated dishes.

1 Serving: Calories 240; Total Fat 11g (Saturated Fat 2.5g, Trans Fat 0g); Cholesterol 65mg; Sodium 1160mg; Total Carbohydrate 10g (Dietary Fiber 0g); Protein 26g **Exchanges:** ½ Other Carbohydrate, 4 Very Lean Meat, 2 Fat **Carbohydrate Choices:** ½

Spicy Korean Beef Kabobs
Prepare recipe as directed through Step 2. Heat gas or charcoal grill. Remove beef from marinade; reserve marinade. Onto 4 (12-inch) metal skewers, alternately thread beef pieces, 1 red bell pepper, cut into 8 (2-inch) pieces, ½ red onion, cut into 8 wedges, and 8 medium whole mushrooms, leaving about ¼-inch space between each piece. Place skewers on grill over medium heat. Cover grill; cook 15 to 18 minutes, turning occasionally, until beef is of desired doneness and vegetables are tender. During last 2 to 3 minutes of cooking, brush kabobs generously with reserved marinade and turn frequently. Discard any remaining marinade. Serve beef and vegetables over rice or noodles.

Slow-Cooker Beef Stew Adobo

5 servings | Prep Time: 30 Minutes | Start to Finish: 8 Hours 15 Minutes

• • •

STEW

1½	lb beef stew meat
4	small red potatoes, cut into quarters
2	medium sweet potatoes, peeled, cut into 2-inch pieces
1	cup chopped onion (1 large)
½	cup packed brown sugar
½	teaspoon salt
¼	teaspoon crushed red pepper flakes
8	cloves garlic, finely chopped
3	dried bay leaves
1	cup beef broth
½	cup cider vinegar

TO THICKEN

¼	cup beef broth
2	tablespoons all-purpose flour

1 In 1-gallon resealable freezer plastic bag, mix all stew ingredients; seal bag.

2 Lay bag flat in freezer. Freeze up to 3 months. Thaw 12 to 24 hours in refrigerator until completely thawed.

3 Spray 4- to 5-quart slow cooker with cooking spray. Pour stew mixture into slow cooker. Cover; cook on Low heat setting 7 hours 30 minutes to 8 hours 30 minutes (or High heat setting 3 hours 30 minutes to 4 hours 30 minutes) or until beef and vegetables are tender.

4 Increase heat setting to High. In small bowl, mix ¼ cup broth and the flour; stir into beef mixture. Cover; cook 15 minutes longer or until slightly thickened. Remove and discard bay leaves.

1 Serving: Calories 280; Total Fat 8g (Saturated Fat 2g, Trans Fat 0g); Cholesterol 155mg; Sodium 1880mg; Total Carbohydrate 17g (Dietary Fiber 0g); Protein 36g **Exchanges:** 1 Other Carbohydrate, 5 Very Lean Meat, 1 Fat **Carbohydrate Choices:** 1

In a Flash With this clever freezer-to fridge-to slow cooker bag, no morning is too busy to get dinner ready. Coming home to this zesty home-cooked stew is wonderful at the end of a long day.

Beer-Roasted Rib-Eye

12 servings | Prep Time: 30 Minutes | Start to Finish: 10 Hours 20 Minutes

• • •

MARINADE

- 1 bottle or can (12 oz) beer
- 2 white onions, chopped (2 cups)
- 2 cloves garlic, finely chopped
- ¼ cup packed brown sugar
- 2 teaspoons salt
- 1 teaspoon dried thyme leaves
- ½ teaspoon freshly ground pepper
- 2 dried bay leaves

BEEF ROAST

- 1 boneless beef rib-eye roast (3 lb), trimmed of fat

SAUCE

- 3 tablespoons butter, softened
- 3 tablespoons all-purpose flour
- 1 bottle or can (12 oz) beer
- 1½ cups beef broth
- 2 tablespoons packed brown sugar
- 2 tablespoons Dijon mustard
- 2 teaspoons balsamic vinegar

1 In large glass bowl, mix all marinade ingredients. Place beef in 2-gallon resealable freezer plastic bag. Add marinade; seal bag. Turn bag to coat beef with marinade.

2 Lay bag flat in refrigerator. Refrigerate up to 8 hours, turning beef occasionally. Or freeze up to 3 months. Thaw 12 to 24 hours in refrigerator until completely thawed.

3 Heat oven to 375°F. Remove beef and onions from marinade; place in 13x9-inch (3-quart) glass baking dish. Discard marinade and bay leaves.

4 Roast uncovered 1 hour to 1 hour 30 minutes or until meat thermometer inserted in center reads 125°F to 135°F. Cover; let stand 20 minutes.

5 Meanwhile, in 3-quart saucepan, melt butter over medium-high heat. Beat in flour with whisk until smooth. Gradually stir in beer and broth. Stir in remaining sauce ingredients. Heat to boiling; reduce heat. Simmer, stirring occasionally, until sauce thickens slightly. Cut beef across grain into thin slices. Serve with sauce.

1 Serving: Calories 240; Total Fat 11g (Saturated Fat 5g, Trans Fat 0g); Cholesterol 90mg; Sodium 330mg; Total Carbohydrate 6g (Dietary Fiber 0g); Protein 28g **Exchanges:** ½ Other Carbohydrate, 4 Lean Meat **Carbohydrate Choices:** ½

Slow-Cooker Asian Beef Short Ribs

8 servings | Prep Time: 45 Minutes | Start to Finish: 9 Hours 45 Minutes

• • •

TO FREEZE/COOK

1	tablespoon vegetable oil
3	lb beef short ribs, cut into individual ribs
⅓	cup soy sauce
⅓	cup packed brown sugar
⅓	cup hoisin sauce
⅓	cup chili garlic sauce
2	tablespoons Dijon mustard
1	bulb garlic, cloves peeled
1	piece (2 inches) gingerroot, peeled, chopped

TO SERVE

½	cup rice vinegar
¼	cup granulated sugar
2	teaspoons soy sauce
1	English (hothouse) cucumber, halved crosswise, then shaved with vegetable peeler
3	carrots, peeled, then shaved with vegetable peeler
4	cups hot cooked white rice
½	cup chopped fresh cilantro, if desired
½	cup thinly sliced green onions, if desired
8	lime wedges, if desired

Fresh Idea **For other toppings, consider chopped cashews, ponzu sauce, Sriracha sauce or additional chili garlic sauce.**

1 In 12-inch skillet, heat oil over medium-high heat. Cook ribs in two batches on all sides, 2 to 3 minutes per side, or until browned. Remove from skillet to plate; cool 15 minutes. Discard fat and pan drippings. Place ribs in 1-gallon freezer plastic bag. Pour ⅓ cup soy sauce over ribs; seal bag, pressing out as much air as possible. Lay flat in freezer. Freeze up to 3 months.

2 In medium bowl, mix brown sugar, hoisin sauce, chili garlic sauce and mustard with whisk. Stir in garlic and gingerroot. Pour into freezer container; seal tightly. Freeze up to 3 months.

3 Thaw ribs and sauce 12 to 24 hours in refrigerator until completely thawed. Spray 3½- to 4-quart slow cooker with cooking spray. Pour ribs and sauce into slow cooker. Cover; cook on Low heat setting 8 to 9 hours.

4 Meanwhile, in medium bowl, mix vinegar, granulated sugar and 2 teaspoons soy sauce with whisk. Stir in cucumber and carrots. Cover; refrigerate at least 1 hour but no longer than 3 hours. Drain before serving.

5 Remove ribs from slow cooker to cutting board. Remove ½ cup liquid from slow cooker to medium bowl. Remove bones and any pieces of fat from ribs and discard. Shred meat with 2 forks; place in bowl with reserved cooking liquid. Discard remaining cooking liquid.

6 To serve, divide rice among 8 bowls. Top with shredded beef and marinated vegetables. Garnish with cilantro, onions and lime.

1 Serving: Calories 350; Total Fat 12g (Saturated Fat 4g, Trans Fat 0g); Cholesterol 45mg; Sodium 1360mg; Total Carbohydrate 46g (Dietary Fiber 2g); Protein 16g **Exchanges:** 1½ Starch, 1½ Other Carbohydrate, 1½ Lean Meat, 1½ Fat **Carbohydrate Choices:** 3

Make-Ahead Oven-Roasted Pulled Pork

10 cups | Prep Time: 15 Minutes | Start to Finish: 8 Hours 15 Minutes

• • •

1	boneless pork shoulder roast (5 lb)
20	cloves garlic, peeled
¼	cup olive oil
2	teaspoons salt
2	teaspoons pepper

1 Heat oven to 325°F. In 13x9-inch (3-quart) glass baking dish, place pork, fat side up. With sharp knife, cut (20) 1-inch slits in fat; tuck 1 clove garlic into each slit. Rub pork with oil. Sprinkle with salt and pepper; rub into meat.

2 Cover tightly with foil. Roast 5 hours 30 minutes to 6 hours 30 minutes or until meat thermometer inserted in center of roast reads 190°F. Let stand until cool enough to handle, about 30 minutes.

3 Shred meat with 2 forks; discard garlic. Toss shredded pork in some of the pan juices (if any) to coat. Divide pork into 2-cup portions; place in freezer containers or resealable freezer plastic bags. Seal tightly; refrigerate until completely cooled, at least 1 hour. Freeze up to 3 months.

½ Cup: Calories 160; Total Fat 12g (Saturated Fat 4g, Trans Fat 0g); Cholesterol 45mg; Sodium 270mg; Total Carbohydrate 0g (Dietary Fiber 0g); Protein 12g **Exchanges:** 1½ Medium-Fat Meat, 1 Fat **Carbohydrate Choices:** 0

Fresh Idea **We recommended freezing the pork in 2-cup portions, but make it work for you by packaging in whatever size portion you need to feed your family for one meal.**

Creamy Pulled Pork Pasta

8 servings (1¼ cups each) | Prep Time: 35 Minutes | Start to Finish: 35 Minutes

• • •

1   box (16 oz) campanelle pasta

2   tablespoons butter

1   cup thinly sliced onion

½   teaspoon salt

1   package (8 oz) sliced fresh mushrooms (about 3 cups)

¼   cup sherry vinegar

Freezer Short-cut

2   cups frozen Make-Ahead Oven-Roasted Pulled Pork (recipe on page 83), thawed

1   cup whipping cream

1   package (5 oz) baby arugula

½   cup shredded Parmesan cheese (2 oz)

Additional sherry vinegar, if desired

1   In Dutch oven or stockpot, cook pasta as directed on package. Drain, reserving ¼ cup cooking water. Return pasta to Dutch oven; cover to keep warm.

2   Meanwhile, in 10-inch skillet, melt butter over medium heat. Add onion and salt; cook 5 to 7 minutes, stirring frequently, until edges of onion slices are browned and soft. Add mushrooms; cook 5 to 7 minutes or until mushrooms release juices, liquid evaporates and mushrooms are browned.

3   Add vinegar; scrape up any bits from bottom of pan and stir until liquid is almost completely evaporated. Stir in pork. Add whipping cream and reserved pasta cooking water; cook 2 to 3 minutes or until thickened. Add pork mixture to pasta in Dutch oven; toss to coat. Fold in arugula; stir until arugula wilts.

4   Divide pasta mixture among 8 bowls. Top each with cheese. Drizzle with a few drops vinegar.

1 Serving: Calories 500; Total Fat 24g (Saturated Fat 12g, Trans Fat 0.5g); Cholesterol 75mg; Sodium 660mg; Total Carbohydrate 52g (Dietary Fiber 3g); Protein 19g **Exchanges:** 2½ Starch, 1 Other Carbohydrate, 1½ Lean Meat, 3½ Fat **Carbohydrate Choices:** 3½

Fresh Idea Can't find campanelle? Try bow-tie (farfalle), penne or ziti. A sturdy pasta shape will work well with this hearty onion-mushroom sauce.

Jamaican Loaded Baked Sweet Potatoes

4 servings | Prep Time: 20 Minutes | Start to Finish: 1 Hour 45 Minutes

• • •

SWEET POTATOES

- 4 large dark-orange sweet potatoes
- ¼ teaspoon salt

MANGO-RUM SALSA

- 1 tablespoon packed brown sugar
- 1 tablespoon lime juice
- 1½ teaspoons dark rum*
- 2 teaspoons finely chopped gingerroot
- 1 tablespoon finely chopped seeded jalapeño chile
- ¼ cup diced red onion
- 1 cup diced mango
- 2 tablespoons chopped fresh cilantro

TOPPINGS

Freezer Short-cut

- 2 cups frozen Make-Ahead Oven-Roasted Pulled Pork (recipe on page 83), thawed

- 1 tablespoon olive oil
- 1½ teaspoons jerk seasoning
- ¼ cup crumbled queso fresco cheese (1 oz)

1 Heat oven to 400°F. Line cookie sheet with sides with foil; spray foil with cooking spray. Poke sweet potatoes all over with fork; place on cookie sheet.

2 Bake 1 hour to 1 hour 15 minutes or until completely tender when pierced all the way through with knife. Cool about 10 minutes or until easy to handle.

3 Meanwhile, in small bowl, stir together brown sugar, lime juice, rum and gingerroot until sugar is dissolved. Add chile, onion and mango; toss to coat. Stir in cilantro. Cover; refrigerate until serving time.

4 In medium microwavable bowl, mix pork, oil and jerk seasoning. Microwave uncovered on High 1 to 2 minutes or until steaming hot.

5 Cut open sweet potatoes; using fork, mash potato flesh. Sprinkle salt over potato flesh; stir in with fork. Top each potato with ½ cup pork mixture, ¼ cup mango-rum salsa and 1 tablespoon cheese.

*The rum can be omitted, if desired.

1 Serving: Calories 400; Total Fat 18g (Saturated Fat 6g, Trans Fat 0g); Cholesterol 50mg; Sodium 670mg; Total Carbohydrate 43g (Dietary Fiber 5g); Protein 16g **Exchanges:** 2 Starch, 1 Other Carbohydrate, 1½ Lean Meat, 2½ Fat **Carbohydrate Choices:** 3

Fresh Idea Want less bite from the red onion? Just wash the raw onion in a strainer with cold water, and pat dry to lessen the onion zing.

Pulled Pork Tomato Mole Enchiladas

8 enchiladas | Prep Time: 20 Minutes | Start to Finish: 50 Minutes

• • •

Freezer Short-cut

2 cups frozen Make-Ahead Roasted Roma Tomato Sauce (recipe on page 194), thawed

1 tablespoon chopped chipotle chiles in adobo sauce (from 7-oz can)

4 teaspoons unsweetened baking cocoa

Freezer Short-cut

2 cups frozen Make-Ahead Oven-Roasted Pulled Pork (recipe on page 83), thawed, coarsely chopped

8 flour tortillas (8 inch)

1½ cups crumbled queso fresco cheese (6 oz)

¼ cup chopped green onions (4 medium)

¼ cup chopped fresh cilantro

1 Heat oven to 400°F. Spray 13x9-inch (3-quart) glass baking dish with cooking spray.

2 In 4-quart saucepan, heat tomato sauce, chiles and cocoa to simmering over medium heat. Reduce heat to medium-low; cook 5 minutes longer to blend flavors. Remove 1 cup mole sauce to small bowl; set aside. Add pork to sauce in pan; toss to coat.

3 Spoon pork mixture down center of tortillas; sprinkle evenly with ½ cup of the cheese. Roll up; place enchiladas, seam sides down, in baking dish. Top with reserved 1 cup sauce. Spray sheet of foil with cooking spray; cover baking dish with foil, sprayed side down.

4 Bake 25 to 30 minutes or until hot and bubbly. Top with remaining 1 cup cheese, the onions and cilantro.

1 Enchilada: Calories 300; Total Fat 16g (Saturated Fat 6g, Trans Fat 1.5g); Cholesterol 40mg; Sodium 640mg; Total Carbohydrate 24g (Dietary Fiber 1g); Protein 14g **Exchanges:** 1 Starch, ½ Other Carbohydrate, 1½ Lean Meat, 2 Fat **Carbohydrate Choices:** 1½

Fresh Idea Like it hot? Double the chipotles or add a little more of the adobo sauce to the mole.

Slow-Cooker Herbed Pork and Red Potatoes

8 servings | Prep Time: 30 Minutes | Start to Finish: 6 Hours 30 Minutes

* * *

1   boneless pork shoulder (3 lb), trimmed of visible fat, cut into 2-inch chunks

2   lb small red potatoes

3   medium carrots, coarsely chopped (1 cup)

1   large onion, coarsely chopped (1½ cups)

1   bulb garlic, cloves peeled

1   sprig fresh thyme

¼   cup honey

1   tablespoon salt

1   teaspoon crushed red pepper flakes

2   tablespoons chopped fresh thyme leaves

1   Place pork in 1-gallon resealable freezer plastic bag. Add remaining ingredients except chopped thyme; seal bag.

2   Lay bag flat in freezer. Freeze up to 3 months. Thaw 12 to 24 hours in refrigerator until completely thawed.

3   Spray 6-quart slow cooker with cooking spray. Pour pork mixture into slow cooker. Cover; cook on Low heat setting 6 to 7 hours or until potatoes are tender when pierced with paring knife and pork shreds easily.

4   Remove pork from slow cooker to plate; shred with 2 forks. Remove potatoes to cutting board; cut into quarters. Divide mixture among 8 bowls; sprinkle with chopped thyme.

1 Serving: Calories 470; Total Fat 21g (Saturated Fat 7g, Trans Fat 0g); Cholesterol 110mg; Sodium 980mg; Total Carbohydrate 33g (Dietary Fiber 3g); Protein 39g **Exchanges:** 2 Starch **Carbohydrate Choices:** 2

Fresh Idea To add a little zip, double up on the red pepper flakes.

SLOW-COOKER-READY FREEZER BAGS

How do you handle dinner on your busiest days when you're craving a home-cooked meal? Arm yourself for days like this with frozen meals you've prepped in advance and stashed in your freezer for your slow cooker. When it's going to be a crazy day, simply empty one into your slow cooker, turn it on and boom —dinner cooks while you're off taking care of life. They're the perfect solution for getting dinner on the table when there isn't time or you don't feel like cooking.

Select Sure-Winning Recipes

This book contains many recipes specifically designed to freeze and cook in your slow cooker, turning them into delicious meals you'll be proud to serve your family. But not all slow-cooker recipes will translate well into yumminess when frozen first. Some ingredients don't freeze well, leaving less-than-desirable textures and colors when cooked (see Unfriendly Freezer Foods, page 9). Also, some recipes have great flavor when cooked fresh, but if frozen first, the flavors die, as some ingredients can lose or change their flavor when frozen. Use the Freezer-Friendly Foods chart on page 8 to help you select slow-cooker recipes that will freeze well before cooking.

Mapping Out a Plan

SET ASIDE PREP TIME: If you plan to make several recipes in advance at one time, you can be ready on those hectic days. Consider making a double batch of the same recipe.

MAKE A LIST, CHECK IT TWICE: Decide how many recipes you'd like to make on one prep occasion. Be realistic about the time you have to devote to this meal prep session—don't bite off more than you can chew! Make a grocery list from your meal-planning list, highlighting common ingredients and being sure to double all ingredients needed to make double batches.

COMBINE TASKS: Now that you've shopped and are ready to get started, look through your recipes at the common ingredients you've highlighted, such as onions and garlic. Save time by chopping them all at the same time. Enlist the help of your kitchen gadgets like food processors or food choppers to help slash time.

ONE RECIPE AT A TIME: Once all the common ingredients are ready, focus on finishing all the remaining prep for one recipe at a time. Once it's ready for the freezer, follow the Top Tips for Freezing, page 6, using resealable freezer plastic bags and storing them flat to save space in the freezer and help them thaw quickly.

ADD FINAL STEPS: Write the cooking time, temperature and any last preparation steps needed right on the bag with a permanent marker. This way, you won't have to reference the recipe when you want to cook it.

THAW THE NIGHT BEFORE: Place the frozen bag in your refrigerator the night before you want to use it, allowing enough time for the mixture to thaw completely. If the bag contains liquid that could leak when thawed, place the frozen bag in a 13x9-inch pan to catch any drips and avoid a mess in your refrigerator.

DUMP AND FORGET: In the morning, simply dump the ingredients from the freezer bag into your slow cooker, turn it on and let it cook. You'll come home to dinner already done (or nearly done, if there are any final quick steps needed to finish it) with little effort at all!

Maple-Dijon Pork Chops

4 servings | Prep Time: 20 Minutes | Start to Finish: 25 Minutes

• • •

MARINADE

¼	cup olive oil
¼	cup real maple syrup
¼	cup Dijon mustard
1	tablespoon water
½	teaspoon dried thyme leaves
¼	teaspoon coarse ground black pepper
¼	teaspoon salt

MEAT

4	bone-in pork loin chops, ¾ inch thick (about 1¾ lb)

1 In medium bowl, mix all marinade ingredients with whisk until smooth. Place pork chops in 1-gallon resealable freezer plastic bag; add marinade. Seal bag; turn bag to coat pork with marinade.

2 Lay bag flat in freezer. Freeze up to 3 months. Thaw 12 to 24 hours in refrigerator until completely thawed.

3 Heat gas or charcoal grill. Remove pork from marinade; reserve marinade. Place pork chops on grill over medium heat. Cover grill; cook 8 to 10 minutes, turning frequently and brushing with reserved marinade, until pork is no longer pink and meat thermometer inserted in center reads 145°F. Let stand at least 3 minutes before serving. Discard any remaining marinade.

1 Serving: Calories 280; Total Fat 12g (Saturated Fat 3g, Trans Fat 0g); Cholesterol 110mg; Sodium 220mg; Total Carbohydrate 4g (Dietary Fiber 0g); Protein 41g **Exchanges:** 6 Very Lean Meat, 2 Fat **Carbohydrate Choices:** 0

Fresh Idea Four boneless pork loin chops, ½ to ¾ inch thick (about 1 pound), trimmed of fat, can be substituted for the bone-in chops.

In a Flash While you have the grill going, add some sweet potatoes, corn on the cob or asparagus spears to serve on the side. All three taste great grilled.

Beer-Cheese Mac and Sausages

8 servings | Prep Time: 25 Minutes | Start to Finish: 1 Hour 5 Minutes

• • •

1 **box (7 oz) elbow macaroni (2½ cups)**

3 **tablespoons butter**

1 **small onion, finely chopped (¼ cup)**

3 **tablespoons all-purpose flour**

2 **cups half-and-half**

1 **teaspoon ground mustard**

½ **teaspoon red pepper sauce**

¼ **teaspoon salt**

1 **cup regular or nonalcoholic beer**

2 **cups shredded Colby–Monterey Jack cheese blend (8 oz)**

1 **package (1 lb) cocktail-size smoked link sausages (about 48 sausages)**

2 **cups popped popcorn**

1 Spray 2½-quart casserole with cooking spray. Cook and drain macaroni as directed on package, using minimum cook time. Return macaroni to saucepan.

2 Meanwhile, in 3-quart saucepan, melt butter over medium heat. Cook onion in butter 2 to 3 minutes, stirring frequently, until softened. Stir in flour; cook 1 minute, stirring constantly. Gradually stir in half-and-half, mustard, pepper sauce and salt; cook about 5 minutes longer, stirring constantly, until thickened and bubbly. Stir in beer.

3 Remove from heat; let stand 2 to 3 minutes. Stir in cheese until melted. Add sausages to cooked macaroni; stir in cheese sauce. Spoon macaroni mixture into casserole.

4 Cover casserole tightly. Freeze up to 3 months. Thaw in refrigerator overnight.

5 Heat oven to 350°F. Uncover casserole. Bake 30 to 40 minutes or until bubbly and top begins to brown. Top individual servings with popcorn.

1 Serving: Calories 500; Total Fat 34g (Saturated Fat 16g, Trans Fat 1g); Cholesterol 80mg; Sodium 1130mg; Total Carbohydrate 30g (Dietary Fiber 1g); Protein 16g **Exchanges:** 2 Starch, 1½ High-Fat Meat, 4 Fat **Carbohydrate Choices:** 2

Fresh Idea This casserole is perfect for a football game-day watching party! Serve with warm soft pretzels and fresh veggies, such as carrots and celery sticks, bell pepper strips and cucumber slices.

Italian Sausage Lasagna

8 servings | Prep Time: 45 Minutes | Start to Finish: 2 Hours 30 Minutes

- - -

1 lb bulk Italian pork sausage

1 medium onion, chopped (½ cup)

1 clove garlic, finely chopped

3 tablespoons chopped fresh parsley

1 tablespoon chopped fresh or 1 teaspoon dried basil leaves

1 teaspoon sugar

2 cups diced tomatoes (from 28-oz can), undrained

1 can (15 oz) tomato sauce

12 uncooked lasagna noodles

1 container (15 oz) ricotta cheese or small-curd cottage cheese

½ cup grated Parmesan cheese

1 tablespoon chopped fresh or 1½ teaspoons dried oregano leaves

2 cups shredded mozzarella cheese (8 oz)

1 In 12-inch skillet, cook sausage, onion and garlic over medium heat, stirring occasionally, until sausage is no longer pink; drain. Stir in 2 tablespoons of the parsley, the basil, sugar, tomatoes and tomato sauce. Heat to boiling, stirring occasionally. Reduce heat to low; simmer uncovered about 45 minutes or until slightly thickened.

2 Meanwhile, cook and drain noodles as directed on package.

3 Heat oven to 350°F. In medium bowl, mix ricotta cheese, ¼ cup of the Parmesan cheese, remaining 1 tablespoon parsley and the oregano.

4 Spread 1 cup of the sauce mixture in ungreased 13x9-inch (3-quart) glass baking dish. Top with 4 cooked noodles. Spread 1 cup of the cheese mixture over noodles; spread 1 cup of the sauce mixture over cheese mixture. Sprinkle with ⅔ cup of the mozzarella cheese. Repeat with 4 noodles, the remaining cheese mixture, 1 cup of the sauce mixture and ⅔ cup of the mozzarella cheese. Top with remaining noodles and sauce mixture. Sprinkle with remaining mozzarella cheese and ¼ cup Parmesan cheese.

5 Cover; bake 30 minutes. Uncover; bake about 15 minutes longer or until hot and bubbly. Let stand 15 minutes before cutting.

6 To freeze, cool completely. Cover baking dish tightly. Freeze up to 3 months. Thaw in refrigerator overnight. Reheat lasagna covered at 350°F for 30 minutes or until thoroughly heated.

1 Serving: Calories 490; Total Fat 24g (Saturated Fat 11g, Trans Fat 0g); Cholesterol 65mg; Sodium 1380mg; Total Carbohydrate 40g (Dietary Fiber 3g); Protein 29g **Exchanges:** 2 Starch, 1½ Vegetable, 1 Medium-Fat Meat, 2 High-Fat Meat, ½ Fat **Carbohydrate Choices:** 2½

In a Flash To save time, instead of making the meat sauce, use 5 cups (40 ounces) of your favorite regular spaghetti sauce with meat instead of the first eight ingredients. Just be sure not to use thick or extra-thick varieties.

Bacon-Pepper Mac and Cheese

6 servings (1 cup each) | Prep Time: 35 Minutes | Start to Finish: 1 Hour

* * *

3   cups uncooked penne pasta (9 oz)

¼   cup butter

1   medium red bell pepper, thinly sliced (about 1 cup)

4   medium green onions, sliced (¼ cup)

¼   cup all-purpose flour

½   teaspoon salt

¼   teaspoon pepper

1   teaspoon Dijon mustard

2¼   cups milk

10   slices packaged precooked bacon (from 2.2-oz package), cut into ½-inch pieces

4   oz sharp Cheddar cheese, shredded (1 cup)

4   oz Muenster cheese, shredded (1 cup)

2   oz Gruyère cheese, shredded (½ cup)

¼   cup Italian bread crumbs

1   tablespoon butter, melted

1 Spray 2-quart casserole with cooking spray. Cook and drain pasta as directed on package, using minimum cook time.

2 Meanwhile, in 3-quart saucepan, melt butter over medium heat. Cook bell pepper and onions in butter 1 minute, stirring constantly. Stir in flour, salt, pepper and mustard. Cook and stir until mixture is bubbly. Increase heat to medium-high. Gradually add milk, stirring constantly until mixture boils and thickens, about 5 minutes. Gently stir in bacon and pasta. Remove from heat; stir in cheeses. Pour into casserole. Cool completely.

3 Cover casserole tightly. Freeze up to 3 months. Thaw in refrigerator overnight.

4 Heat oven to 350°F. Uncover casserole. In small bowl, mix bread crumbs and melted butter; sprinkle over pasta mixture.

5 Bake 20 to 25 minutes or until hot and edges are bubbly.

1 Serving: Calories 1010; Total Fat 51g (Saturated Fat 29g, Trans Fat 1.5g); Cholesterol 145mg; Sodium 1790mg; Total Carbohydrate 91g (Dietary Fiber 5g); Protein 45g **Exchanges:** 5½ Starch, ½ Other Carbohydrate, 4 High-Fat Meat, 3 Fat **Carbohydrate Choices:** 6

Fresh Idea Go ahead and use the classic elbow macaroni in place of the penne. You can also use Swiss cheese instead of the Gruyère. Gruyère has a more pronounced nutty flavor than regular Swiss, so use whichever you prefer.

Pepperoni Pizza Pasta Bake

6 servings (1½ cups each) | Prep Time: 15 Minutes | Start to Finish: 55 Minutes

● ● ●

4 cups uncooked large elbow macaroni (12 oz)

1 package (5 oz) miniature sliced pepperoni (about 1 cup)

2 cans (18 oz each) fire-roasted tomato cooking sauce

1 can (3.8 oz) sliced ripe olives, drained

1 cup shredded mozzarella cheese (4 oz)

1 Cook and drain macaroni as directed on package, using minimum cook time. In ungreased 3-quart casserole, mix macaroni, pepperoni, cooking sauce and olives.

2 Cover casserole tightly. Freeze up to 3 months. Thaw in refrigerator overnight.

3 Heat oven to 350°F. Bake casserole covered 30 to 35 minutes or until hot in center. Sprinkle with cheese; bake uncovered about 5 minutes longer or until cheese is melted.

1 Serving: Calories 560; Total Fat 18g (Saturated Fat 6g, Trans Fat 0g); Cholesterol 30mg; Sodium 1040mg; Total Carbohydrate 75g (Dietary Fiber 7g); Protein 24g **Exchanges:** 4½ Starch, ½ Other Carbohydrate, 1½ Medium-Fat Meat, 1½ Fat **Carbohydrate Choices:** 5

Baked Sausage and Penne

6 servings | Prep Time: 25 Minutes | Start to Finish: 55 Minutes

* * *

2⅔ cups uncooked penne pasta (8 oz)

1 lb bulk Italian pork sausage

1 large onion, chopped (1 cup)

3 cloves garlic, finely chopped

1 jar (24 oz) marinara sauce

¼ cup chopped fresh basil leaves

1 cup ricotta cheese

¼ cup grated Parmesan cheese

1 egg

1 cup shredded Italian cheese blend (4 oz)

Thinly sliced fresh basil leaves, if desired

1. Spray 11x7-inch (2-quart) glass baking dish with cooking spray. In Dutch oven or 3-quart saucepan, cook pasta as directed on package, using minimum cook time; drain and return to Dutch oven.

2. Meanwhile, in 10-inch skillet, cook sausage, onion and garlic over medium-high heat 5 to 7 minutes, stirring occasionally, until sausage is no longer pink; drain. Add sausage, marinara sauce and chopped basil to cooked pasta in Dutch oven; stir well. Spoon into baking dish.

3. In small bowl, mix ricotta cheese, Parmesan cheese and egg. Spoon over pasta mixture. Sprinkle with cheese blend.

4. Cover baking dish tightly. Freeze up to 3 months. Thaw in refrigerator overnight.

5. Heat oven to 375°F. Bake covered 20 minutes. Uncover; bake 10 minutes longer or until hot and bubbly and cheese is melted. Sprinkle with sliced basil.

1 Serving: Calories 580; Total Fat 27g (Saturated Fat 11g, Trans Fat 0g); Cholesterol 0mg; Sodium 1260mg; Total Carbohydrate 50g (Dietary Fiber 5g); Protein 31g **Exchanges:** 3 Starch, 1 Vegetable, 3 High-Fat Meat **Carbohydrate Choices:** 3

Fresh Idea The fresh basil really adds nice flavor and color to the dish. All you need to make this a meal is to serve it with a salad. You can add some of the fresh basil in the salad as well.

Spicy Chorizo-Stuffed Peppers

8 servings | Prep Time: 15 Minutes | Start to Finish: 1 Hour 15 Minutes

• • •

1⅓ cups water

⅔ cup uncooked regular long-grain white rice

2 smoked chorizo sausage links (3 oz each), diced (1¼ cups)

1 can (15 oz) black beans, drained, rinsed

1 can (14.5 oz) fire-roasted tomatoes with chipotle peppers, undrained

1½ cups shredded Mexican cheese blend (6 oz)

4 medium red or green bell peppers or 2 of each, cut in half lengthwise, seeds and membranes removed

4 medium green onions, chopped (¼ cup)

1 In 2-quart saucepan, heat water to boiling over medium-high heat. Stir in rice. Reduce heat to low. Cover; simmer 15 minutes or until liquid is absorbed and rice is tender.

2 In medium bowl, mix sausage, beans, tomatoes, 1 cup of the cheese and the cooked rice. Place pepper halves, cut sides up, in ungreased 13x9-inch (3-quart) glass baking dish. Spoon about ⅔ cup rice mixture into each pepper half, mounding as necessary.

3 Cover baking dish tightly. Freeze up to 3 months. Thaw in refrigerator overnight.

4 Heat oven to 375°F. Bake covered 35 to 40 minutes or until peppers are crisp-tender and filling is thoroughly heated. Uncover; sprinkle tops of peppers with remaining ½ cup cheese and the onions. Bake 5 minutes longer or until cheese is melted.

1 Serving: Calories 340; Total Fat 15g (Saturated Fat 7g, Trans Fat 0g); Cholesterol 40mg; Sodium 540mg; Total Carbohydrate 34g (Dietary Fiber 7g); Protein 17g **Exchanges:** 2 Starch, 1 Vegetable, 1 Medium-Fat Meat, 2 Fat **Carbohydrate Choices:** 2

Fresh Idea You can substitute diced tomatoes with green chiles or plain fire-roasted tomatoes for the fire-roasted tomatoes with chipotle peppers.

chapter three

Chicken & Turkey

Make-Ahead Shredded Chicken Breast

6 cups | Prep Time: 25 Minutes | Start to Finish: 1 Hour 35 Minutes

• • •

4 lb bone-in skin-on chicken breasts (6 to 8)
1 teaspoon garlic salt
1 teaspoon lemon-pepper seasoning
1 teaspoon dried basil leaves
1 tablespoon olive or vegetable oil

1 Heat oven to 400°F. Line 15x10x1-inch pan with foil; spray foil with cooking spray.

2 Trim excess fat from chicken. Loosen skin without removing from breasts. In small bowl, mix garlic salt, lemon-pepper seasoning and basil; rub under skin on chicken breast meat. Brush chicken skin with oil. Place in pan.

3 Bake uncovered 45 to 55 minutes or until juice of chicken is clear when thickest part is cut to bone (at least 165°F).

4 Cool 15 minutes. Remove skin and bones; shred chicken with 2 forks. Cool completely. Place 2 cups of chicken in each of 3 freezer containers or resealable freezer plastic bags; seal tightly. Freeze up to 3 months. Thaw 12 to 24 hours in refrigerator until completely thawed.

½ **Cup:** Calories 130; Total Fat 4.5g (Saturated Fat 1g, Trans Fat 0g); Cholesterol 65mg; Sodium 170mg; Total Carbohydrate 0g (Dietary Fiber 0g); Protein 23g **Exchanges:** 3 Very Lean Meat, ½ Fat **Carbohydrate Choices:** 0

Fresh Idea To make Mexican-flavored chicken, omit garlic salt, lemon-pepper seasoning and basil. In small bowl, mix 2 teaspoons chili powder, 1 teaspoon garlic powder, 1 teaspoon ground cumin and 1 teaspoon salt. Rub on chicken as directed.

SHREDDED CHIX BREAST 3/14

Chicken Salad Club Sandwich Stackers

4 servings (½ sandwich each) | Prep Time: 15 Minutes | Start to Finish: 15 Minutes

• • •

⅓ cup mayonnaise

1 teaspoon honey mustard

Freezer Short-cut

2 cups frozen Make-Ahead Shredded Chicken Breast (recipe on page 110), thawed

⅓ cup finely chopped celery

6 slices whole-grain bread, toasted

8 slices tomato

4 slices bacon, cooked, drained and cut in half

4 leaves romaine or leaf lettuce

4 tiny dill or sweet gherkins

1 In medium bowl, mix mayonnaise and mustard. Stir in chicken and celery until well mixed.

2 Spread ½ cup chicken mixture on one side of 2 bread slices. Layer each with 2 tomato slices, 2 half slices of bacon and 1 lettuce leaf. Top each with another bread slice. Repeat layers, starting with chicken mixture. Top each with third bread slice.

3 Thread pickles on toothpicks; insert 2 into each sandwich. Cut each sandwich in half to serve.

1 Serving: Calories 420; Total Fat 22g (Saturated Fat 4.5g, Trans Fat 0g); Cholesterol 75mg; Sodium 620mg; Total Carbohydrate 25g (Dietary Fiber 5g); Protein 29g **Exchanges:** 1 Starch, ½ Other Carbohydrate, ½ Vegetable, 3½ Lean Meat, 2 Fat **Carbohydrate Choices:** 1½

Taco-Spiced Chicken

4 servings | Prep Time: 30 Minutes | Start to Finish: 45 Minutes

• • •

2 tablespoons taco seasoning mix (from 1-oz package)

1 teaspoon dried oregano leaves

4 boneless skinless chicken breasts (about 1¼ lb)

1 tablespoon olive or vegetable oil

¼ cup barbecue sauce

2 tablespoons chili sauce

½ teaspoon ground cumin

1 Heat gas or charcoal grill. In small bowl, mix taco seasoning mix and oregano. Brush chicken with oil; sprinkle with taco seasoning mixture.

2 Place chicken on grill over medium heat. Cover grill; cook 15 to 20 minutes, turning once, until juice of chicken is clear when center of thickest part is cut (at least 165°F).

3 Cool 15 minutes. Cut chicken into strips or cubes, shred with 2 forks, or leave whole. Cool completely. Place in freezer containers or resealable freezer plastic bags and seal tightly, or wrap tightly if freezing whole. Freeze up to 3 months. Thaw in refrigerator overnight.

4 In small microwavable bowl, mix barbecue sauce, chili sauce and cumin. Cover; microwave on High 30 to 60 seconds or until hot. Serve chicken with sauce. Or reheat sliced, cubed or shredded chicken in the sauce.

1 Serving: Calories 240; Total Fat 8g (Saturated Fat 2g, Trans Fat 0g); Cholesterol 85mg; Sodium 780mg; Total Carbohydrate 11g (Dietary Fiber 0g); Protein 31g **Exchanges:** ½ Other Carbohydrate, 4½ Very Lean Meat, 1 Fat **Carbohydrate Choices:** 1

Oven Directions: Heat oven to 375°F. Line shallow baking pan with foil or spray with cooking spray. Place coated chicken in pan. Bake uncovered 25 to 30 minutes until juice of chicken is clear when center of thickest part is cut (at least 165°F).

In a Flash **For zesty, make-your-own wrap sandwiches, slice the warm chicken into strips and serve with tortillas, shredded lettuce, sliced avocado and the sauce.**

Cheese-Stuffed Buffalo Chicken Rolls

4 servings | Prep Time: 25 Minutes | Start to Finish: 1 Hour

• • •

4   boneless skinless chicken breasts (about 1¼ lb)

¼   teaspoon salt

¼   cup finely crumbled blue cheese (1 oz)

¼   cup finely shredded Cheddar cheese (1 oz)

2   tablespoons butter, melted

2   tablespoons Buffalo wing sauce

⅓   cup unseasoned dry bread crumbs

   Blue cheese dressing, if desired

   Celery sticks, if desired

1 Between pieces of plastic wrap or waxed paper, place each chicken breast smooth side down; gently pound with flat side of meat mallet or rolling pin until about ¼ inch thick. Sprinkle with salt.

2 Place 1 tablespoon blue cheese and 1 tablespoon Cheddar cheese in center of each chicken breast to within ½ inch of short sides. Fold short sides about 1 inch toward center. Starting at long side, roll chicken over cheese, tucking in sides as needed. Secure ends with toothpicks.

3 Cover and refrigerate up to 24 hours before baking, or wrap tightly and freeze up to 3 months. Thaw in refrigerator overnight.

4 Heat oven to 375°F. Spray 15x10x1-inch pan with cooking spray. In shallow dish, mix melted butter and Buffalo wing sauce until well blended. Place bread crumbs in another shallow dish. Coat chicken rolls with butter mixture; roll in crumbs. Place in pan.

5 Bake 25 to 35 minutes or until chicken is no longer pink in center. Remove toothpicks. Serve chicken with blue cheese dressing and celery.

1 Serving: Calories 350; Total Fat 17g (Saturated Fat 9g, Trans Fat 0g); Cholesterol 130mg; Sodium 620mg; Total Carbohydrate 7g (Dietary Fiber 0g); Protein 42g **Exchanges:** ½ Other Carbohydrate, 5½ Very Lean Meat, ½ High-Fat Meat, 2 Fat **Carbohydrate Choices:** ½

Oven Chicken Cordon Bleu

4 servings | Prep Time: 20 Minutes | Start to Finish: 50 Minutes

• • •

4 boneless skinless chicken breasts (about 1¼ lb)

2 teaspoons Dijon mustard

4 teaspoons chopped fresh chives

4 thin slices (about ¾ oz each) lean cooked ham

4 thin slices (about ¾ oz each) reduced-fat Swiss cheese

1 egg white

1 tablespoon water

⅓ cup finely crushed corn flakes or bran flakes cereal

¼ teaspoon paprika

1 Between pieces of plastic wrap or waxed paper, place each chicken breast smooth side down; gently pound with flat side of meat mallet or rolling pin until about ¼ inch thick. Spread each chicken breast with ½ teaspoon mustard; sprinkle with 1 teaspoon chives.

2 Cut ham and cheese slices to fit chicken. Top each chicken breast with 1 ham and 1 cheese slice. Roll up, tucking ends inside.

3 Wrap tightly. Freeze up to 3 months. Thaw in refrigerator overnight.

4 Heat oven to 375°F. Spray 8-inch square (2 quart) glass baking dish with cooking spray. In shallow dish, slightly beat egg white and water. Place cereal crumbs in another shallow dish. Coat chicken rolls with egg white mixture; roll in crumbs. Place in baking dish. Sprinkle with paprika.

5 Bake uncovered 25 to 30 minutes or until chicken is no longer pink in center.

1 Serving: Calories 150; Total Fat 4g (Saturated Fat 1.5g, Trans Fat 0g); Cholesterol 60mg; Sodium 440mg; Total Carbohydrate 2g (Dietary Fiber 0g); Protein 25g **Exchanges:** 3 Lean Meat **Carbohydrate Choices:** 0

Fresh Idea Continue the French theme with French bread and a tossed salad with vinaigrette—homemade is particularly nice.

Mexican Chicken Casserole

8 servings | Prep Time: 20 Minutes | Start to Finish: 55 Minutes

· · ·

Freezer Short-cut

2   cups Make-Ahead Shredded Chicken Breast (recipe on page 110)

1   can (15.5 oz) pinto beans, drained, rinsed

½   cup chunky-style salsa

3   teaspoons chili powder

¼   teaspoon garlic powder

½   loaf (16-oz size) prepared cheese product, cut into cubes

1   cup Original Bisquick mix

¾   cup milk

2   tablespoons butter, melted

1   cup shredded lettuce

1   plum (Roma) tomato, diced (½ cup)

4   medium green onions, sliced (¼ cup)

Guacamole, sour cream and pickled sliced jalapeño chiles, if desired

1 Spray round 2-quart casserole or 11x7-inch (2-quart) glass baking dish with cooking spray. In large bowl, mix chicken, beans, salsa, chili powder and garlic powder; stir in cheese. Spoon into casserole.

2 In small bowl, stir together Bisquick mix, milk and butter. Pour and spoon evenly over chicken mixture.

3 Cover casserole tightly. Refrigerate up to 24 hours.

4 Heat oven to 425°F. Uncover casserole. Bake 30 to 35 minutes or until crust is golden brown.

5 Top with lettuce, tomato and onions. Serve with guacamole, sour cream and chiles.

1 Serving: Calories 350; Total Fat 16g (Saturated Fat 9g, Trans Fat 1g); Cholesterol 65mg; Sodium 610mg; Total Carbohydrate 28g (Dietary Fiber 6g); Protein 24g **Exchanges:** 1½ Starch, ½ Vegetable, 2½ Medium-Fat Meat, ½ Fat **Carbohydrate Choices:** 2

Fresh Idea Try 1 can (15 ounces) black beans, drained and rinsed, in place of the pinto beans.

Slow-Cooker Wild Rice and Rosemary Chicken

4 servings | Prep Time: 15 Minutes | Start to Finish: 4 Hours 5 Minutes

• • •

CHICKEN AND VEGETABLES

4	boneless skinless chicken breasts (about 1¼ lb)
¼	teaspoon salt
¼	teaspoon pepper
1	cup uncooked wild rice
5	medium carrots, diagonally sliced (2 cups)
1	bag (12 oz) frozen cut green beans
4	slices thick-sliced bacon, crisply cooked, crumbled

TO COOK

2¼	cups chicken broth
1½	teaspoons chopped fresh rosemary leaves
2	tablespoons all-purpose flour

1 Sprinkle both sides of chicken evenly with salt and pepper; rub into chicken. Place chicken in 1-gallon resealable freezer plastic bag. Add wild rice, carrots, green beans and bacon; seal bag.

2 Lay bag flat in freezer. Freeze up to 3 months. Thaw 12 to 24 hours in refrigerator until completely thawed.

3 Spray 4- to 5-quart slow cooker with cooking spray. Pour chicken mixture into slow cooker; add 2 cups of the broth and the rosemary. Cover; cook on Low heat setting 3 hours 30 minutes to 4 hours or until chicken, vegetables and rice are tender. Remove chicken mixture with slotted spoon to serving plate; cover to keep warm.

4 Increase heat setting to High. In small bowl, mix remaining ¼ cup broth and the flour; gradually stir into cooking liquid. Cover; cook 20 minutes or until slightly thickened. Serve gravy with chicken, vegetables and rice.

1 Serving: Calories 500; Total Fat 11g (Saturated Fat 3g, Trans Fat 0g); Cholesterol 115mg; Sodium 1020mg; Total Carbohydrate 50g (Dietary Fiber 7g); Protein 50g **Exchanges:** 2½ Starch, ½ Other Carbohydrate, 1 Vegetable, 5½ Very Lean Meat, 1½ Fat **Carbohydrate Choices:** 3

Fresh Ideas To add a hint of sweetness, stir in ½ cup dried cranberries or cherries with the broth and rosemary.

Garnish with additional crisply cooked bacon, toasted chopped pecans and rosemary sprigs.

Chicken Biscuit Pot Pie

5 servings | Prep Time: 30 Minutes | Start to Finish: 55 Minutes

• • •

1	tablespoon olive oil
3/4	lb boneless skinless chicken breasts, cut into 1/2-inch pieces
1	large onion, chopped (1 cup)
3/4	cup frozen mixed vegetables (from 12-oz bag), thawed
1/2	cup sour cream
1	jar (12 oz) chicken gravy
2	tablespoons cornstarch
1/4	teaspoon dried thyme leaves
1/4	teaspoon pepper
1	can (12 oz) refrigerated flaky biscuits
1/2	cup grated Parmesan cheese
	Crumbled cooked bacon, if desired
	Chopped fresh chives, if desired

1. In 10-inch skillet, heat oil over medium-high heat. Cook chicken in oil about 4 minutes, stirring frequently, until no longer pink in center. Add onion; cook until crisp-tender. Stir in mixed vegetables.

2. In medium bowl, mix sour cream, gravy, cornstarch, thyme and pepper until blended. Stir into chicken mixture; cook until hot. Spoon into ungreased 13x9-inch (3-quart) glass baking dish.

3. Cover baking dish tightly. Freeze up to 3 months. Thaw in refrigerator overnight.

4. Heat oven to 350°F. Uncover baking dish. Separate dough into 10 biscuits; arrange over chicken mixture. Sprinkle with cheese.

5. Bake 15 to 23 minutes or until filling is bubbly and biscuits are golden brown. Sprinkle with bacon and chives.

1 Serving: Calories 450; Total Fat 19g (Saturated Fat 7g, Trans Fat 0g); Cholesterol 0mg; Sodium 1240mg; Total Carbohydrate 42g (Dietary Fiber 1g); Protein 24g **Exchanges:** 2 Starch, 1/2 Other Carbohydrate, 1 Vegetable, 2 Very Lean Meat, 1/2 Medium-Fat Meat, 3 Fat **Carbohydrate Choices:** 2 1/2

Super-Easy Chicken Manicotti

7 servings | Prep Time: 15 Minutes | Start to Finish: 1 Hour 20 Minutes

* * *

1 jar (26 oz) tomato pasta sauce

¾ cup water

1 teaspoon garlic salt

1½ lb uncooked chicken breast tenders (not breaded)

14 uncooked manicotti pasta shells

2 cups shredded mozzarella cheese (8 oz)

Chopped fresh basil leaves, if desired

1 Serving: Calories 370; Total Fat 8g (Saturated Fat 4.5g, Trans Fat 0g); Cholesterol 60mg; Sodium 710mg; Total Carbohydrate 38g (Dietary Fiber 3g); Protein 35g **Exchanges:** 2 Starch, ½ Other Carbohydrate, 4 Very Lean Meat, 1 Fat **Carbohydrate Choices:** 2½

Fresh Idea Try stirring a tablespoon or two of red wine or beef broth into the pasta sauce for a deeper flavor. Or, use Make-Ahead Roasted Roma Tomato Sauce (recipe on page 194) for the pasta sauce.

1 In medium bowl, mix pasta sauce and water. Spread about one-third of the mixture in ungreased 13x9-inch (3-quart) glass baking dish.

2 Sprinkle garlic salt on chicken. Insert chicken into uncooked pasta shells, stuffing from each end of shell to fill if necessary. Place shells in baking dish. Pour remaining pasta sauce mixture evenly over shells, covering completely.

3 Cover baking dish tightly. Freeze up to 3 months. Thaw in refrigerator overnight.

4 Heat oven to 350°F. Bake manicotti covered about 1 hour or until chicken is no longer pink in center and shells are tender. Sprinkle with cheese. Bake uncovered about 5 minutes longer or until cheese is melted. Sprinkle with basil.

Cheesy Barbecue Chicken Lasagna Roll-Ups

16 roll-ups | Prep Time: 50 Minutes | Start to Finish: 2 Hours 20 Minutes

· · ·

ROLL-UPS

16   uncooked lasagna noodles

1   package (8 oz) cream cheese, softened

2   cups shredded sharp Cheddar cheese (8 oz)

1   teaspoon Cajun seasoning

2   eggs, slightly beaten

3½   cups chopped cooked chicken

1   cup finely chopped green onions

TOPPINGS

2   cups barbecue sauce

2   cups shredded sharp Cheddar cheese (8 oz)

¼   cup sliced green onions

¼   cup ranch dressing, if desired

1 Line 15x10x1-inch pan with foil. Cook and drain noodles as directed on package. Rinse with hot water; drain well.

2 In large bowl, beat cream cheese, 2 cups Cheddar cheese and the Cajun seasoning with electric mixer on medium speed until blended. On low speed, beat in eggs, one at a time. Stir in chicken and finely chopped onions. Spread slightly less than ⅓ cup chicken mixture down center of each cooked noodle to within 1 inch of one short end. Roll up firmly toward unfilled end.

3 Place roll-ups, seam sides down, in pan; cover loosely with foil. Freeze about 30 minutes or until firm. Wrap tightly. Freeze up to 3 months. Thaw in refrigerator at least 8 hours but no longer than 24 hours.

4 Heat oven to 350°F. Spray two 13x9-inch (3-quart) glass baking dishes with cooking spray. Place 8 roll-ups in each baking dish. Pour 1 cup barbecue sauce over and around roll-ups in each dish.

5 Cover tightly; bake 40 to 50 minutes or until hot and bubbly. Uncover; sprinkle each dish with 1 cup Cheddar cheese. Bake 3 to 5 minutes longer or until cheese is melted. Sprinkle with sliced onions. Let stand 5 minutes before serving. Drizzle with ranch dressing.

1 Roll-Up: Calories 370; Total Fat 18g (Saturated Fat 10g, Trans Fat 0g); Cholesterol 95mg; Sodium 760mg; Total Carbohydrate 33g (Dietary Fiber 1g); Protein 20g **Exchanges:** 1 Starch, 1 Other Carbohydrate, 1½ Lean Meat, 1 High-Fat Meat, 1 Fat **Carbohydrate Choices:** 2

Chicken Enchilada Lasagna Roll-Ups

16 roll-ups | Prep Time: 50 Minutes | Start to Finish: 2 Hours 20 Minutes

• • •

ROLL-UPS

- 16 uncooked lasagna noodles
- 1 package (8 oz) cream cheese, softened
- 2 cups shredded pepper Jack cheese (8 oz)
- ¾ cup chopped green onions
- 1 can (10 oz) enchilada sauce
- 1 can (4.5 oz) chopped green chiles
- 4 cups diced cooked chicken

TOPPINGS

- 2 cans (10 oz each) enchilada sauce
- 2 cups shredded sharp Cheddar cheese (8 oz)
- 2 cups chopped tomatoes
- 1 cup sour cream
  - Chopped fresh cilantro, if desired
  - Sliced olives, if desired

Fresh Idea **Have fun with the toppings—change it up with guacamole for the sour cream, sliced jalapeño chiles for the tomatoes, and crumbled queso fresco or shredded taco-flavored cheese.**

1 Line 15x10x1-inch pan with foil. Cook and drain noodles as directed on package. Rinse with hot water; drain well.

2 In large bowl, beat cream cheese, pepper Jack cheese and onions with electric mixer on medium speed 1 to 2 minutes or until blended. Add 1 can enchilada sauce and green chiles; beat on low speed until combined. Stir in chicken. Spread heaping ⅓ cup chicken mixture down center of each cooked noodle to within 1 inch of one short end. Roll up firmly toward unfilled end.

3 Place roll-ups, seam sides down, in pan; cover loosely with foil. Freeze about 30 minutes or until firm. Wrap tightly. Freeze up to 3 months. Thaw in refrigerator at least 8 hours but no longer than 24 hours.

4 Heat oven to 350°F. Spray two 13x9-inch (3-quart) glass baking dishes with cooking spray. Place 8 roll-ups in each baking dish. Divide 1 of the remaining cans of enchilada sauce between baking dishes, pouring over and down sides of roll-ups.

5 Cover tightly; bake 40 to 50 minutes or until hot and bubbly. Uncover; sprinkle each dish with 1 cup Cheddar cheese. Bake 3 to 5 minutes longer or until cheese is melted. Let stand 5 minutes before serving.

6 Meanwhile, in 1½-quart saucepan, heat remaining can of enchilada sauce over medium-low heat until hot. Spoon sauce over roll-ups. Top with tomatoes, sour cream, cilantro and olives.

1 Roll-Up: Calories 360; Total Fat 20g (Saturated Fat 11g, Trans Fat 0.5g); Cholesterol 80mg; Sodium 590mg; Total Carbohydrate 23g (Dietary Fiber 1g); Protein 21g **Exchanges:** 1 Starch, ½ Other Carbohydrate, 1½ Lean Meat, 1 High-Fat Meat, 1½ Fat **Carbohydrate Choices:** 1½

Chicken and Spinach Stuffed Shells

6 servings | Prep Time: 30 Minutes | Start to Finish: 1 Hour 20 Minutes

• • •

18 uncooked jumbo pasta shells

1 container (15 oz) whole milk ricotta cheese

1 egg, slightly beaten

¼ cup grated Parmesan cheese

2 cups frozen cut-leaf spinach, thawed, squeezed to drain

1 cup chopped cooked chicken

1 jar (26 oz) tomato pasta sauce

2 cups shredded Italian cheese blend (8 oz)

1 Cook and drain pasta shells as directed on package. Rinse with cold water to cool; drain. Meanwhile, in medium bowl, mix ricotta cheese, egg, Parmesan cheese, spinach and chicken.

2 Spread 1 cup of the pasta sauce in bottom of ungreased 13x9-inch (3-quart) glass baking dish. Spoon about 2 tablespoons ricotta mixture into each pasta shell. Arrange shells, filled sides up, on sauce in baking dish. Spoon remaining sauce over stuffed shells.

3 Cover baking dish tightly. Refrigerate up to 24 hours, or freeze up to 3 months. Thaw in refrigerator overnight.

4 Heat oven to 350°F. Bake covered 35 minutes. Uncover; sprinkle with Italian cheese blend. Bake 10 to 15 minutes longer or until sauce is bubbly and cheese is melted.

1 Serving: Calories 570; Total Fat 28g (Saturated Fat 15g, Trans Fat 0.5g); Cholesterol 120mg; Sodium 1330mg; Total Carbohydrate 48g (Dietary Fiber 4g); Protein 33g **Exchanges:** 3 Starch, 1 Vegetable, 3 Medium-Fat Meat, 2 Fat **Carbohydrate Choices:** 3

White Chicken Chili

6 servings (1⅓ cups each) | Prep Time: 20 Minutes | Start to Finish: 45 Minutes

• • •

1 tablespoon vegetable oil

1 large onion, chopped (1 cup)

2 cloves garlic, finely chopped

3 cups chicken broth

1 can (11 oz) vacuum-packed white shoepeg or whole kernel sweet corn, drained

1 can (15.5 oz) great northern beans, drained

1 can (15.5 oz) butter beans, drained

2 tablespoons chopped fresh cilantro

2 tablespoons lime juice

1 teaspoon ground cumin

½ teaspoon dried oregano leaves

¼ teaspoon red pepper sauce

¼ teaspoon salt

2 cups chopped cooked chicken breast

1 In 3-quart saucepan or 4-quart Dutch oven, heat oil over medium heat. Cook onion and garlic in oil 4 to 6 minutes, stirring occasionally, until onion is tender.

2 Stir in remaining ingredients except chicken. Heat to boiling; reduce heat. Simmer uncovered 20 minutes. Stir in chicken. Simmer about 5 minutes longer or until hot.

3 To freeze, cool completely. Transfer individual portions to freezer containers; seal tightly. Freeze up to 3 months. Thaw in refrigerator overnight. Reheat in microwave or on stove.

1 Serving: Calories 360; Total Fat 6g (Saturated Fat 1.5g, Trans Fat 0g); Cholesterol 40mg; Sodium 920mg; Total Carbohydrate 46g (Dietary Fiber 11g); Protein 31g **Exchanges:** 2 Starch, 3 Vegetable, 2 Lean Meat **Carbohydrate Choices:** 3

Fresh Idea **If you like shredded chicken in your chili, try adding Make-Ahead Shredded Chicken Breast (recipe on page 110). Just thaw it before using in this recipe.**

HOST A FREEZER MEAL PARTY

Think of it as a productive Ladies Night Out or a cookie exchange, gone main dish. As you sip wine, nibble on snacks and catch up — you are also making meals to take home and freeze for future use. The work goes fast when you're in the company of fun friends. Use these great tips to get your own Meal Party started!

How to Plan the Party

CHOOSE A VENUE Much of the work of a freezer meal party is chopping and assembling — an enormous kitchen is not required. Anywhere you can spread out will work — a dining room, breakfast nook or even a makeshift station on a card table. Consider other places as well — a room rented at your local rec center, a conference room at the office or a condo party-room of one of the guests.

DETERMINE THE PARTY SIZE Decide what a comfortable number of guests and meals to make would be: 8 attendees means each person goes home with 8 meals for their freezer.

SELECT RECIPES Choose recipes for the party that will freeze well, using recipes from this book as a starting point. Select a variety of recipes with a range of prep difficulty, as some guests may be more kitchen savvy than others. If you select recipes that each use a meat, veggies and a few other ingredients, then the recipes will be roughly the same cost for each participant.

PARTY LENGTH The length of your party will be based on the type you choose:

Prep Party — 4 hours: All ingredients are prepared and assembled at the party (chop veggies, brown ground beef, etc.). Plan for enough room for each person to prep their recipe, using the stove top and sink as needed.

Assemble Party — 2 hours: Less prep, more conversation. Prep is done by guests at home before they attend. Simply assemble the meals at the party while enjoying snacks and beverages you provide.

INTERACTIVE INVITATIONS If possible, create an event on social media or a free event-planning site to have a central location, including all the details of the event. Have a few additional people on a wait list, if you wish, so that should someone drop out, your party will stay the same size.

List the details of how the party will work: Have each guest select a recipe that they will be responsible for. If you are having 6 guests, have each person purchase all the groceries for the recipe, 6 times, so that each person will go home with one meal of each type.

Let guests know how much to prep their ingredients before they arrive. Ask them to bring the necessary utensils to make their recipe and appropriate totable containers for their meals, such as resealable freezer plastic bags, foil pans or inexpensive plastic containers. Have them bring their ingredients in a cooler with ice packs — they will use the cooler and ice packs again to bring home the prepared meals that everyone made.

SET THE STAGE Set up a station at the party for each person to prep their meals. Label each meal with recipe name, number of servings, thawing/cooking instructions and any last-minute prep steps right on the bags or containers.

PARTY WITH A GIVING PURPOSE Turn this party into a way help those around you — whether it be a new mom, a sick neighbor or a family that just lost a loved one — what could be a better way to show you care than delivering a homemade meal, ready for them to cook?

You can join with friends or neighbors, making meals solely for the recipient or plan for each guest to bring all the ingredients for a recipe for the number of party guests + one. That way, each guest goes home with meals for themselves and there's one more of each meal for the recipient!

Gather friends to make meals for families dealing with difficult circumstances, labeling them as directed above. Store the meals in your charity of choice's freezer (check first to see if they can accept frozen homemade items) so as a family is in need, they can drop by and pick one out to bring home.

Jill: chop herbs
cube meat
Dana: saute
veggies
Susan: measure
spice
___: pour
wine!

Slow-Cooker Rotisserie Spiced Chicken

4 servings | Prep Time: 10 Minutes | Start to Finish: 4 Hours 25 Minutes

• • •

SPICE RUB

- 2 teaspoons paprika
- 1 teaspoon garlic salt
- 1 teaspoon onion powder
- 1 teaspoon sugar
- 1 teaspoon chili powder
- ½ teaspoon dried thyme leaves, crushed
- ½ teaspoon dried marjoram leaves, crushed
- ½ teaspoon pepper

CHICKEN

- 1 whole chicken (3½ to 4½ lb)

1 Spray 5- to 6-quart oval slow cooker with cooking spray. In small bowl, mix all spice rub ingredients until well blended.

2 Rub spice mixture on all sides of chicken. Do not tie legs. Place chicken in slow cooker, making sure it fits loosely (leave at least 1 inch of space around chicken).

3 Cover; cook on Low heat setting 4 to 5 hours or until instant-read meat thermometer inserted in thickest part of inside thigh muscle and not touching bone reads at least 165°F and legs move easily when lifted or twisted. Do not remove lid before 4 hours.

4 Remove chicken from slow cooker to plate or cutting board; cool 15 minutes. Cut chicken into serving pieces; or remove bones and shred chicken with 2 forks. Cool completely. Transfer to freezer containers or resealable freezer plastic bags; seal tightly. Freeze up to 3 months.

1 Serving: Calories 270; Total Fat 11g (Saturated Fat 3g, Trans Fat 0g); Cholesterol 125mg; Sodium 370mg; Total Carbohydrate 3g (Dietary Fiber 1g); Protein 40g **Exchanges:** 5½ Very Lean Meat, 1½ Fat **Carbohydrate Choices:** 0

Fresh Idea For a smoky flavor, use 1 teaspoon smoked paprika and 1 teaspoon regular paprika in the spice rub.

Slow-Cooker Chicken Paprikash

8 servings | Prep Time: 20 Minutes | Start to Finish: 4 Hours 20 Minutes

• • •

TO FREEZE/COOK

1	can (28 oz) fire-roasted diced tomatoes, undrained
1	tablespoon smoked paprika
2	teaspoons salt
4	cloves garlic, peeled
20	oz boneless skinless chicken thighs
3	red and/or yellow bell peppers, cut into large strips
1	large onion, halved, cut into ½-inch slices

TO SERVE

4	cups hot cooked white rice
½	cup sour cream
4	teaspoons chopped fresh dill weed

1 In large bowl, mix tomatoes, paprika, salt and garlic. Add chicken, bell peppers and onion; mix well. Transfer to large freezer container; seal tightly.

2 Freeze up to 3 months. Thaw 12 to 24 hours in refrigerator until completely thawed.

3 Spray 5-quart slow cooker with cooking spray. Pour chicken mixture into slow cooker. Cover; cook on Low heat setting 4 to 5 hours.

4 To serve, place ½ cup rice in each of 8 bowls. Top each with chicken mixture, 1 tablespoon sour cream and ½ teaspoon dill.

1 Serving: Calories 260; Total Fat 6g (Saturated Fat 2.5g, Trans Fat 0g); Cholesterol 75mg; Sodium 1110mg; Total Carbohydrate 32g (Dietary Fiber 2g); Protein 18g **Exchanges:** 1½ Starch, ½ Other Carbohydrate, 2 Lean Meat **Carbohydrate Choices:** 2

Fresh Idea Like it hot? Use 1 teaspoon hot Hungarian paprika and 2 teaspoons smoked paprika.

Slow-Cooker Asian Peach Chicken Thighs

4 servings | Prep Time: 20 Minutes | Start to Finish: 4 Hours 25 Minutes

• • •

TO FREEZE/COOK

- ¼ cup honey
- ¼ cup soy sauce
- 2 tablespoons butter, melted
- 2 tablespoons chili garlic sauce
- 20 oz boneless skinless chicken thighs
- 1 bag (12 oz) frozen sliced peaches

TO SERVE

- 2 tablespoons cornstarch
- 2 tablespoons cold water
- 2 cups hot cooked white rice
- ½ cup sliced green onions
- ¼ cup chopped fresh cilantro
- ¼ cup chopped roasted salted cashews
- 1 lime, cut into wedges

1 In 1-gallon resealable freezer plastic bag, place honey, soy sauce, melted butter and chili garlic sauce; seal bag. Knead bag to mix well. Add chicken and frozen peaches; turn bag to thoroughly coat chicken and peaches with sauce.

2 Lay bag flat in freezer. Freeze up to 3 months. Thaw 12 to 24 hours in refrigerator until completely thawed.

3 Spray 3½- to 4-quart slow cooker with cooking spray. Pour chicken mixture into slow cooker. Cover; cook on Low heat setting 4 to 5 hours.

4 Increase heat setting to High. In small bowl, beat cornstarch and cold water. Quickly stir into chicken mixture in slow cooker. Cover; cook 5 to 10 minutes longer or until thickened.

5 To serve, place ½ cup rice in each of 4 bowls. Top with chicken mixture, onions, cilantro and cashews. Serve with lime.

1 Serving: Calories 510; Total Fat 16g (Saturated Fat 6g, Trans Fat 0g); Cholesterol 150mg; Sodium 1480mg; Total Carbohydrate 55g (Dietary Fiber 3g); Protein 35g **Exchanges:** 1½ Starch, 1 Fruit, 1 Other Carbohydrate, 4½ Lean Meat, ½ Fat **Carbohydrate Choices:** 3½

Fresh Idea **Not crazy about cilantro? Try Thai or Italian basil instead.**

Coconut-Curry Chicken

4 servings | Prep Time: 35 Minutes | Start to Finish: 35 Minutes

• • •

CURRY SAUCE

1   can (13.66 oz) coconut milk (not cream of coconut)

2   tablespoons red or green Thai curry paste

2   tablespoons fish sauce or soy sauce*

1   tablespoon packed brown sugar

1   teaspoon curry powder

1   cup frozen sweet peas (from 12-oz bag)

CHICKEN AND ONIONS

1¼   lb boneless skinless chicken breasts, cut into 1-inch pieces

1   medium onion, chopped (½ cup)

1   tablespoon coconut oil or butter

SERVE-WITH, IF DESIRED

Hot cooked basmati or regular long-grain rice

Chopped fresh cilantro

Chopped dry-roasted peanuts

1   In medium bowl, mix coconut milk, curry paste, fish sauce, brown sugar and curry powder with whisk until smooth. Pour sauce into 1-gallon resealable freezer plastic bag. Add peas; seal bag.

2   Place chicken and onions in another 1-gallon resealable freezer plastic bag; seal bag.

3   Lay bags flat in freezer. Freeze up to 3 months. Thaw 12 to 24 hours in refrigerator until completely thawed.

4   In 12-inch skillet, heat oil over medium-high heat. Cook chicken and onion in oil 3 to 4 minutes, stirring frequently, until chicken turns white on outside. Pour sauce over chicken. Heat to boiling; reduce heat. Simmer 15 to 18 minutes, stirring occasionally, until chicken is no longer pink in center. Serve over rice; garnish with cilantro and peanuts.

*Soy sauce can be substituted, but the sauce will not have the same authentic Thai flavor.

1 Serving: Calories 290; Total Fat 10g (Saturated Fat 6g, Trans Fat 0g); Cholesterol 90mg; Sodium 950mg; Total Carbohydrate 15g (Dietary Fiber 2g); Protein 34g **Exchanges:** 1 Other Carbohydrate, 5 Very Lean Meat, 1½ Fat **Carbohydrate Choices:** 1

Buffalo–Blue Cheese Chicken Burgers

6 burgers | Prep Time: 35 Minutes | Start to Finish: 35 Minutes

• • •

1¾   **lb ground chicken**

¼   **cup Buffalo wing sauce**

½   **teaspoon salt**

1   **to 3 drops red pepper sauce**

¼   **cup refrigerated chunky blue cheese dressing**

¼   **cup crumbled blue cheese (1 oz)**

6   **burger buns, split**

6   **leaves green leaf lettuce**

1 In large bowl, mix chicken, Buffalo wing sauce, salt and pepper sauce. Shape mixture into 6 patties, ½ inch thick.

2 Wrap patties tightly. Freeze up to 3 months. Thaw in refrigerator overnight.

3 Heat gas or charcoal grill. In small bowl, stir together dressing and cheese.

4 Carefully brush oil on grill rack. Place patties on grill over medium heat. Cover grill; cook 10 to 12 minutes, turning once, until thermometer inserted in center of patties reads 165°F. During last 2 minutes of cooking, add buns, cut sides down, to grill.

5 On bun bottoms, place lettuce and burgers. Top with blue cheese mixture. Cover with bun tops.

1 Burger: Calories 330; Total Fat 17g (Saturated Fat 4.5g, Trans Fat 0g); Cholesterol 85mg; Sodium 890mg; Total Carbohydrate 23g (Dietary Fiber 1g); Protein 22g **Exchanges:** 1½ Starch, 2½ Medium-Fat Meat, ½ Fat **Carbohydrate Choices:** 1½

In a Flash **If you like, grill up the patties, then cool and freeze them on a waxed paper–lined cookie sheet. When frozen, transfer them to a resealable freezer plastic bag. Just thaw and reheat to have summer-grilled burgers whenever you want them!**

Freezer-Friendly Turkey Meatballs

64 meatballs | Prep Time: 40 Minutes | Start to Finish: 3 Hours 50 Minutes

• • •

3	eggs, beaten
1½	cups milk
8	slices white bread, crusts removed, cubed (about 5 cups)
2½	lb ground turkey
2	teaspoons salt
1	large onion, finely chopped (about 2 cups)
6	cloves garlic, finely chopped
1	tablespoon Dijon mustard
1	teaspoon Worcestershire sauce
½	cup olive oil

1 Line 2 cookie sheets with sides with cooking parchment paper. In large bowl, mix eggs and milk; add bread cubes. Cover; refrigerate 20 minutes.

2 Drain and reserve ¾ cup of the egg mixture; discard remaining egg mixture. Stir bread and the ¾ cup egg mixture with spoon until smooth. Add turkey, salt, onion, garlic, mustard and Worcestershire sauce; stir gently until combined. Using wet hands, shape meatballs into 64 (1½-inch) balls.

3 Place meatballs on cookie sheets; cover with plastic wrap. Freeze until firm, at least 2 hours. Transfer meatballs to freezer containers or resealable freezer plastic bags; seal tightly. Freeze up to 3 months.

4 Heat oven to 400°F. Line cookie sheets with foil; place metal cooling racks on cookie sheets. Spray racks with cooking spray. Dip or brush bottoms of frozen meatballs with oil; place 1 inch apart on racks.

5 Bake 45 to 50 minutes or until instant-read thermometer inserted in center of meatball reads 165°F.

2 Meatballs: Calories 110; Total Fat 7g (Saturated Fat 1.5g, Trans Fat 0g); Cholesterol 40mg; Sodium 220mg; Total Carbohydrate 4g (Dietary Fiber 0g); Protein 8g **Exchanges:** 1 Very Lean Meat, 1½ Fat **Carbohydrate Choices:** 0

In a Flash Warm pizza sauce (from a jar or can) is perfect for these meatballs. If serving them as an appetizer, use the sauce for dipping, or use the sauce for reheating already cooked meatballs on the stove.

Mediterranean Turkey Meatball Taco Boats

4 servings | Prep Time: 15 Minutes | Start to Finish: 50 Minutes

• • •

MEATBALLS AND SHELLS

Freezer Short-cut

8   **frozen uncooked Freezer-Friendly Turkey Meatballs (recipe on page 146)**

1   tablespoon olive oil

½   teaspoon curry powder

⅛   teaspoon ground red pepper (cayenne)

4   boat-shaped flour tortillas

TOPPINGS

⅓   cup Greek plain yogurt

¼   cup diced red onion

¼   cup diced cucumber

⅛   teaspoon salt

1   cup shredded romaine lettuce

¼   cup diced tomato

¼   cup crumbled feta cheese (1 oz)

1   Heat oven to 400°F. Line cookie sheet with foil; place metal cooling rack on cookie sheet. Spray rack with cooking spray.

2   In resealable food-storage plastic bag, place frozen meatballs, oil, curry powder and red pepper; seal bag and toss to coat. Place meatballs on half of rack; bake 30 minutes.

3   Place tortillas on other half of rack. Bake about 3 minutes longer or until tortillas are golden brown on edges and instant-read thermometer inserted in meatball reads 165°F.

4   Meanwhile, in small bowl, stir together yogurt, onion, cucumber and salt. Cut meatballs in half.

5   To serve, place ¼ cup lettuce in each tortilla boat. Top each with 4 meatball halves, the yogurt mixture, tomato and cheese.

1 Serving: Calories 270; Total Fat 16g (Saturated Fat 4.5g, Trans Fat 0g); Cholesterol 50mg; Sodium 570mg; Total Carbohydrate 20g (Dietary Fiber 1g); Protein 13g **Exchanges:** 1 Starch, ½ Vegetable, 1½ Very Lean Meat, 3 Fat **Carbohydrate Choices:** 1

Turkey Meatball Tacos

4 tacos | Prep Time: 15 Minutes | Start to Finish: 50 Minutes

• • •

Freezer Short-cut

8 **frozen uncooked Freezer-Friendly Turkey Meatballs (recipe on page 146)**

1 **tablespoon olive oil**

¾ **teaspoon ground cumin**

¾ **teaspoon ground coriander**

4 **taco shells**

1 **cup shredded lettuce**

12 **very thin slices jalapeño chiles**

¼ **cup salsa**

½ **avocado, diced**

¼ **cup crumbled queso fresco cheese (1 oz)**

¼ **cup chopped fresh cilantro**

1 Heat oven to 400°F. Line cookie sheet with foil; place metal cooling rack on cookie sheet. Spray rack with cooking spray.

2 In resealable food-storage plastic bag, place frozen meatballs, oil, cumin and coriander; seal bag and toss to coat. Place meatballs on half of rack; bake 30 minutes.

3 Place taco shells on other half of rack. Bake about 3 minutes longer or until instant-read thermometer inserted in meatball reads 165°F. Cut meatballs in half.

4 To serve, place ¼ cup lettuce in each taco shell. Top each with 4 meatball halves, the chiles, salsa, avocado, cheese and cilantro.

1 Taco: Calories 280; Total Fat 18g (Saturated Fat 4.5g, Trans Fat 0g); Cholesterol 45mg; Sodium 460mg; Total Carbohydrate 16g (Dietary Fiber 2g); Protein 11g **Exchanges:** 1 Starch, 1 Lean Meat, 3 Fat **Carbohydrate Choices:** 1

Creamy Meatballs and Potatoes

4 servings (1⅓ cups each) | Prep Time: 25 Minutes | Start to Finish: 25 Minutes

· · ·

2 cups refrigerated cooked potato wedges (from 20-oz bag)

1 can (10¾ oz) condensed cream of onion soup

¼ cup water

2 cups frozen broccoli florets (from 12-oz bag)

Freezer Short-cut

24 frozen Freezer-Friendly Turkey Meatballs (recipe on page 146), cooked

¼ cup sour cream

1 In 12-inch nonstick skillet, gently stir potatoes, soup and water. Heat to boiling; reduce heat to low. Simmer 5 minutes, stirring occasionally.

2 Stir in broccoli and cooked meatballs. Simmer 10 to 15 minutes, stirring occasionally, until broccoli and potatoes are tender. Add sour cream; cook and stir just until hot.

1 Serving: Calories 520; Total Fat 23g (Saturated Fat 7g, Trans Fat 0g); Cholesterol 190mg; Sodium 1550mg; Total Carbohydrate 39g (Dietary Fiber 5g); Protein 39g **Exchanges:** 1 Starch, 1 Other Carbohydrate, 1 Vegetable, 1½ Fat **Carbohydrate Choices:** 2½

Fresh Idea **If your family likes green beans or peas, go ahead and substitute either for the broccoli. You can also substitute condensed cream of mushroom for the onion soup.**

Slow-Cooker Turkey Mole Chili

6 servings (1½ cups each) | Prep Time: 15 Minutes | Start to Finish: 8 Hours 15 Minutes

• • •

2½	lb lean ground turkey
1	large onion, chopped (1 cup)
2	medium carrots, chopped (about 1 cup)
1	can (28 oz) diced tomatoes, undrained
1	can (15 oz) black beans, drained, rinsed
1	jar (8¼ oz) mole
1¾	cups chicken broth
½	cup sour cream
½	cup crumbled cotija (white Mexican) cheese (2 oz)

1 In 12-inch nonstick skillet, cook turkey over medium-high heat 5 to 7 minutes, stirring occasionally, until no longer pink; drain.

2 Spray 4- to 5-quart slow cooker with cooking spray. In slow cooker, mix turkey, onion, carrots, tomatoes, beans, mole and broth.

3 Cover; cook on Low heat setting 8 to 10 hours. Stir well before serving. Top individual servings with sour cream and cheese.

4 To freeze, cool completely. Transfer individual portions to freezer containers; seal tightly. Freeze up to 3 months. Thaw 12 to 24 hours in refrigerator until completely thawed. Reheat in microwave or on stove.

1 Serving: Calories 610; Total Fat 26g (Saturated Fat 7g, Trans Fat 0g); Cholesterol 0mg; Sodium 1840mg; Total Carbohydrate 32g (Dietary Fiber 6g); Protein 47g **Exchanges:** ½ Starch, 1 Other Carbohydrate, 2 Vegetable, 5½ Lean Meat, 4 Fat **Carbohydrate Choices:** 1½

Fresh Ideas Cotija cheese is a hard, white cheese made from cow's milk. Look for it in small rounds or large blocks in the dairy or cheese aisle of your grocery store. If you can't find it, try crumbled Feta.

Mole, pronounced "MOH-lay," is a dark reddish-brown Mexican sauce made from chiles, onion, garlic, chocolate, ground sesame or pumpkin seeds and other spices. Prepared mole is a thicker paste, which cooks with the ingredients in this recipe to make a savory sauce perfect for chili.

Cheesy Grilled Turkey Burgers

12 burgers | Prep Time: 40 Minutes | Start to Finish: 40 Minutes

- - -

- **3** lb ground turkey breast
- **1** or 2 jalapeño chiles, seeded, chopped
- **1** cup diced pepper Jack cheese
- **¾** teaspoon pepper
- **1½** cups chunky-style salsa
- **12** burger buns, split
- **12** slices tomato

  Additional chunky-style salsa, if desired

1 In large bowl, mix turkey, chiles, cheese, pepper and 1½ cups salsa. Shape mixture into 12 patties, about ¾ inch thick.

2 Wrap patties tightly. Freeze up to 3 months. Thaw in refrigerator overnight.

3 Heat gas or charcoal grill. Place patties on grill over medium heat. Cover grill; cook 12 to 15 minutes, turning once, until thermometer inserted in center of patties reads 165°F. During last 2 minutes of cooking, add buns, cut sides down, to grill.

4 Serve burgers on buns with tomato slices and additional salsa.

1 Burger: Calories 350; Total Fat 15g (Saturated Fat 5g, Trans Fat 0.5g); Cholesterol 95mg; Sodium 560mg; Total Carbohydrate 25g (Dietary Fiber 1g); Protein 29g **Exchanges:** 1½ Starch, 3½ Lean Meat, ½ Fat **Carbohydrate Choices:** 1½

In a Flash These grilled burgers also freeze well; just thaw and reheat these easy burgers for nights when you need dinner on the table really fast.

White Lasagna Roll-Ups with Turkey and Prosciutto

16 roll-ups | Prep Time: 50 Minutes | Start to Finish: 2 Hours 30 Minutes

• • •

ROLL-UPS

16	uncooked lasagna noodles
2	tablespoons olive oil
1¼	lb ground turkey
1	teaspoon salt
1	package (8 oz) sliced fresh mushrooms (about 3 cups), finely chopped
1	box (9 oz) frozen chopped spinach, thawed, squeezed to drain
1	container (15 oz) ricotta cheese
2	eggs, slightly beaten
1	teaspoon Italian seasoning
1	teaspoon crushed red pepper flakes
3	oz prosciutto, torn into small strips

TOPPINGS

1	jar (15 oz) Alfredo pasta sauce
1	cup shredded Italian cheese blend (4 oz)
½	cup shredded fresh basil leaves

Fresh Idea Not a fan of prosciutto? Feel free to leave it out — the roll-ups will be just as delicious without it. And, shredded Parmesan cheese makes a nice substitute for the Italian cheese blend.

1. Line 15x10x1-inch pan with foil. Cook and drain lasagna noodles as directed on package. Rinse with hot water; drain well.

2. Meanwhile, in 12-inch nonstick skillet, heat oil over medium-high heat. Add turkey and salt; cook 5 to 6 minutes, stirring occasionally, until turkey is no longer pink. Add mushrooms; cook 5 to 8 minutes or until browned. Transfer to medium bowl; cool 10 minutes.

3. Add spinach, ricotta cheese, eggs, Italian seasoning and pepper flakes to turkey mixture; stir well. Spread slightly less than ⅓ cup mixture down center of each cooked noodle to within 1 inch of one short end. Top evenly with prosciutto strips. Roll up firmly toward unfilled end.

4. Place roll-ups, seam sides down, in pan; cover loosely with foil. Freeze about 30 minutes or until firm. Wrap tightly. Freeze up to 3 months. Thaw in refrigerator at least 8 hours but no longer than 24 hours.

5. Heat oven to 350°F. Spray two 13x9-inch (3-quart) glass baking dishes with cooking spray. Place 8 roll-ups in each baking dish. Pour Alfredo sauce over and down sides of roll-ups in each baking dish.

6. Cover tightly; bake 40 to 50 minutes or until hot and bubbly. Uncover; sprinkle each dish with ½ cup cheese. Bake 3 to 5 minutes longer or until cheese is melted. Let stand 5 minutes before serving. Top with basil.

1 Roll-Up: Calories 330; Total Fat 19g (Saturated Fat 9g, Trans Fat 0g); Cholesterol 95mg; Sodium 530mg; Total Carbohydrate 22g (Dietary Fiber 1g); Protein 19g **Exchanges:** 1 Starch, ½ Other Carbohydrate, 1½ Lean Meat, ½ High-Fat Meat, 2 Fat **Carbohydrate Choices:** 1½

Cheesy Turkey-Spinach Lasagna Roll-Ups

16 roll-ups | Prep Time: 50 Minutes | Start to Finish: 2 Hours 30 Minutes

• • •

ROLL-UPS

- 16 uncooked lasagna noodles
- 1 tablespoon olive oil
- 1¼ lb ground turkey
- 4 cloves garlic, chopped
- 1 tablespoon Italian seasoning
- 1 jar (26 oz) Italian herb tomato pasta sauce
- 2 boxes (9 oz each) frozen chopped spinach, thawed, squeezed to drain
- 1 cup shredded carrots, if desired
- 1 container (15 oz) whole milk ricotta cheese
- 2 eggs

TOPPINGS

- 1 jar (26 oz) Italian herb tomato pasta sauce
- 2 cups shredded mozzarella cheese (8 oz)
- ½ cup julienne-cut fresh basil leaves

Fresh Idea Try bulk Italian sausage or ground chicken in place of the turkey, and roasted garlic or tomato basil pasta sauce instead of Italian herb sauce.

1 Line 15x10x1-inch pan with foil. Cook and drain lasagna noodles as directed on package. Rinse with hot water; drain well.

2 Meanwhile, in 12-inch nonstick skillet, heat oil over medium-high heat. Add turkey, garlic and Italian seasoning; cook 5 to 6 minutes, stirring occasionally, until turkey is no longer pink. Stir in 1 jar pasta sauce; heat to boiling. Reduce heat to low; cook 10 minutes, stirring occasionally. Transfer to medium bowl; cool 10 minutes.

3 In medium bowl, mix spinach, carrots, ricotta cheese and eggs. Spread slightly less than ¼ cup ricotta mixture down center of each cooked noodle. Spread ¼ cup turkey mixture over ricotta mixture to within 1 inch of one short end. Roll up firmly toward unfilled end.

4 Place roll-ups, seam sides down, in pan; cover loosely with foil. Freeze about 30 minutes or until firm. Wrap tightly. Freeze up to 3 months. Thaw in refrigerator at least 8 hours but no longer than 24 hours.

5 Heat oven to 350°F. Spray two 13x9-inch (3-quart) glass baking dishes with cooking spray. Place 8 roll-ups in each baking dish. Pour 1 jar pasta sauce over and down sides of roll-ups.

6 Cover tightly; bake 40 to 50 minutes or until hot and bubbly. Uncover; sprinkle each dish with 1 cup mozzarella cheese. Bake 3 to 5 minutes longer or until cheese is melted. Let stand 5 minutes before serving. Top with basil.

1 Roll-Up: Calories 290; Total Fat 12g (Saturated Fat 5g, Trans Fat 0g); Cholesterol 70mg; Sodium 490mg; Total Carbohydrate 27g (Dietary Fiber 3g); Protein 20g **Exchanges:** 1 Starch, ½ Other Carbohydrate, 1 Vegetable, 2 Lean Meat, 1 Fat **Carbohydrate Choices:** 2

chapter four

Fish & Seafood

Fresh Flounder Rolls

12 sandwiches | Prep Time: 35 Minutes | Start to Finish: 35 Minutes

* * *

FISH AND BUNS

- 2 lb fresh flounder, halibut or cod fillets, skin removed
- ½ cup milk
- 1 egg
- 1 cup panko crispy bread crumbs
- 1 teaspoon salt
- 2 tablespoons vegetable oil
- 2 tablespoons butter, melted
- 12 hot dog buns, split

  Lemon slices, if desired

  Fresh dill weed sprigs, if desired

CUCUMBER SAUCE

- 1 container (6 oz) Greek plain yogurt
- 3 tablespoons mayonnaise
- 1 medium cucumber, peeled, seeded and coarsely grated
- 3 tablespoons chopped fresh dill weed
- 1 tablespoon chopped green onion (1 medium)
- 1 tablespoon lemon juice
- ½ teaspoon salt

1 Cut fish into 12 serving pieces. In pie plate, mix milk and egg. In another pie plate, mix bread crumbs and salt. Dip fish into milk mixture; roll in bread crumbs. Shake off excess crumbs.

2 In 12-inch skillet, heat oil over medium-high heat. Cook fish in oil 10 to 12 minutes, turning once, until fish flakes easily with fork.

3 To freeze, cool fish completely. Wrap tightly. Freeze up to 3 months. Thaw in refrigerator overnight.

4 Reheat fish in hot oven. Meanwhile, in small bowl, mix all sauce ingredients.

5 Heat 10-inch skillet over medium heat. Brush melted butter on cut sides of buns. Place buns, cut sides down, in skillet; cook about 3 minutes or until toasted. Serve fish on buns with sauce. Garnish with lemon and dill sprigs.

1 Sandwich: Calories 280; Total Fat 11g (Saturated Fat 3g, Trans Fat 0g); Cholesterol 55mg; Sodium 630mg; Total Carbohydrate 30g (Dietary Fiber 1g); Protein 15g **Exchanges:** 1½ Starch, ½ Other Carbohydrate, 1½ Very Lean Meat, 2 Fat **Carbohydrate Choices:** 2

Fresh Idea For food truck–inspired sandwiches, start with bigger buns for more filling — substitute French bread for the hot dog buns. Then top the fish with a slice of cheddar cheese, coleslaw or sliced avocado and cucumber.

Fish Sticks Marinara

6 servings | Prep Time: 10 Minutes | Start to Finish: 40 Minutes

● ● ◑

2 boxes (9 oz each) frozen broccoli spears, thawed, drained

1 tablespoon olive or vegetable oil

½ teaspoon dried basil leaves

1 clove garlic, chopped

12 frozen breaded fish sticks

Freezer Short-cut

2 cups Make-Ahead Roasted Roma Tomato Sauce (recipe on page 194)

¼ cup shredded Parmesan cheese (1 oz)

6 slices (1 oz each) mozzarella cheese

1 Heat oven to 350°F. Arrange broccoli in ungreased 8-inch square (2-quart) glass baking dish. Drizzle with oil; sprinkle with basil and garlic.

2 Place fish sticks on broccoli. Spoon tomato sauce over fish. Sprinkle with Parmesan cheese. Arrange mozzarella cheese on top.

3 Bake uncovered about 30 minutes or until thoroughly heated.

1 Serving: Calories 330; Total Fat 17g (Saturated Fat 6g, Trans Fat 1g); Cholesterol 30mg; Sodium 700mg; Total Carbohydrate 26g (Dietary Fiber 3g); Protein 17g **Exchanges:** 1½ Other Carbohydrate, 1 Vegetable, 2 Medium-Fat Meat, 1½ Fat **Carbohydrate Choices:** 2

In a Flash No Make-Ahead Roma sauce in the freezer? Use 2 cups of purchased marinara sauce.

Pecan-Crusted Fish Fillets

4 servings | Prep Time: 25 Minutes | Start to Finish: 25 Minutes

· · ·

1 lb sole, orange roughy, walleye or other delicate-to medium-texture fish fillets (about ½ inch thick), skin removed

½ teaspoon salt

¼ teaspoon pepper

1 cup finely chopped pecans (not ground)

¼ cup unseasoned dry bread crumbs

2 teaspoons grated lemon peel

1 egg

1 tablespoon milk

2 tablespoons vegetable oil

Lemon wedges

1 Cut fish into 4 serving pieces. Sprinkle both sides with salt and pepper. In shallow dish, mix pecans, bread crumbs and lemon peel. In another shallow dish, beat egg and milk with fork or whisk until blended.

2 Dip fish into egg mixture, then coat well with pecan mixture, pressing lightly into fish.

3 In 12-inch nonstick skillet, heat oil over medium heat. Add fish. Reduce heat to medium-low. Cook 6 to 10 minutes, carefully turning once with 2 pancake turners, until fish flakes easily with fork and is browned. Serve with lemon wedges.

4 To freeze, cool fillets completely. Wrap tightly. Freeze up to 3 months. Thaw in refrigerator overnight. Reheat in hot oven.

1 Serving: Calories 350; Total Fat 25g (Saturated Fat 3g, Trans Fat 0g); Cholesterol 105mg; Sodium 450mg; Total Carbohydrate 9g (Dietary Fiber 3g); Protein 24g **Exchanges:** ½ Starch, 3 Lean Meat, 3 Fat **Carbohydrate Choices:** ½

Fish Sandwiches with Lemon-Basil Mayo

6 sandwiches | Prep Time: 15 Minutes | Start to Finish: 35 Minutes

• • •

SANDWICHES

- 1 cup Fiber One™ original bran cereal
- 1 teaspoon grated lemon peel
- ¼ teaspoon salt
- ¼ cup reduced-fat mayonnaise
- 2 tablespoons fat-free (skim) milk
- 6 cod fillets (4 oz each), patted dry
- Cooking spray
- 6 leaves lettuce
- 6 whole wheat burger buns, split
- 12 slices tomato

LEMON-BASIL MAYO

- ½ cup reduced-fat mayonnaise
- 3 tablespoons chopped fresh basil leaves
- ½ teaspoon grated lemon peel

1 Heat oven to 400°F. Spray large cookie sheet with sides with cooking spray.

2 Place cereal in resealable food-storage plastic bag; seal bag and finely crush with rolling pin or meat mallet (or finely crush in food processor).

3 In shallow dish, mix cereal, 1 teaspoon lemon peel and the salt; mix well. In another shallow dish, beat ¼ cup mayonnaise and the milk with whisk until smooth. Dip each fillet into mayonnaise mixture, coating all sides. Coat thoroughly with crumb mixture. Place on cookie sheet. Spray fillets with cooking spray.

4 Bake about 20 minutes or until fish flakes easily with fork and crust is golden brown. To freeze, cool fillets completely. Wrap tightly. Freeze up to 3 months. Thaw 12 to 24 hours in refrigerator until completely thawed. Reheat in hot oven.

5 Meanwhile, in small bowl, mix ½ cup mayonnaise, the basil and ½ teaspoon lemon peel. (Mayo can be made up to 2 days ahead; cover and refrigerate.) For each sandwich, place lettuce leaf on bun bottoms. Top with fish, 2 slices tomato and 1 rounded tablespoon lemon-basil mayo. Cover with bun tops.

1 Sandwich: Calories 310; Total Fat 6g (Saturated Fat 1g, Trans Fat 0g); Cholesterol 70mg; Sodium 710mg; Total Carbohydrate 34g (Dietary Fiber 8g); Protein 28g **Exchanges:** 1½ Starch, ½ Other Carbohydrate, ½ Vegetable, 3 Very Lean Meat, 1 Fat **Carbohydrate Choices:** 2

Fresh Idea If you don't have fresh basil on hand, you can use fresh chives.

Salmon Patties with Sour Cream–Dill Sauce

4 servings | Prep Time: 25 Minutes | Start to Finish: 25 Minutes

• • •

PATTIES

- 1 egg
- 2 tablespoons milk
- 1 can (14¾ oz) salmon, drained, skin and bones removed, flaked
- 2 medium green onions, chopped (2 tablespoons)
- 1 cup soft bread crumbs (about 1½ slices bread)
- ¼ teaspoon salt
- 1 tablespoon vegetable oil

SOUR CREAM–DILL SAUCE

- ⅓ cup sour cream
- 3 tablespoons mayonnaise or salad dressing
- ¾ teaspoon dried dill weed

1 In medium bowl, beat egg and milk with fork or whisk. Stir in salmon, onions, bread crumbs and salt. Shape mixture into 4 patties, about 4 inches in diameter.

2 Wrap patties tightly. Freeze up to 3 months. Thaw in refrigerator overnight.

3 In 10-inch nonstick skillet, heat oil over medium heat. Cook patties in oil about 8 minutes, turning once, until golden brown.

4 Meanwhile, in small bowl, stir all sauce ingredients until well mixed. Serve patties with sauce.

1 Serving: Calories 300; Total Fat 22g (Saturated Fat 6g, Trans Fat 0g); Cholesterol 120mg; Sodium 750mg; Total Carbohydrate 6g (Dietary Fiber 0g); Protein 20g **Exchanges:** ½ Starch, 2½ Lean Meat, 3 Fat **Carbohydrate Choices:** ½

In a Flash Need dinner on the run? Turn these patties into fantastic burgers by serving in hamburger buns topped with cucumber and tomato slices.

Lemon-Herb Salmon

4 servings | Prep Time: 25 Minutes | Start to Finish: 25 Minutes

• • •

MARINADE

- ¼ **cup vegetable oil**
- 1 **teaspoon grated lemon peel**
- ¼ **cup fresh lemon juice**
- 1 **teaspoon dried marjoram leaves**
- ½ **teaspoon dried tarragon leaves**
- ¼ **teaspoon dried thyme leaves**
- ¼ **teaspoon salt**

FISH

- 1 **salmon fillet (1 lb and about 1 inch thick), cut into 4 serving pieces***

1 In 1-gallon resealable freezer plastic bag, place all marinade ingredients; seal bag and knead to combine. Add salmon; seal bag. Turn bag to coat salmon with marinade.

2 Lay bag flat in freezer. Freeze up to 3 months. Thaw 12 to 24 hours in refrigerator until completely thawed.

3 Heat gas or charcoal grill. Remove salmon from marinade; reserve marinade. Carefully brush oil on grill rack. Place salmon on grill over medium heat (if salmon has skin, place skin side down). Cover grill; cook 10 to 12 minutes, brushing 2 or 3 times with reserved marinade, until fish flakes easily with fork. Discard any remaining marinade.

*Center-cut salmon fillets are evenly shaped and not tapered, making them perfect for cutting into crosswise serving pieces. If your salmon is thinner or thicker than 1 inch, adjust the cooking time accordingly.

1 Serving: Calories 210; Total Fat 14g (Saturated Fat 2.5g, Trans Fat 0g); Cholesterol 55g; Sodium 90mg; Total Carbohydrate 0g (Dietary Fiber 0g); Protein 19g **Exchanges:** 3 Lean Meat, 1 Fat **Carbohydrate Choices:** 0

To Broil: Set oven control to broil. Remove salmon from marinade; reserve marinade. Place salmon on rack in broiler pan (if salmon has skin, place skin side down). Broil with tops 4 to 6 inches from heat 10 to 14 minutes, brushing 2 or 3 times with reserved marinade, until fish flakes easily with fork. Discard any remaining marinade.

Creamy Seafood Lasagna

8 servings | Prep Time: 40 Minutes | Start to Finish: 1 Hour 40 Minutes

• • •

9   uncooked lasagna noodles

¼   cup butter

1   medium onion, finely chopped (½ cup)

2   cloves garlic, finely chopped

¼   cup all-purpose flour

2   cups half-and-half

1   cup chicken broth

⅓   cup dry sherry or chicken broth

½   teaspoon salt

¼   teaspoon pepper

1   container (15 oz) ricotta cheese

½   cup grated Parmesan cheese

1   egg, slightly beaten

¼   cup chopped fresh parsley

2   packages (8 oz each) frozen salad-style imitation crabmeat, thawed, drained and chopped

2   packages (4 oz each) frozen cooked salad shrimp, thawed, drained

3   cups shredded mozzarella cheese (12 oz)

1   tablespoon chopped fresh parsley, if desired

1   Cook and drain noodles as directed on package. Meanwhile, in 3-quart saucepan, melt butter over medium heat. Cook onion and garlic in butter 2 to 3 minutes, stirring occasionally, until onion is crisp-tender. Stir in flour; cook and stir until bubbly. Gradually stir in half-and-half, broth, sherry, salt and pepper. Heat to boiling, stirring constantly. Boil and stir 1 minute; remove from heat.

2   In medium bowl, mix ricotta cheese, Parmesan cheese, egg and ¼ cup parsley.

3   In ungreased 13x9-inch (3-quart) glass baking dish, spread ¾ cup of the white sauce. Top with 3 noodles. Spread half of the imitation crabmeat and shrimp over noodles; spread with ¾ cup of the sauce. Sprinkle with 1 cup of the mozzarella cheese; top with 3 noodles. Spread ricotta mixture over noodles; spread with ¾ cup of the sauce. Sprinkle with 1 cup of the mozzarella cheese; top with remaining noodles. Spread with remaining crabmeat, shrimp and sauce. Sprinkle with remaining 1 cup mozzarella cheese.

4   Cover baking dish tightly. Freeze up to 3 months. Thaw in refrigerator overnight.

5   Heat oven to 350°F. Uncover baking dish. Bake 40 to 45 minutes or until cheese is light golden brown. Let stand 15 minutes before cutting. Sprinkle with 1 tablespoon parsley.

1 Serving: Calories 560; Total Fat 29g (Saturated Fat 17g, Trans Fat 1g); Cholesterol 180mg; Sodium 1400mg; Total Carbohydrate 33g (Dietary Fiber 2g); Protein 41g **Exchanges:** 2 Starch, 5 Medium-Fat Meat, ½ Fat **Carbohydrate Choices:** 2

Biscuit Tuna Melts

8 servings (½ sandwich each) | Prep Time: 15 Minutes | Start to Finish: 35 Minutes

• • •

2 cans (5 oz each) tuna in water, well drained

⅓ cup chopped onion

⅓ cup mayonnaise

⅛ teaspoon salt

⅛ teaspoon pepper

1 can (16.3 oz) large refrigerated flaky biscuits

1 cup shredded Cheddar cheese (4 oz)

Sour cream, if desired

Chopped tomato, if desired

Shredded lettuce, if desired

1 Heat oven to 350°F. Spray cookie sheet with cooking spray. In medium bowl, mix tuna, onion, mayonnaise, salt and pepper.

2 Separate dough into 8 biscuits. Place 4 of the biscuits on cookie sheet; press or roll each to form 5-inch round. Spoon tuna mixture onto center of biscuits. Top with cheese. Press or roll remaining 4 biscuits to form 5-inch rounds. Place over filling; press edges to seal.

3 Bake 15 to 20 minutes or until golden brown. Cut each sandwich in half. Top with sour cream, tomato and lettuce.

4 To freeze, cool sandwiches completely. Wrap tightly. Freeze up to 3 months. Thaw in refrigerator overnight. Reheat in hot oven.

1 Serving: Calories 350; Total Fat 21g (Saturated Fat 6g, Trans Fat 3.5g); Cholesterol 30mg; Sodium 840mg; Total Carbohydrate 25g (Dietary Fiber 0g); Protein 15g **Exchanges:** 1½ Starch, 1½ Lean Meat, 3 Fat **Carbohydrate Choices:** 1½

Fresh Idea Top the tuna mixture with a few slices of jalapeño before adding the cheese for an extra kick of flavor.

Impossibly Easy Tuna, Tomato and Cheddar Pie

6 servings | Prep Time: 20 Minutes | Start to Finish: 1 Hour

• • •

1 tablespoon butter

1 large onion, chopped (1 cup)

1 can (5 oz) tuna in water, drained

1 cup shredded Cheddar cheese (4 oz)

½ cup Original Bisquick mix

1 cup milk

⅛ teaspoon pepper

2 eggs

1 medium tomato, thinly sliced

1   Spray 9-inch pie plate with cooking spray. In 10-inch skillet, melt butter over low heat. Cook onion in butter, stirring occasionally, until tender. Sprinkle tuna, ½ cup of the cheese and the onion in pie plate.

2   In medium bowl, stir Bisquick mix, milk, pepper and eggs with whisk or fork until blended. Pour into pie plate.

3   Cover tightly; refrigerate up to 24 hours.

4   Heat oven to 400°F. Uncover pie. Bake 30 minutes or until knife inserted in center comes out clean. Top with tomato slices and remaining ½ cup cheese. Bake 3 to 5 minutes longer or until cheese is melted. Let stand 5 minutes before serving.

1 Serving: Calories 210; Total Fat 12g (Saturated Fat 7g, Trans Fat 0.5g); Cholesterol 1C5mg; Sodium 340mg; Total Carbohydrate 12g (Dietary Fiber 1g); Protein 13g **Exchanges:** ½ Starch, 1 Vegetable, 1½ Lean Meat, 1½ Fat **Carbohydrate Choices:** 1

Tuna Burgers

4 burgers | Prep Time: 25 Minutes | Start to Finish: 25 Minutes

• • •

1   **cup soft bread crumbs (about 2 slices bread)**

½   **cup Original Bisquick mix**

1   **tablespoon Dijon mustard**

¼   **teaspoon pepper**

2   **eggs, slightly beaten**

8   **medium green onions, finely chopped (½ cup)**

2   **pouches (about 7 oz each) light tuna in water, drained, flaked**

2   **tablespoons butter**

4   **burger buns, split**

4   **tablespoons dill dip**

1 In medium bowl, mix bread crumbs, Bisquick mix, mustard, pepper, eggs, onions and tuna. Shape mixture into 4 patties, 3½ inches in diameter.

2 Wrap patties tightly. Freeze up to 3 months. Thaw in refrigerator overnight.

3 In 12-inch nonstick skillet, melt butter over medium heat. Cook patties in butter 10 to 12 minutes, turning once, until browned and thoroughly cooked. Serve on buns with dill dip.

1 Burger: Calories 440; Total Fat 16g (Saturated Fat 7g, Trans Fat 1g); Cholesterol 155mg; Sodium 1090mg; Total Carbohydrate 39g (Dietary Fiber 2g); Protein 34g **Exchanges:** 2½ Starch, 4 Very Lean Meat, 2½ Fat **Carbohydrate Choices:** 2½

Crab Cake Burgers
Substitute two 5-ounce cans of crabmeat for the tuna.

Fresh Idea **For added crunch, top burgers with thinly sliced cucumber and sliced red onion.**

Classic Crab Cakes

6 crab cakes | Prep Time: 25 Minutes | Start to Finish: 25 Minutes

- - -

⅓ cup mayonnaise or salad dressing

1 egg

1¼ cups soft white bread crumbs (about 2 slices bread)

1 teaspoon ground mustard

¼ teaspoon salt

¼ teaspoon ground red pepper (cayenne), if desired

⅛ teaspoon black pepper

2 medium green onions, chopped (2 tablespoons)

1 can (1 lb) or 2 refrigerated containers (8 oz each) pasteurized lump crabmeat, well drained, cartilage removed*

2 tablespoons vegetable oil

¼ cup unseasoned dry bread crumbs

1 In medium bowl, mix mayonnaise and egg with whisk. Gently stir in soft bread crumbs, mustard, salt, red pepper, black pepper, onions and crabmeat so that crabmeat doesn't break apart into small pieces. Shape mixture into 6 patties, about 3 inches in diameter (mixture will be moist).

2 Wrap patties tightly. Freeze up to 3 months. Thaw in refrigerator overnight.

3 In 12-inch nonstick skillet, heat oil over medium heat. Coat patties with dry bread crumbs. Cook patties in oil about 10 minutes, gently turning once, until golden brown and hot in center. Reduce heat if crab cakes become brown too quickly.

*3 cans (6 ounces each) lump crabmeat can be substituted for the 1-pound can or the refrigerated crabmeat.

1 Crab Cake: Calories 330; Total Fat 18g (Saturated Fat 3g, Trans Fat 0g); Cholesterol 120mg; Sodium 690mg; Total Carbohydrate 20g (Dietary Fiber 0g); Protein 22g **Exchanges:** 1 Starch, 3 Lean Meat, 2 Fat **Carbohydrate Choices:** 1

Salmon Cakes Substitute

1 can (15 ounces) red salmon, drained, for the lump crabmeat.

Easy Shrimp Tacos

8 tacos | Prep Time: 20 Minutes | Start to Finish: 20 Minutes

• • •

SHRIMP

1	teaspoon ground cumin
1	teaspoon chili powder
½	teaspoon salt
¼	teaspoon smoked paprika
2	tablespoons vegetable oil
1	lb uncooked medium fresh shrimp, peeled, deveined

TACOS

8	flour tortillas (6 inch), heated as directed on package
1	cup thinly sliced cabbage
½	cup shredded Monterey Jack cheese (2 oz)
½	cup chunky-style salsa
1	large avocado, pitted, peeled and cubed
½	cup sour cream

1 In 1-gallon resealable freezer plastic bag, place cumin, chili powder, salt and paprika; seal bag and shake to mix ingredients. Add oil and shrimp; seal bag. Turn bag to coat shrimp with oil and seasonings.

2 Lay bag flat in freezer. Freeze up to 3 months. Thaw 12 to 24 hours in refrigerator until completely thawed.

3 Heat 10-inch nonstick skillet over medium heat. Add shrimp mixture; cook 3 to 4 minutes, stirring frequently, until shrimp are pink.

4 To serve, divide shrimp among warm tortillas. Top evenly with cabbage, cheese, salsa, avocado and sour cream.

1 Taco: Calories 240; Total Fat 13g (Saturated Fat 4.5g, Trans Fat 0.5g); Cholesterol 90mg; Sodium 570mg; Total Carbohydrate 16g (Dietary Fiber 2g); Protein 14g **Exchanges:** ½ Starch, ½ Other Carbohydrate, 2 Very Lean Meat, 2½ Fat **Carbohydrate Choices:** 1

Fresh Idea You can substitute shredded lettuce for the cabbage, if you like.

Shrimp Creole

6 servings | Prep Time: 30 Minutes | Start to Finish: 1 Hour

· · ·

¼ cup butter

3 medium onions, chopped (1½ cups)

2 medium green bell peppers, finely chopped (2 cups)

2 medium stalks celery, finely chopped (1 cup)

2 cloves garlic, finely chopped

1 can (15 oz) tomato sauce

1 cup water

2 teaspoons chopped fresh parsley

1½ teaspoons salt

¼ teaspoon ground red pepper (cayenne)

2 dried bay leaves

2 lb frozen (do not thaw) uncooked medium shrimp, peeled, deveined (tail shells removed)

3 cups hot cooked rice

1 In 3-quart saucepan, melt butter over medium heat. Cook onions, bell peppers, celery and garlic in butter about 10 minutes, stirring occasionally, until onions are tender. Stir in remaining ingredients except shrimp and rice. Heat to boiling; reduce heat to low. Simmer uncovered 10 minutes. Remove from heat.

2 Cool completely. Transfer to freezer container; seal tightly. Freeze up to 3 months. Thaw in refrigerator overnight.

3 Transfer Creole mixture to 3-quart saucepan. Heat to boiling; reduce heat to medium. Rinse frozen shrimp in hot water; add to saucepan. Cover; cook 4 to 6 minutes, stirring occasionally, until shrimp are pink. Remove and discard bay leaves. Serve shrimp mixture over rice.

1 Serving: Calories 350; Total Fat 10g (Saturated Fat 6g, Trans Fat 0g); Cholesterol 255mg; Sodium 2380mg; Total Carbohydrate 36g (Dietary Fiber 3g); Protein 29g **Exchanges:** 1½ Starch, ½ Other Carbohydrate, 1 Vegetable, 3 Very Lean Meat, 1½ Fat **Carbohydrate Choices:** 2½

Corn and Shrimp Chowder

7 servings (1⅓ cups each) | Prep Time: 35 Minutes | Start to Finish: 50 Minutes

● ● ○

4 slices bacon, cut into ½-inch pieces

1 medium onion, coarsely chopped (½ cup)

1 medium stalk celery, coarsely chopped (½ cup)

6 small red potatoes, cut into ½-inch pieces

2 cups frozen whole kernel corn

¼ teaspoon dried thyme leaves

1 carton (32 oz) chicken broth (4 cups)

¼ cup quick-mixing flour

12 oz frozen (do not thaw) uncooked medium shrimp, peeled, deveined (tail shells removed)

2 cups half-and-half

½ teaspoon salt

⅛ teaspoon pepper

1. In 4-quart Dutch oven or stockpot, cook bacon over medium-high heat 5 to 6 minutes, stirring frequently, until crisp. Stir in onion, celery, potatoes, frozen corn and thyme. Cook 5 to 6 minutes, stirring frequently, until onion and celery are softened.

2. With whisk, beat in broth and flour. Heat to boiling; reduce heat to medium. Cover; cook about 15 minutes, stirring occasionally, or until potatoes are tender and soup is slightly thickened. Remove from heat.

3. Cool completely. Transfer to freezer container; seal tightly. Freeze up to 3 months. Thaw in refrigerator overnight.

4. Transfer chowder to 4-quart Dutch oven or stockpot. Heat to boiling; reduce heat to medium. Rinse frozen shrimp in hot water; add to Dutch oven. Stir in half-and-half, salt and pepper. Cover; cook 4 to 6 minutes, stirring occasionally, until shrimp are pink.

1 Serving: Calories 420; Total Fat 19g (Saturated Fat 11g, Trans Fat 0.5g); Cholesterol 125mg; Sodium 890mg; Total Carbohydrate 45g (Dietary Fiber 5g); Protein 18g **Exchanges:** 2½ Starch, ½ Other Carbohydrate, 1½ Lean Meat, 2½ Fat **Carbohydrate Choices:** 3

New England Clam Chowder

4 servings (1¼ cups each) | Prep Time: 20 Minutes | Start to Finish: 35 Minutes

. . .

- 4 slices bacon, cut into ½-inch pieces
- 1 medium onion, chopped (½ cup)
- 1 medium stalk celery, sliced (½ cup)
- 2 cans (6½ oz each) minced or chopped clams, drained, ¼ cup liquid reserved*
- 2¾ cups milk or half-and-half
- 2 medium potatoes, peeled, diced (2 cups)
- ¼ teaspoon salt
- Dash pepper
- ¼ cup all-purpose flour
- Chopped fresh parsley, if desired

1 In 3-quart saucepan, cook bacon, onion and celery over medium heat, stirring occasionally, until bacon is crisp and onion is tender; drain.

2 Stir in clams, reserved clam liquid, ¾ cup of the milk, the potatoes, salt and pepper. Heat to boiling; reduce heat. Cover; simmer about 15 minutes or until potatoes are tender.

3 To freeze, cool chowder completely. Transfer to freezer container; seal tightly. Freeze up to 3 months. Thaw 12 to 24 hours in refrigerator until completely thawed. Reheat in saucepan.

4 In medium bowl, mix remaining 2 cups milk and the flour with whisk until smooth and blended. Stir into clam mixture. Heat to boiling, stirring frequently. Boil and stir 1 minute until thickened. Garnish with parsley just before serving.

*1 pint shucked fresh clams with their liquid can be substituted for the canned clams. Chop the clams and stir in with the potatoes in Step 2.

1 Serving: Calories 240; Total Fat 5g (Saturated Fat 1.5g, Trans Fat 0g); Cholesterol 75mg; Sodium 490mg; Total Carbohydrate 19g (Dietary Fiber 1g); Protein 29g **Exchanges:** ½ Starch, ½ Low-Fat Milk, 1 Vegetable, 3 Very Lean Meat, 1 Fat **Carbohydrate Choices:** 1

chapter five

Meatless

Make-Ahead
Roasted Roma Tomato Sauce

8 cups | Prep Time: 25 Minutes | Start to Finish: 2 Hours 10 Minutes

• • •

24 plum (Roma) tomatoes, stem end trimmed off, halved lengthwise

¼ cup olive oil

1 tablespoon salt

½ teaspoon crushed red pepper flakes

2 large onions, thickly sliced (¾ inch), not separated into rings

2 bulbs garlic, root end sliced off

1 Heat oven to 425°F. Line 2 cookie sheets with sides with foil; spray foil with cooking spray.

2 In large bowl, toss tomatoes, oil, salt and pepper flakes. Place tomatoes, cut sides up, in single layer on 1 cookie sheet, tightly packed in rows. Place onions on second cookie sheet. Press cut side of garlic into oil mixture remaining in bowl; place on cookie sheet with onions. Scrape remaining oil mixture from bowl onto onions.

3 Roast 55 minutes to 1 hour 15 minutes or until tomatoes are charred on edges and onions are browned.

4 Squeeze garlic pulp from skins into blender. Working in batches, add tomatoes, onions and pan juices to blender. Cover; blend until smooth, starting on low speed and working up to high speed, 30 to 60 seconds. Transfer to large glass or stainless steel bowl. Cover loosely with plastic wrap; refrigerate about 30 minutes or until lukewarm.

5 Spoon 1-cup portions into freezer containers or 1-quart resealable freezer plastic bags; seal tightly. Freeze up to 3 months. Thaw overnight in refrigerator or in microwave on Medium (50%) 3 to 5 minutes or until completely thawed, then use immediately.

¼ **Cup:** Calories 40; Total Fat 2g (Saturated Fat 0g, Trans Fat 0g); Cholesterol 0mg; Sodium 230mg; Total Carbohydrate 5g (Dietary Fiber 0g); Protein 1g **Exchanges:** 1 Vegetable, ½ Fat **Carbohydrate Choices:** ½

Fresh Idea We chose Roma tomatoes because they are delicious and available all year, but feel free to use your garden surplus or farmers' market tomatoes in this recipe as well. Use about 10 large tomatoes (about 4½ lbs) in place of the 24 plum tomatoes.

Easy Caprese Soup

4 servings (1½ cups each) | Prep Time: 15 Minutes | Start to Finish: 15 Minutes

• • • •

Freezer Short-cut

| 4 | cups frozen Make-Ahead Roasted Roma Tomato Sauce (recipe on page 194), thawed |

2	cups reduced-sodium vegetable or chicken broth
4	slices rustic bread (1 inch), cut from a round loaf
8	oz fresh mozzarella cheese, cut into ¼-inch rounds, patted dry
12	large fresh basil leaves, shredded

1. In 3-quart saucepan, heat tomato sauce and broth to simmering over medium heat. Cook 5 minutes or until hot.

2. Meanwhile, line cookie sheet with foil. Set oven control to broil. Place bread on cookie sheet; broil with tops 6 inches from heat 1 to 2 minutes, turning once, until edges start to brown.

3. Top each slice of bread with 3 pieces of cheese. Broil with tops 6 inches from heat 1 to 2 minutes or until cheese melts and begins to bubble.

4. Divide soup among 4 bowls. Top each with 1 slice of toasted bread; sprinkle with basil.

1 Serving: Calories 480; Total Fat 22g (Saturated Fat 10g, Trans Fat 0g); Cholesterol 50mg; Sodium 1670mg; Total Carbohydrate 48g (Dietary Fiber 4g); Protein 22g **Exchanges:** 2 Starch, 1 Other Carbohydrate, 1 Vegetable, 2 High-Fat Meat, 1 Fat **Carbohydrate Choices:** 3

Fresh Idea If you want smaller portions, use baguette slices, and serve the soup in ramekins or mugs. And, for a tasty garnish, drizzle a few drops of balsamic vinegar on top of the soup.

Slow-Cooker Smoky Chipotle Soft Tacos

18 tacos | Prep Time: 20 Minutes | Start to Finish: 4 Hours 20 Minutes

· · ·

1 large onion, chopped (1 cup)

1 Anaheim chile, chopped (⅓ cup)

Cooking spray

6 cups frozen soy-protein crumbles (from two 12-oz packages)

¾ cup chili sauce

1½ cups water

½ cup mole sauce (from 8.25-oz jar)

1 tablespoon chopped chipotle chiles in adobo sauce (from 7-oz can)

1 teaspoon ground cumin

¾ teaspoon salt

18 flour tortillas (6 inch), heated as directed on package

2 cups shredded Cheddar cheese (8 oz)

3 medium tomatoes, chopped (2¼ cups)

1 Generously spray 8-inch skillet with cooking spray. Add onion and Anaheim chile; spray onion and chile with cooking spray. Cook over medium heat 4 to 5 minutes, stirring occasionally, until onion is crisp-tender.

2 Spray 3½- to 4-quart slow cooker with cooking spray. In slow cooker, stir together onion mixture, burger crumbles, chili sauce, water, mole sauce, chipotle chiles, cumin and salt.

3 Cover; cook on Low heat setting 4 to 5 hours.

4 To freeze, cool mixture completely. Transfer desired portions to freezer containers or resealable freezer plastic bags; seal tightly. Freeze up to 3 months. Thaw 12 to 24 hours in refrigerator until completely thawed. Reheat in microwave or on stove.

5 To serve, spoon ⅓ cup mixture down center of each tortilla; top with 1 heaping tablespoon cheese and 2 tablespoons tomatoes. Roll tortilla around filling.

1 Taco: Calories 250; Total Fat 10g (Saturated Fat 3.5g, Trans Fat 0g); Cholesterol 15mg; Sodium 730mg; Total Carbohydrate 24g (Dietary Fiber 4g); Protein 15g **Exchanges:** 1½ Starch, 1½ Lean Meat, 1 Fat **Carbohydrate Choices:** 1½

Cheese Enchiladas

4 servings (2 enchiladas each) | Prep Time: 25 Minutes | Start to Finish: 55 Minutes

• • • •

2 cups shredded Monterey Jack cheese (8 oz)

1 cup shredded Cheddar cheese (4 oz)

½ cup sour cream

1 medium onion, chopped (½ cup)

2 tablespoons chopped fresh parsley

¼ teaspoon pepper

1 can (15 oz) tomato sauce

1 small green bell pepper, chopped (½ cup)

1 can (4.5 oz) chopped green chiles, drained

1 clove garlic, finely chopped

⅔ cup water

1 tablespoon chili powder

1½ teaspoons chopped fresh or ½ teaspoon dried oregano leaves

¼ teaspoon ground cumin

TORTILLAS AND TOPPINGS

8 soft corn tortillas (5 or 6 inch)

Chopped green onions, if desired

Additional sour cream, if desired

1 In medium bowl, mix cheeses, sour cream, onion, parsley and pepper; set aside.

2 In 2-quart saucepan, heat tomato sauce, bell pepper, chiles, garlic, water, chili powder, oregano and cumin to boiling, stirring occasionally; reduce heat. Simmer uncovered 5 minutes. Pour into ungreased 9-inch glass pie plate.

3 Dip each tortilla into sauce to coat both sides. Spoon about ¼ cup cheese mixture onto each tortilla; roll tortilla around filling. In ungreased 11x7-inch (2-quart) glass baking dish, place enchiladas, seam sides down. Pour remaining sauce over top.

4 Cover baking dish tightly. Freeze up to 3 months. Thaw in refrigerator overnight.

5 Heat oven to 350°F. Uncover baking dish. Bake 25 to 30 minutes or until bubbly. Garnish with chopped green onions and additional sour cream.

1 Serving: Calories 530; Total Fat 34g (Saturated Fat 20g, Trans Fat 1g); Cholesterol 100mg; Sodium 1310mg; Total Carbohydrate 31g (Dietary Fiber 5g); Protein 26g **Exchanges:** 1 Starch, ½ Other Carbohydrate, 1 Vegetable, 3 High-Fat Meat, 2 Fat **Carbohydrate Choices:** 2

Veggie Burritos

8 burritos | Prep Time: 45 Minutes | Start to Finish: 1 Hour 10 Minutes

. . .

VEGETABLE MIXTURE

2	tablespoons vegetable oil
1	medium onion, chopped (½ cup)
2	medium red or green bell peppers, seeded, chopped (about 2 cups)
1½	cups shredded carrots (2 medium)
2	cloves garlic, finely chopped
1	jalapeño chile, seeded, finely chopped
1	teaspoon dried oregano leaves
1	teaspoon ground cumin
½	teaspoon salt
2	tablespoons water

BEANS, CHEESE AND TOPPINGS

1	can (16 oz) vegetarian refried beans
8	flour tortillas (9 or 10 inch)
2	cups shredded Cheddar, Colby–Monterey Jack cheese blend or Mexican cheese blend (8 oz)
⅓	cup chunky-style salsa
	Additional chunky-style salsa, if desired
	Sour cream, if desired

1 In 12-inch skillet, heat oil over medium-high heat. Cook onion in oil about 5 minutes, stirring frequently, until tender. Stir in bell peppers, carrots, garlic, chile, oregano, cumin and salt. Cook 5 minutes, stirring frequently. Stir in water. Reduce heat to low. Cover; steam 5 to 10 minutes or until vegetables are crisp-tender.

2 Spread about 3 tablespoons refried beans on each tortilla. Spoon about ⅓ cup vegetable mixture and ¼ cup cheese onto each tortilla. Fold sides up over filling; roll up tortilla.

3 Wrap burritos in foil. Place in freezer container; seal tightly. Freeze up to 3 months. Thaw in refrigerator overnight.

4 Heat oven to 350°F. Place unwrapped burritos, seam sides down, about 1 inch apart on ungreased cookie sheet. Brush tops and sides with salsa.

5 Bake 18 to 22 minutes or until thoroughly heated. Serve topped with additional salsa and sour cream.

1 Burrito: Calories 220; Total Fat 13g (Saturated Fat 7g, Trans Fat 0g); Cholesterol 30mg; Sodium 660mg; Total Carbohydrate 14g (Dietary Fiber 4g); Protein 10g **Exchanges:** ½ Starch, ½ Vegetable, 1 Medium-Fat Meat, 1½ Fat **Carbohydrate Choices:** 1

In a Flash Want burritos on hand to serve up (literally) in a minute? Wrap each unbaked burrito in plastic wrap and refrigerate up to 5 days. When ready to serve, remove plastic wrap and wrap a burrito in microwavable paper towel. Microwave 1 burrito on High 45 to 60 seconds or until hot and cheese is melted.

Cheesy Broccoli and Brown Rice Patties

4 servings | Prep Time: 10 Minutes | Start to Finish: 45 Minutes

• • •

1 box (10 oz) frozen broccoli and cheese sauce

2 tablespoons grated Parmesan cheese

½ teaspoon garlic salt

¼ teaspoon red pepper sauce

2 cups cooked brown rice

½ cup marinara sauce, heated

1 Cook broccoli as directed on box; pour into medium bowl. With kitchen scissors, cut broccoli into ¼- to ½-inch pieces. Add cheese, garlic salt and pepper sauce; mix well. Stir in cooked rice. Shape mixture into 4 patties, about ½ inch thick.

2 Wrap patties tightly. Freeze up to 3 months. Thaw in refrigerator overnight.

3 Heat oven to 400°F. Line cookie sheet with foil; spray foil with cooking spray. Unwrap patties; place on cookie sheet.

4 Bake 20 minutes; turn. Bake 15 minutes longer or until light golden brown. Serve with marinara sauce.

1 Serving: Calories 410; Total Fat 6g (Saturated Fat 2g, Trans Fat 0g); Cholesterol 0mg; Sodium 600mg; Total Carbohydrate 79g (Dietary Fiber 10g); Protein 11g **Exchanges:** 3 Starch, 2 Other Carbohydrate, 1 Vegetable, 1 Fat **Carbohydrate Choices:** 5

Fresh Idea Be creative with toppings for these tasty patties. Why not try pico de gallo or black bean salsa for a Tex-Mex twist? Or the tartness of sour cream or yogurt will play nicely against the flavor of these savory patties.

In a Flash Instant brown rice cooks in 10 minutes, rather than the 45 minutes for regular brown rice. You can also find frozen precooked brown rice in the freezer section of your supermarket.

Falafel

4 servings | Prep Time: 30 Minutes | Start to Finish: 4 Hours

• • •

2	cups water
1	cup dried garbanzo beans
3	tablespoons chopped fresh parsley
2	tablespoons all-purpose flour
2	teaspoons finely chopped garlic
1	teaspoon salt
1	teaspoon ground coriander
¾	teaspoon ground cumin
¼	teaspoon baking powder
⅛	teaspoon ground red pepper (cayenne)
1	egg
1	small red onion, finely chopped
	Vegetable oil, for frying

1 In 2-quart saucepan, heat water and beans to boiling. Boil 2 minutes; remove from heat. Cover; let stand 1 hour.

2 Add enough water to cover beans if necessary. Heat to boiling; reduce heat. Cover; simmer 1 hour to 1 hour 30 minutes or until tender. Drain, reserving liquid.

3 Mash beans with fork; add 2 to 3 tablespoons reserved liquid if necessary. (Do not puree beans in blender or food processor.) Stir in remaining ingredients except oil (mixture should be thick). Cover; let stand 1 hour.

4 Pinch off 1-inch pieces of bean mixture; shape into rounds and flatten. Wrap tightly. Freeze up to 3 months. Thaw in refrigerator overnight.

5 In 3-quart saucepan, heat oil (2 inches) to 375°F. Fry 4 or 5 rounds at a time in oil 2 to 3 minutes, turning once, until golden brown. Remove with slotted spoon; drain on paper towels.

1 Serving: Calories 230; Total Fat 11g (Saturated Fat 2g, Trans Fat 0g); Cholesterol 55mg; Sodium 650mg; Total Carbohydrate 24g (Dietary Fiber 5g); Protein 9g **Exchanges:** 1 Starch, 1½ Vegetable, ½ Very Lean Meat, 2 Fat **Carbohydrate Choices:** 1½

In a Flash If you don't have time to start with dried beans, use 2 cans (15 to 16 ounces each) garbanzo beans, drained and liquid reserved. You can add the reserved liquid as needed in Step 3.

Fresh Idea The falafel are great as is, or try them in pita bread with tomato, lettuce and a little plain yogurt.

Slow-Cooker Veggie Joes

16 sandwiches | Prep Time: 10 Minutes | Start to Finish: 4 Hours 10 Minutes

• • •

4	cups frozen soy-protein crumbles (from two 12-oz packages)
1	medium onion, finely chopped (½ cup)
1½	cups ketchup
½	cup water
2	tablespoons packed brown sugar
2	tablespoons white vinegar
1	tablespoon yellow mustard
½	teaspoon pepper
¼	teaspoon salt
16	burger buns, split

1 Spray 3½- to 4-quart slow cooker with cooking spray. In slow cooker, mix all ingredients except buns.

2 Cover; cook on Low heat setting 4 to 6 hours. (If slow cooker has black liner, do not cook longer than 6 hours or mixture may burn around edge.)

3 To freeze, cool mixture completely. Transfer desired portions to freezer/microwavable containers or resealable freezer plastic bags; seal tightly. Freeze up to 3 months. Thaw 12 to 24 hours in refrigerator until completely thawed.

4 Reheat in microwave or on stove. Spoon ⅓ cup mixture into each bun.

1 Sandwich: Calories 190; Total Fat 3g (Saturated Fat 0.5g, Trans Fat 0g); Cholesterol 0mg; Sodium 640mg; Total Carbohydrate 30g (Dietary Fiber 3g); Protein 10g **Exchanges:** 1½ Starch, ½ Other Carbohydrate, 1 Very Lean Meat, ½ Fat **Carbohydrate Choices:** 2

Fresh Idea **Skip the buns and try spooning the mixture over tortilla chips, pasta or rice instead.**

Veggie and Bean Burgers

4 burgers | Prep Time: 25 Minutes | Start to Finish: 25 Minutes

• • •

½   **cup small fresh broccoli florets**

2   **oz fresh mushrooms (about 4 medium)**

½   **small red bell pepper, cut into large pieces**

½   **cup cooked instant white or brown rice**

1   **can (15 to 16 oz) garbanzo beans, drained, rinsed**

1   **egg**

1   **clove garlic**

½   **teaspoon seasoned salt**

1   **teaspoon dried chopped onion**

⅓   **cup seasoned dry bread crumbs**

3   **tablespoons vegetable oil**

4   **whole wheat burger buns, split**

   Toppings (Cheddar cheese slices, lettuce, sliced tomato, sliced onion and mayonnaise), if desired

1   In food processor, place broccoli, mushrooms and bell pepper. Cover; process, using quick on-and-off motions, to finely chop vegetables (do not puree). Remove vegetables to medium bowl; stir in rice.

2   Add beans, egg, garlic and seasoned salt to food processor. Cover; process until smooth. Stir bean mixture, dried chopped onion and bread crumbs into vegetable mixture. Shape mixture into 4 patties, about ½ inch thick.

3   Wrap patties tightly. Freeze up to 3 months. Thaw in refrigerator overnight.

4   In 10-inch nonstick skillet, heat oil over medium-high heat. Cook patties in oil 8 to 10 minutes, turning once, until browned and crisp. Serve in buns with toppings.

1 Burger: Calories 460; Total Fat 16g (Saturated Fat 2.5g, Trans Fat 0g); Cholesterol 55mg; Sodium 540mg; Total Carbohydrate 61g (Dietary Fiber 9g); Protein 17g **Exchanges:** 3½ Starch, 2 Vegetable, 2 Fat **Carbohydrate Choices:** 4

Veggie and Bean "Meatballs"

Heat oven to 400°F. Generously spray 15x10x1-inch pan with cooking spray. Shape vegetable mixture into 16 balls; place in pan. Generously spray tops of balls with cooking spray. Bake about 20 minutes or until crisp. Serve with cheese sauce, tomato pasta sauce (any meatless variety) or Make-Ahead Roasted Roma Tomato Sauce (recipe on page 194).

Spicy Chili Bean Burgers

5 burgers | Prep Time: 25 Minutes | Start to Finish: 25 Minutes

• • •

1   cup Fiber One original bran cereal

1   can (15 or 16 oz) spicy chili beans in sauce, undrained

½   cup quick-cooking oats

¼   cup chopped green onions (4 medium)

1   egg, slightly beaten

1¼   cups fresh baby spinach leaves

5   slices tomato

5   whole wheat burger buns, split

1   Place cereal in resealable food-storage plastic bag; seal bag and crush with rolling pin or meat mallet (or crush in food processor).

2   In medium bowl, mash beans with fork until no whole beans remain. Add crushed cereal, oats, onions and egg; mix well. Shape mixture into 5 patties, about 3½ inches in diameter.

3   Wrap patties tightly. Freeze up to 3 months. Thaw in refrigerator overnight.

4   Spray 12-inch skillet with cooking spray. Add patties; cook over medium heat about 10 minutes, turning once, until browned.

5   Place ¼ cup spinach leaves and 1 tomato slice on each bun bottom; top with bean burger and bun top.

1 Burger: Calories 280; Total Fat 4.5g (Saturated Fat 1g, Trans Fat 0g); Cholesterol 40mg; Sodium 800mg; Total Carbohydrate 48g (Dietary Fiber 12g); Protein 11g **Exchanges:** 2½ Starch, ½ Other Carbohydrate, ½ Vegetable, ½ Fat **Carbohydrate Choices:** 3

Veggie-Fried Grains

6 servings | Prep Time: 30 Minutes | Start to Finish: 1 Hour

• • •

FARRO AND EGG MIXTURE

1¼	cups uncooked farro
2¼	cups water
1	teaspoon vegetable oil
2	eggs, slightly beaten

VEGETABLES

1	cup small fresh cauliflower florets, separated into mini florets (about ¼ inch)
1	cup small fresh broccoli florets, separated into mini florets (about ¼ inch)
1	cup coarsely shredded carrots
1	cup frozen sugar snap peas (from 12-oz bag)
½	cup diced red bell pepper
4	medium green onions, sliced (¼ cup)

TO COOK

1	tablespoon vegetable oil
¼	cup soy sauce

1. In 2-quart saucepan, heat farro and water to boiling; reduce heat to low. Cover; simmer 25 to 30 minutes or until tender. Rinse with cold water; drain well.

2. In 8-inch skillet, heat 1 teaspoon oil over medium heat. Cook eggs in oil, stirring constantly, until thickened throughout but still moist. Stir eggs into farro. Spoon mixture into 1-gallon resealable freezer plastic bag; seal bag.

3. Place vegetables in another 1-gallon resealable freezer plastic bag; seal bag.

4. Lay bags flat in freezer. Freeze up to 3 months. Thaw 12 to 24 hours in refrigerator until completely thawed.

5. In 12-inch nonstick skillet, heat 1 tablespoon oil over medium-high heat. Cook vegetables in oil 2 to 3 minutes, stirring frequently, until crisp-tender. Add farro mixture; stir to combine. Cook and stir until thoroughly heated. Stir in soy sauce.

1 Serving: Calories 250; Total Fat 6g (Saturated Fat 1g, Trans Fat 0g); Cholesterol 60mg; Sodium 630mg; Total Carbohydrate 38g (Dietary Fiber 7g); Protein 10g **Exchanges:** 2 Starch, 1 Vegetable, ½ Medium-Fat Meat, ½ Fat **Carbohydrate Choices:** 2½

Fresh Idea Make this yummy dish the base of some fantastic "rice" bowls. Top the warm grains with sliced avocado, chopped tomato, black beans and lettuce or whatever combination of fresh toppings you have on hand.

Barley can be substituted for the farro. Cook 45 to 50 minutes.

QUICK FREEZER IDEAS

Making foods to freeze can be a fun and creative weekend experience. Get a jump-start on weeknight meals by preparing and freezing ingredients so it will be short work to finish meals later, and take advantage of sales at the grocery store or preserve food so it doesn't get wasted. Nothing beats food that's already been prepped when you're short on time.

Plan Ahead

STOCK UP: Stock up on sale items that can be used for future meals. It's easy to subdivide large amounts of meat, rewrap and store in the freezer. Refer to the Freezer-Friendly Foods storage chart on page 8, for how long foods can be frozen. Write the date the food should be used by on the package.

COOK ONCE, USE TWICE: It's easy to brown up a big batch of ground beef, drain, cool and then divide it into portions and freeze for future meals.

READY BACON: If you love adding bacon to recipes but hate having to cook up one or two slices at a time, why not cook up an entire package of bacon and then freeze it for those times when you need just a few slices? Done in the oven, you can cook it all at once—line bottom and sides of 15x10x1 inch pans with cooking parchment paper or aluminum foil. Arrange bacon in pans with edges touching. Bake 15 to 20 minutes or until it's crisp.

SLICE AND DICE: When you have time, chop a lot of onions and garlic and place them in resealable freezer plastic bags to pull from for future recipes that need these items: 1 medium onion = ½ cup and 1 clove garlic =½ teaspoon finely chopped garlic.

MAKE TWO, FREEZE ONE: When making a casserole for dinner, why not make two and freeze one for another meal? The time it takes to make the second casserole is less when you are making two at the same time.

BIG-BATCH BREAKFASTS: When making pancakes or waffles on the weekend, make a big batch so you'll have extras for fast weekday breakfasts. Cool them completely in a single layer on a cooling rack; move to a resealable freezer plastic bag and freeze. To reheat pancakes, place 3 on a microwavable plate; microwave uncovered on High 1 minute or until hot. To reheat waffles, toast in toaster until heated through.

FRESH HERBS, ANYTIME: Place herbs such as chopped thyme, chives and rosemary leaves in ice-cube trays or mini muffin cups. Cover with water, broth or olive or vegetable oil. Cover and freeze until firm. Put frozen cubes in a resealable freezer plastic bag to add to simmering soups, stews and sauces. Or soft herbs such as basil, sage or thyme leaves can be frozen in a single layer on a cookie sheet and then transferred to a resealable freezer plastic bag (press all the air out) or made into pesto before placing in ice cube trays.

SOUP SAVVY: Make a batch of soup or chili and freeze it in individual portions to take with you to work—saving you the time and money of going out to eat. Most broth-based soups and red chilis freeze well. Soups made with cream may separate after freezing. If you wish to freeze this kind of soup, skip the cream while making it and add it instead after reheating thoroughly.

FREEZE FOR EASY USE: For foods that stick together when frozen or get mushy when frozen (think meatballs, bacon, berries or rice), freeze individually first, then wrap and store for later. Wrap the bottom of a cooling rack with foil and place the food to be frozen on top. Place cooling rack in freezer 15 to 30 minutes or until the pieces are frozen. Then move the frozen pieces to a resealable freezer plastic bag or container. The pieces will stay separate, making it easy to pull out only the amount you wish to use at one time.

Bulgur Pilaf

4 servings | Prep Time: 15 Minutes | Start to Finish: 30 Minutes

• • •

2 tablespoons butter

1 medium onion, chopped (½ cup)

1 medium carrot, chopped (½ cup)

1¾ cups vegetable or chicken broth

1 cup uncooked bulgur

¼ teaspoon lemon-pepper seasoning salt or black pepper

½ cup slivered almonds

¼ cup chopped fresh parsley

1 In 2-quart saucepan, melt 1 tablespoon of the butter. Cook onion and carrot in butter about 3 minutes, stirring occasionally, until crisp-tender.

2 Stir in broth, bulgur and lemon-pepper seasoning salt. Heat to boiling; reduce heat. Cover; simmer about 15 minutes or until liquid is absorbed and bulgur is tender. Remove from heat; cool completely.

3 Spoon pilaf into freezer container; seal tightly. Freeze up to 3 months. Thaw in refrigerator overnight.

4 Transfer pilaf to saucepan; reheat on stove. (Add additional broth, if necessary, for desired consistency.) Meanwhile, in 8-inch skillet, melt remaining 1 tablespoon butter over medium-high heat. Cook almonds in butter 2 to 3 minutes, stirring constantly, until golden brown.

5 Sprinkle pilaf with parsley and toasted almonds.

1 Serving: Calories 190; Total Fat 9g (Saturated Fat 3g, Trans Fat 0g); Cholesterol 10mg; Sodium 330mg; Total Carbohydrate 23g (Dietary Fiber 6g); Protein 5g **Exchanges:** 1½ Starch, 1½ Fat **Carbohydrate Choices:** 1½

Moroccan Garbanzo Beans with Raisins

8 servings | Prep Time: 25 Minutes | Start to Finish: 25 Minutes

. . .

2 tablespoons peanut or vegetable oil

1 large onion, sliced

1 medium onion, chopped (½ cup)

2 cloves garlic, finely chopped

2 cups diced seeded peeled acorn or butternut squash

½ cup raisins

2 cups vegetable broth

2 teaspoons ground turmeric

2 teaspoons ground cinnamon

1 teaspoon ground ginger

2 cans (15 oz each) garbanzo beans, drained, rinsed

Hot cooked rice or couscous, if desired

1. In 4-quart saucepan, heat oil over medium heat. Add sliced onion, chopped onion and garlic; cook about 7 minutes, stirring occasionally, until onions are tender. Stir in remaining ingredients except garbanzo beans and rice.

2. Heat to boiling; reduce heat. Cover; simmer about 8 minutes, stirring occasionally, until squash is tender. Remove from heat; cool completely.

3. Spoon into freezer container; seal tightly. Freeze up to 3 months. Thaw in refrigerator overnight.

4. Transfer mixture to 4-quart saucepan. Heat to boiling; reduce heat. Stir in beans; cook until hot. Serve over rice.

1 Serving: Calories 220; Total Fat 6g (Saturated Fat 1g, Trans Fat 0g); Cholesterol 0mg; Sodium 410mg; Total Carbohydrate 35g (Dietary Fiber 8g); Protein 6g **Exchanges:** 2 Starch, ½ Other Carbohydrate, 1 Fat **Carbohydrate Choices:** 2

Apple-Cinnamon–Butternut Squash Soup

8 servings (1 cup each) | Prep Time: 25 Minutes | Start to Finish: 45 Minutes

• • •

8 cups cubed seeded peeled butternut squash (2 medium)

1 large apple, peeled, chopped

1 large onion, cut into 1-inch pieces

2 tablespoons packed brown sugar

¾ teaspoon salt

¾ teaspoon ground cinnamon

⅛ teaspoon pepper

3 cups vegetable or chicken broth

¾ cup milk

1 container (6 oz) fat-free Greek plain yogurt

2 tablespoons chopped fresh chives

1 In 4-quart Dutch oven or stockpot, mix squash, apple, onion, brown sugar, salt, cinnamon and pepper. Add broth. Heat to boiling over medium-high heat; reduce heat. Cover; simmer about 20 minutes or until squash is tender.

2 In blender or food processor, place one-third of squash mixture at a time. Cover; blend until smooth. Pour into freezer containers; cool completely.

3 Seal tightly. Freeze up to 3 months. Thaw in refrigerator overnight.

4 Transfer soup to 3-quart saucepan. Heat to boiling; reduce heat to low. Stir in milk and yogurt. Cook and stir just until thoroughly heated. Sprinkle individual servings with chives.

1 Serving: Calories 130; Total Fat 0.5g (Saturated Fat 0g, Trans Fat 0g); Cholesterol 0mg; Sodium 570mg; Total Carbohydrate 25g (Dietary Fiber 2g); Protein 4g **Exchanges:** ½ Starch, 1 Other Carbohydrate, 1 Vegetable **Carbohydrate Choices:** 1½

Bean and Barley Chili with Cilantro Sour Cream

6 servings (1⅓ cups each) | Prep Time: 15 Minutes | Start to Finish: 1 Hour 15 Minutes

* * *

CHILI

1	tablespoon olive oil
1	large onion, chopped (1 cup)
2	cloves garlic, finely chopped
½	cup uncooked pearl barley
2	tablespoons chili powder
1½	teaspoons ground cumin
	Salt and pepper to taste
2	cups water
2	cans (14.5 oz each) diced tomatoes, undrained
1	can (15 oz) black beans, drained, rinsed
1	can (15 oz) dark red kidney beans, drained, rinsed
¾	cup chunky-style salsa

CILANTRO SOUR CREAM

½	cup reduced-fat sour cream
2	tablespoons finely chopped fresh cilantro

1 In 4-quart Dutch oven or stockpot, heat oil over medium-high heat. Cook onion and garlic in oil 5 minutes, stirring frequently, until tender. Stir in barley, chili powder, cumin, salt, pepper, water and tomatoes. Reduce heat. Cover; simmer 30 minutes.

2 Stir in black beans, kidney beans and salsa. Cover; simmer about 30 minutes longer or until barley is tender.

3 Cool completely. Transfer to freezer containers; seal tightly. Freeze up to 3 months. Thaw in refrigerator overnight.

4 Reheat soup in microwave or on stove. Meanwhile, in small bowl, mix sour cream and cilantro until blended. Top individual servings with cilantro sour cream.

1 Serving: Calories 300; Total Fat 6g (Saturated Fat 2g, Trans Fat 0g); Cholesterol 10mg; Sodium 960mg; Total Carbohydrate 48g (Dietary Fiber 11g); Protein 12g **Exchanges:** 2 Starch, 1 Other Carbohydrate, 1 Vegetable, ½ Very Lean Meat, 1 Fat **Carbohydrate Choices:** 3

Chili Blanco

4 servings | Prep Time: 30 Minutes | Start to Finish: 30 Minutes

- - -

1 cup chopped onions
(2 medium)

2 cloves garlic, finely chopped

2 cans (15.5 oz each) great
northern beans, drained,
rinsed

1 can (11 oz) white shoepeg
corn, undrained

1 can (4.5 oz) chopped green
chiles, undrained

1 extra-large vegetarian
vegetable bouillon cube

2 teaspoons ground cumin

¼ teaspoon salt

¼ teaspoon pepper

2½ cups water

¼ cup chopped fresh cilantro

½ cup shredded Monterey Jack
cheese (2 oz), if desired

½ cup broken tortilla chips, if
desired

1 Spray 3-quart saucepan with cooking spray; heat over medium-high heat. Add onions and garlic; cook 1 minute, stirring constantly.

2 Stir in beans, corn, chiles, bouillon, cumin, salt, pepper and water. Heat to boiling; reduce heat. Cover; simmer about 15 minutes, stirring occasionally. Remove from heat; cool completely.

3 Transfer to freezer container; seal tightly. Freeze up to 3 months. Thaw in refrigerator overnight.

4 Reheat in microwave or on stove. Stir in cilantro. Place 2 tablespoons cheese in each individual soup bowl. Spoon chili over cheese; top with tortilla chips.

1 Serving: Calories 430; Total Fat 1.5g (Saturated Fat 0g, Trans Fat 0g); Cholesterol 0mg; Sodium 800mg; Total Carbohydrate 79g (Dietary Fiber 16g); Protein 24g **Exchanges:** 1 Starch, 3½ Other Carbohydrate, 2½ Vegetable, 2 Very Lean Meat **Carbohydrate Choices:** 5

Bean and Vegetable Stew
with Polenta

4 servings (1½ cups each) | Prep Time: 1 Hour 15 Minutes | Start to Finish: 1 Hour 15 Minutes

• • •

1 tablespoon olive or
vegetable oil

1 medium yellow or green bell
pepper, coarsely chopped
(1 cup)

1 medium onion, coarsely
chopped (½ cup)

2 teaspoons finely
chopped garlic

2 medium carrots, cut into
¼-inch slices (1 cup)

2 cans (14.5 oz each) diced
tomatoes with basil,
undrained

1 can (15 oz) black-eyed peas,
drained, rinsed

1 can (19 oz) cannellini (white
kidney) beans, drained,
rinsed

1 cup water

1 teaspoon Italian seasoning

½ teaspoon salt

¼ teaspoon pepper

1 cup frozen cut green beans
(from 12-oz bag)

1 roll (16 oz)
refrigerated polenta

1 In 4-quart Dutch oven or stockpot, heat oil over medium heat. Cook bell pepper, onion and garlic in oil 5 to 6 minutes, stirring frequently, until onion is softened.

2 Stir in remaining ingredients except polenta and green beans. Heat to boiling; reduce heat to medium-low. Cover; cook 35 to 40 minutes, stirring occasionally, until carrots are tender. Remove from heat; cool completely.

3 Transfer to freezer container; seal tightly. Freeze up to 3 months. Thaw in refrigerator overnight.

4 Reheat stew on stove, adding frozen green beans during last 5 minutes, until hot. Meanwhile, cook polenta as directed on package. To serve, spoon stew over polenta.

1 Serving: Calories 780; Total Fat 4.5g (Saturated Fat 1g, Trans Fat 0g); Cholesterol 0mg; Sodium 2470mg; Total Carbohydrate 149g (Dietary Fiber 22g); Protein 34g **Exchanges:** 9 Starch, 2½ Vegetable **Carbohydrate Choices:** 10

Fresh Idea Any type of canned beans works nicely in this recipe. Experiment with garbanzo, butter, great northern, red or kidney beans— whatever strikes your fancy. And for a special touch, sprinkle each bowl of stew with chopped fresh basil and freshly grated Parmesan cheese.

Spaghetti and Spicy Rice Balls

5 servings | Prep Time: 30 Minutes | Start to Finish: 30 Minutes

• • •

2 **cups cooked regular long-grain white or brown rice***

½ **cup quick-cooking oats**

1 **medium onion, chopped (½ cup)**

¼ **cup unseasoned dry bread crumbs**

¼ **cup milk**

1 **tablespoon chopped fresh or 1 teaspoon dried basil leaves**

2 **teaspoons chopped fresh or ½ teaspoon dried oregano leaves**

¼ **teaspoon ground red pepper (cayenne)**

1 **egg, beaten**

½ **cup wheat germ**

1 **tablespoon vegetable oil**

1 **package (16 oz) spaghetti**

Freezer Short-cut

2 **cups Make-Ahead Roasted Roma Tomato Sauce (recipe on page 194)**

Shredded Parmesan cheese, if desired

*Do not use instant rice.

1 Serving: Calories 740; Total Fat 12g (Saturated Fat 2.5g, Trans Fat 0g); Cholesterol 45mg; Sodium 1180mg; Total Carbohydrate 133g (Dietary Fiber 9g); Protein 24g **Exchanges:** 7½ Starch, 1 Other Carbohydrate, 1 Vegetable, 1½ Fat **Carbohydrate Choices:** 9

1 In medium bowl, mix cooked rice, oats, onion, bread crumbs, milk, basil, oregano, red pepper and egg. Shape mixture into 10 balls; roll in wheat germ to coat.

2 In 10-inch skillet, heat oil over medium heat. Cook rice balls in oil about 10 minutes, turning occasionally, until light golden brown.

3 Place rice balls in single layer on cookie sheet; cool completely. Freeze until firm. Transfer to freezer container or resealable freezer plastic bag; seal tightly. Freeze up to 3 months. Thaw in refrigerator overnight.

4 Cook and drain spaghetti as directed on package. Meanwhile, heat tomato sauce and reheat rice balls separately.

5 Serve rice balls and sauce over spaghetti; sprinkle with cheese.

Bell Pepper–Mac and Cheese with Fondue Cheese Sauce

7 servings (about 1½ cups each) | Prep Time: 30 Minutes | Start to Finish: 1 Hour 10 Minutes

• • •

- 3 medium red, yellow, orange or green bell peppers
- 3 cups uncooked penne pasta (9 oz)
- 10 oz Gruyère cheese, shredded (2½ cups)
- 3 tablespoons all-purpose flour
- 1 cup dry white wine
- ¾ cup whipping cream
- 2 cloves garlic, finely chopped
- ½ teaspoon salt
- ¼ teaspoon ground red pepper (cayenne)
- ⅛ teaspoon ground nutmeg
- 2 tablespoons chopped fresh parsley
- ½ cup Italian-style bread crumbs
- 2 tablespoons butter, melted

1. Set oven control to broil. Broil bell peppers with tops 5 inches from heat about 20 minutes, turning occasionally, until skins are blistered and evenly browned. Place peppers in plastic bag; close tightly. Let stand 20 minutes. Remove skin, stems, seeds and membranes from peppers. Cut peppers into 1-inch pieces; set aside.

2. Cook and drain pasta as directed on package, using minimum cook time. Meanwhile, in medium bowl, toss cheese with flour until cheese is coated. In 3-quart nonreactive saucepan, heat wine, whipping cream and garlic to simmering over medium heat. Reduce heat to low; gradually stir in cheese, salt, pepper and nutmeg until cheese is melted. Cook and stir 2 minutes longer.

3. Spray 3-quart casserole with cooking spray. Stir cooked pasta, roasted peppers and parsley into cheese sauce. Spoon into casserole.

4. Cover casserole tightly. Freeze up to 3 months. Thaw in refrigerator overnight.

5. Heat oven to 350°F. Uncover casserole. In small bowl, stir together bread crumbs and butter. Sprinkle over pasta mixture. Bake uncovered 20 to 30 minutes or until edges are bubbly.

1 Serving: Calories 490; Total Fat 26g (Saturated Fat 14g, Trans Fat 0.5g); Cholesterol 80mg; Sodium 450mg; Total Carbohydrate 39g (Dietary Fiber 2g); Protein 18g **Exchanges:** 2½ Starch, ½ Vegetable, 1½ Medium-Fat Meat, 3½ Fat **Carbohydrate Choices:** 2½

In a Flash If you want to skip roasting the peppers, you can use a 15-oz jar of drained roasted red peppers instead.

Lasagna Cupcakes

12 servings | Prep Time: 15 Minutes | Start to Finish: 1 Hour

• • •

1 cup ricotta cheese

½ cup grated Parmesan cheese

1 egg

1 jar (25.5 oz) tomato pasta sauce (any meatless variety)

½ lb frozen Italian sausage–style soy-protein crumbles (2 cups)

36 pot sticker (gyoza) wrappers

1 cup shredded mozzarella cheese (4 oz)

1 Heat oven to 375°F. Spray 12 regular-size muffin cups with cooking spray. In small bowl, mix ricotta cheese, Parmesan cheese and egg. In another small bowl, mix pasta sauce and soy-protein crumbles.

2 Place 1 pot sticker wrapper in bottom of each muffin cup; top each with 1 heaping tablespoon pasta sauce mixture and 1 tablespoon cheese mixture. Repeat layers twice, ending with pasta sauce mixture. Sprinkle evenly with mozzarella cheese.

3 Spray sheet of foil with cooking spray; place foil, sprayed side down, over pan. Bake 15 minutes. Uncover; bake 15 minutes longer. Let stand 15 minutes before serving.

4 To freeze, cool completely. Wrap tightly. Freeze up to 3 months. To reheat, microwave 1 frozen cupcake uncovered on Medium (50%) 5 to 6 minutes or until hot.

1 Serving: Calories 170; Total Fat 7g (Saturated Fat 3g, Trans Fat 0g); Cholesterol 30mg; Sodium 500mg; Total Carbohydrate 13g (Dietary Fiber 2g); Protein 12g **Exchanges:** 1 Starch, 1 Medium-Fat Meat **Carbohydrate Choices:** 1

In a Flash Once these mini lasagna "cupcakes" are stashed in your freezer, you are only a few minutes from the cutest dinner you'll ever serve—or an after-school snack packed with protein as well as kid appeal.

Roasted-Vegetable Lasagna with Goat Cheese

8 servings | Prep Time: 1 Hour 15 Minutes | Start to Finish: 1 Hour 15 Minutes

• • •

3   **medium bell peppers, cut into 1-inch pieces**

3   **medium zucchini or summer squash, cut in half lengthwise, then cut crosswise into ½-inch slices**

1   **medium onion, cut into 8 wedges, separated into pieces**

1   **package (8 oz) sliced fresh mushrooms (about 3 cups)**

   Cooking spray

½   **teaspoon salt**

¼   **teaspoon pepper**

12   **uncooked lasagna noodles**

1   **package (5 to 6 oz) chèvre (goat) cheese**

1   **container (7 oz) refrigerated basil pesto**

2   **cups tomato pasta sauce**

2   **cups shredded Italian cheese blend (8 oz)**

1   Heat oven to 450°F. Spray 15x10x1-inch pan with cooking spray. In pan, place bell peppers, zucchini, onion and mushrooms in single layer. Spray vegetables with cooking spray; sprinkle with salt and pepper. Roast 15 to 20 minutes, turning vegetables once, until crisp-tender.

2   Meanwhile, cook and drain noodles as directed on package. In medium bowl, crumble chèvre into pesto; stir.

3   Spray 13x9-inch (3-quart) glass baking dish with cooking spray. In baking dish, spread ½ cup of the pasta sauce. Top with 3 noodles; spread with half of the pesto mixture and 2 cups of the roasted vegetables. Layer with 3 noodles, ¾ cup pasta sauce, 1 cup shredded cheese blend and 2 cups vegetables. Layer with 3 noodles, remaining pesto mixture and vegetables. Layer with remaining 3 noodles, remaining ¾ cup pasta sauce and 1 cup shredded cheese.

4   Cover baking dish tightly. Freeze up to 3 months. Thaw in refrigerator overnight.

5   Heat oven to 375°F. Uncover baking dish. Bake 20 to 30 minutes or until hot and bubbly. Let stand 10 minutes before cutting.

1 Serving: Calories 520; Total Fat 26g (Saturated Fat 10g, Trans Fat 0g); Cholesterol 30mg; Sodium 990mg; Total Carbohydrate 47g (Dietary Fiber 5g); Protein 22g **Exchanges:** 1½ Starch, 1 Other Carbohydrate, 2 Vegetable, 2 High-Fat Meat, 2 Fat **Carbohydrate Choices:** 3

Artichoke-Spinach Lasagna

8 servings | Prep Time: 25 Minutes | Start to Finish: 1 Hour 30 Minutes

- - -

1   medium onion, chopped (½ cup)

4   cloves garlic, finely chopped

1¾   cups vegetable broth

1   tablespoon chopped fresh or 1 teaspoon dried rosemary leaves

1   can (14 oz) artichoke hearts, drained, coarsely chopped

1   box (9 oz) frozen chopped spinach, thawed, squeezed to drain

1   jar (15 to 17 oz) Alfredo sauce

9   uncooked lasagna noodles

3   cups shredded mozzarella cheese (12 oz)

1   package (4 oz) crumbled herb-and-garlic feta cheese (1 cup)

Fresh rosemary sprigs, if desired

Lemon wedges, if desired

1 Spray 12-inch skillet with cooking spray; heat over medium-high heat. Add onion and garlic; cook about 3 minutes, stirring occasionally, until onion is crisp-tender. Stir in broth and 1 tablespoon rosemary. Heat to boiling. Stir in artichokes and spinach; reduce heat. Cover; simmer 5 minutes. Stir in pasta sauce.

2 Spray 13x9-inch (3-quart) glass baking dish with cooking spray. Spread one-fourth of the artichoke mixture in baking dish; top with 3 uncooked noodles. Sprinkle with ¾ cup of the mozzarella cheese. Repeat layers twice. Spread with remaining artichoke mixture; sprinkle with remaining ¾ cup mozzarella cheese. Sprinkle with feta cheese.

3 Cover baking dish tightly. Freeze up to 3 months. Thaw in refrigerator overnight.

4 Heat oven to 350°F. Bake lasagna covered 40 minutes. Uncover; bake about 15 minutes longer or until bubbly and noodles are tender. Let stand 10 minutes before cutting. Garnish with rosemary sprigs and lemon wedges.

1 Serving: Calories 520; Total Fat 31g (Saturated Fat 19g, Trans Fat 1g); Cholesterol 95mg; Sodium 960mg; Total Carbohydrate 35g (Dietary Fiber 7g); Protein 24g **Exchanges:** 2½ Starch, 2 Very Lean Meat, 5½ Fat **Carbohydrate Choices:** 2

Fresh Idea Want a Mediterranean flavor? Stir in ½ cup chopped pitted kalamata, Greek or ripe olives with the Alfredo sauce.

Spinach-Stuffed Manicotti with Vodka Blush Sauce

7 servings | Prep Time: 25 Minutes | Start to Finish: 1 Hour

• • •

14 uncooked manicotti pasta shells

2 jars (25.5 oz each) garden vegetable tomato pasta sauce

¼ cup vodka

½ cup whipping cream

2 cups shredded Italian cheese blend (8 oz)

½ cup sun-dried tomatoes in oil, drained, chopped

1 container (15 oz) ricotta cheese

1 box (9 oz) frozen chopped spinach, thawed, squeezed to drain

2 tablespoons julienne-cut fresh basil leaves

1 Cook pasta shells as directed on package. Rinse with cold water to cool; drain.

2 Meanwhile, in 2-quart nonreactive saucepan, heat 1 jar of pasta sauce and the vodka to boiling. Reduce heat; simmer 3 minutes, stirring occasionally. Remove from heat; stir in whipping cream. Set aside.

3 In medium bowl, mix 1 cup of the cheese blend, the sun-dried tomatoes, ricotta and spinach.

4 In 13x9-inch (3-quart) glass baking dish, spread 1 cup of pasta sauce from second jar (save remaining sauce for another use). Fill each pasta shell with about 3 tablespoons ricotta mixture; place over sauce in dish. Pour vodka pasta sauce over filled shells.

5 Cover baking dish tightly. Freeze up to 3 months. Thaw in refrigerator overnight.

6 Heat oven to 375°F. Bake manicotti covered 30 minutes or until sauce is bubbly. Uncover; sprinkle with remaining 1 cup cheese blend. Bake 5 minutes longer or until cheese is melted. Sprinkle with basil.

1 Serving: Calories 420; Total Fat 15g (Saturated Fat 7g, Trans Fat 0g); Cholesterol 35mg; Sodium 880mg; Total Carbohydrate 48g (Dietary Fiber 6g); Protein 19g **Exchanges:** 3 Starch, ½ Vegetable, 1 Medium-Fat Meat, 2 Fat **Carbohydrate Choices:** 3

Fresh Idea The Vodka Blush sauce is delicious, but you can substitute dry white wine for the vodka. Or, if you want to leave out the alcohol, use reduced-sodium vegetable broth.

Texas Tater Casserole

6 servings | Prep Time: 25 Minutes | Start to Finish: 1 Hour 15 Minutes

· · ·

1   large onion, chopped (1 cup)

1   medium stalk celery, chopped (½ cup)

2   cloves garlic, finely chopped

    Cooking spray

2   cups frozen soy-protein crumbles (from 12-oz package)

2   cans (10¾ oz each) condensed Cheddar cheese soup

1   can (11 oz) whole kernel corn with red and green peppers, drained

½   cup chunky-style salsa

2   teaspoons chili powder

¼   teaspoon pepper

4½ cups frozen potato nuggets (from 32-oz bag)

½   cup shredded taco-seasoned cheese blend (2 oz)

1 Generously spray 12-inch skillet with cooking spray. Add onion, celery and garlic to skillet; spray vegetables with cooking spray. Cook over medium heat 8 to 10 minutes, stirring occasionally, until crisp-tender.

2 Stir in veggie crumbles, soup, corn, salsa, chili powder and pepper. Spoon into ungreased 2½-quart casserole. Top with potato nuggets.

3 Cover casserole tightly. Freeze up to 3 months. Thaw in refrigerator overnight.

4 Heat oven to 375°F. Uncover casserole. Bake 40 minutes. Sprinkle with cheese. Bake 5 to 10 minutes longer or until bubbly and cheese is melted.

1 Serving: Calories 470; Total Fat 21g (Saturated Fat 10g, Trans Fat 4g); Cholesterol 25mg; Sodium 2070mg; Total Carbohydrate 51g (Dietary Fiber 7g); Protein 19g **Exchanges:** 3 Starch, ½ Other Carbohydrate, 1½ Lean Meat, 3 Fat **Carbohydrate Choices:** 3½

Baked Tofu and Veggies in Peanut Sauce

4 servings | Prep Time: 15 Minutes | Start to Finish: 1 Hour

• • •

TOFU AND VEGGIES

- 1 package (18 oz) extra-firm tofu, drained
- 1 large red, yellow or orange bell pepper, cut into 1-inch pieces
- 1 bag (12 oz) frozen sugar snap peas

PEANUT SAUCE

- ¼ cup packed brown sugar
- ¼ cup creamy peanut butter
- ¼ cup soy sauce
- 2 tablespoons vegetable oil
- 2 tablespoons toasted sesame oil
- 2 tablespoons rice vinegar or cider vinegar
- 2 tablespoons water
- 2 teaspoons Sriracha sauce

SERVE-WITH

- 2 teaspoons sesame seed, toasted

  Hot cooked Asian noodles or rice, if desired

1 Line cookie sheet with foil. Place drained tofu between layers of paper towels. Place plate on top and weight with a 28-ounce can of vegetables, such as stewed tomatoes. Let stand 15 minutes to drain as much liquid as possible. Cut tofu into 1-inch cubes. Place cubes in single layer on cookie sheet; freeze until firm.

2 Place bell peppers and sugar snap peas in 1-gallon resealable freezer plastic bag; adc frozen tofu cubes. In medium bowl, mix all peanut sauce ingredients with whisk until smooth. Pour sauce into bag; seal bag. Turn bag to coat tofu and vegetables with sauce.

3 Lay bag flat in freezer. Freeze up to 2 months. Thaw 12 to 24 hours in refrigerator until completely thawed.

4 Heat oven to 375°F. Line 15x10x1-inch pan with foil. Arrange tofu and vegetables in single layer in pan.

5 Bake 25 to 30 minutes or until tofu is browned and vegetables are tender. Sprinkle with sesame seed. Serve with noodles or rice.

1 Serving: Calories 510; Total Fat 32g (Saturated Fat 4.5g, Trans Fat 0g); Cholesterol 0mg; Sodium 1010mg; Total Carbohydrate 33mg (Dietary Fiber 3g); Protein 23g **Exchanges:** 1 Starch, 1 Other Carbohydrate, 3 Medium-Fat Meat, 3½ Fat **Carbohydrate Choices:** 2

chapter six

Desserts

Classic Apple Pie

8 servings | Prep Time: 30 Minutes | Start to Finish: 3 Hours 20 Minutes

• • •

1 box refrigerated pie crusts, softened as directed on box

½ cup sugar

¼ cup all-purpose flour

¾ teaspoon ground cinnamon

¼ teaspoon ground nutmeg

Dash salt

6 cups thinly sliced peeled tart apples (6 medium)

2 tablespoons cold butter, if desired

2 teaspoons water

1 tablespoon sugar

1 Heat oven to 425°F. Place 1 pie crust in 9-inch glass pie plate.

2 In large bowl, mix ½ cup sugar, the flour, cinnamon, nutmeg and salt. Stir in apples. Spoon into crust-lined plate. Cut butter into small pieces; sprinkle over apples.

3 Top with second crust; seal and flute. Cut slits in several places in top crust. Brush crust with water; sprinkle with 1 tablespoon sugar. Cover crust edge with pie crust shield ring or strips of foil to prevent excessive browning.

4 Bake 40 to 50 minutes or until crust is golden brown and juice begins to bubble through slits in crust, removing foil during last 15 minutes. Cool on cooling rack at least 2 hours before serving.

5 Freeze tightly wrapped pie unbaked or baked up to 2 months. Thaw at room temperature before baking or serving.

1 Serving: Calories 420; Total Fat 21g (Saturated Fat 7g, Trans Fat 2g); Cholesterol 10mg; Sodium 330mg; Total Carbohydrate 53g (Dietary Fiber 3g); Protein 4g **Exchanges:** 1½ Starch, 2 Fruit, 4 Fat **Carbohydrate Choices:** 3½

French Apple Pie
Heat oven to 400°F. Spoon apple mixture into crust-lined plate. Omit butter, 2 teaspoons water and 1 tablespoon sugar. In small bowl, mix 1 cup all-purpose flour and ½ cup packed brown sugar. Cut in ½ cup cold butter with fork until crumbly. Sprinkle over apple mixture. Bake 35 to 40 minutes or until golden brown. Cover top with foil during last 10 to 15 minutes of baking, if necessary, to prevent excessive browning. Serve warm.

Spiced Gingered Pear Pie

8 servings | Prep Time: 25 Minutes | Start to Finish: 1 Hour 40 Minutes

• • •

CRUST

1 box refrigerated pie crusts, softened as directed on box

FILLING

½ cup packed light brown sugar

¼ cup granulated sugar

2 tablespoons cornstarch

3 tablespoons finely chopped crystallized ginger

1 teaspoon finely grated lemon peel

6 cups thinly sliced peeled pears (about 6 medium)

1 tablespoon cold butter

TOPPING

1 tablespoon water

4 teaspoons granulated sugar

1 Heat oven to 425°F. Place 1 pie crust in 9-inch glass pie plate.

2 In large bowl, mix brown sugar, ¼ cup granulated sugar and the cornstarch. Stir in ginger and lemon peel. Add pears; toss gently. Spoon into crust-lined plate. Cut butter into small pieces; sprinkle over filling.

3 Top with second crust; seal and flute. Cut slits or shapes in several places in top crust. Brush crust with water; sprinkle with 4 teaspoons sugar.

4 Bake 40 to 45 minutes or until pears are tender and crust is golden brown. After 15 to 20 minutes of baking, cover crust edge with strips of foil to prevent excessive browning. Cool on cooling rack at least 30 minutes before serving. Store covered in refrigerator.

5 Freeze tightly wrapped pie unbaked or baked up to 2 months. Thaw at room temperature before baking or serving.

1 Serving: Calories 380; Total Fat 14g (Saturated Fat 6g, Trans Fat 0g); Cholesterol 10mg; Sodium 280mg; Total Carbohydrate 62g (Dietary Fiber 2g); Protein 2g **Exchanges:** 1 Starch, 3 Other Carbohydrate, 2½ Fat **Carbohydrate Choices:** 4

Fresh Ideas Ripe Anjou or Bosc pears work well for pies. Choose fruit that is fragrant and slightly soft to the touch.

For a really luscious dessert, serve the pie warm with a scoop of vanilla ice cream drizzled with caramel sauce.

Golden Pecan Pie

8 servings | Prep Time: 15 Minutes | Start to Finish: 3 Hours 5 Minutes

• • • •

1 refrigerated pie crust, softened as directed on box

⅓ cup packed brown sugar

1½ teaspoons all-purpose flour

1¼ cups light corn syrup

1¼ teaspoons vanilla

3 eggs

1½ cups pecan halves or pieces

2 tablespoons butter, melted

1 Heat oven to 375°F. Place pie crust in 9-inch glass pie plate.

2 In large bowl, mix brown sugar, flour, corn syrup, vanilla and eggs until well blended. Stir in pecans and butter. Pour filling into crust-lined plate.

3 Bake 40 to 50 minutes or until filling is puffed and pie is golden brown. Cool completely on cooling rack, about 2 hours, before serving. Store in refrigerator.

4 To freeze, wrap pie tightly. Freeze up to 3 months. Thaw at room temperature.

1 Serving: Calories 500; Total Fat 24g (Saturated Fat 6g, Trans Fat 0g); Cholesterol 80mg; Sodium 210mg; Total Carbohydrate 65g (Dietary Fiber 2g); Protein 5g **Exchanges:** 1½ Starch, 3 Other Carbohydrate, 4½ Fat **Carbohydrate Choices:** 4

Orange Pecan Pie
Add ½ teaspoon grated orange peel to the filling. Garnish with candied orange peel, if desired.

Fresh Idea You've got Thanksgiving covered with this beautiful pie. Add some fresh whipped cream topped with chocolate shavings for holiday — or any time — flair.

Mini Peach Pies

12 mini pies | Prep Time: 30 Minutes | Start to Finish: 1 Hour 15 Minutes

• • •

1 box refrigerated pie crusts, softened as directed on box

½ cup sugar

¼ cup all-purpose flour

¼ teaspoon ground cinnamon

⅛ teaspoon ground nutmeg

2½ cups cut-up (½-inch pieces) fresh ripe peaches (3 to 5 medium) or 2½ cups cut-up (½-inch pieces) frozen peaches, partially thawed, drained

1 teaspoon sugar

1 Unroll pie crusts on work surface. Cut 12 (3½-inch) rounds, trying to cut as many from one crust as possible (reroll scraps to cut additional rounds) and using part of second crust. Firmly press rounds in bottoms and up sides of ungreased regular-size muffin cups.

2 In large bowl, mix ½ cup sugar, the flour, cinnamon and nutmeg. Stir in peaches. Divide fruit mixture evenly among crust-lined cups.

3 Cut remaining portion of second crust into 3x½-inch strips, rerolling any scraps. Lay 3 strips on top of each fruit-filled cup in lattice or crisscross pattern. Press edges of strips to edge of crust to seal. Sprinkle crust strips with 1 teaspoon sugar.

4 Place muffin pan in freezer until completely frozen. Place in 2-gallon resealable freezer plastic bag; seal bag. Freeze up to 2 months.

5 Heat oven to 400°F. Bake pan of frozen mini pies 28 to 33 minutes or until golden brown. Immediately run knife around edges of each pie to loosen. Cool on cooling rack 10 minutes; carefully remove pies from muffin cups. Serve warm.

6 To bake immediately (without freezing), bake 20 to 25 minutes or until golden brown. Immediately run knife around edges of each pie to loosen. Cool on cooling rack 10 minutes; carefully remove pies from muffin cups. Serve warm.

1 Mini Pie: Calories 200; Total Fat 8g (Saturated Fat 3.5g, Trans Fat 0g); Cholesterol 5g; Sodium 170mg; Total Carbohydrate 30g (Dietary Fiber 0g); Protein 1g **Exchanges:** 1 Starch, ½ Fruit, ½ Other Carbohydrate, 1½ Fat **Carbohydrate Choices:** 2

Berry Ice Cream Pie

8 servings | Prep Time: 25 Minutes | Start to Finish: 2 Hours 50 Minutes

• • • •

FILLING

3	cups vanilla ice cream
2	cups raspberry sherbet
1	box (10 oz) frozen raspberries in syrup, thawed

CRUST

1¼	cups crushed vanilla wafer cookies
½	cup finely chopped pecans
¼	cup butter, melted

SAUCE

3	tablespoons sugar
1	tablespoon cornstarch
	Reserved raspberry liquid
2	tablespoons orange juice
1	container (6 oz) fresh raspberries, if desired

1   Place ice cream and sherbet in refrigerator to soften. Place thawed raspberries in strainer over 2-cup glass measuring cup to drain; reserve liquid for sauce.

2   Heat oven to 375°F. In medium bowl, mix all crust ingredients. Press mixture in bottom and up side of ungreased 9-inch glass pie plate. Bake 5 to 8 minutes or until edge just begins to brown. Cool completely on cooling rack.

3   Stir ice cream until smooth; spoon 1½ cups ice cream into cooled baked crust. In large bowl, fold drained raspberries into sherbet. Spoon evenly over ice cream. Carefully spoon remaining 1½ cups ice cream over top. Freeze at least 2 hours or until firm.

4   In 1-quart saucepan, mix sugar and cornstarch. Stir in reserved raspberry liquid. Cook over medium heat, stirring constantly, until mixture becomes clear and thickened. Stir in orange juice. Cool at room temperature at least 10 minutes before serving.

5   Cut pie into slices; serve with sauce. Garnish with fresh raspberries. Pie can be frozen up to 2 months; make sauce just before serving or up to 3 days ahead.

1 Serving: Calories 390; Total Fat 20g (Saturated Fat 9g, Trans Fat 1g); Cholesterol 40mg; Sodium 160mg; Total Carbohydrate 49g (Dietary Fiber 4g); Protein 4g **Exchanges:** 1 Starch, 2 Other Carbohydrate, 4 Fat **Carbohydrate Choices:** 3

Fresh Idea Instead of layering the ice cream and sherbet, you can fold and swirl them together.

"Jamocha" Ice Cream Pie

8 servings | Prep Time: 15 Minutes | Start to Finish: 4 Hours 25 Minutes

• • •

COFFEE PAT-IN-PAN PIE CRUST

1	cup all-purpose flour
½	cup butter, softened
2	teaspoons instant coffee powder or granules

FILLING

2	pints (4 cups) coffee ice cream, slightly softened
¾	cup hot fudge topping

GARNISH, IF DESIRED

Coffee-flavored chocolate candies or chocolate-covered coffee beans

Fresh Idea **Not a coffee fan? This yummy ice cream pie is also great made with vanilla ice cream and garnished with nuts or your favorite chocolate candies.**

1 Heat oven to 400°F. In medium bowl, mix all crust ingredients with spoon until dough forms. Press dough firmly and evenly in bottom and up side of 9-inch glass pie plate. Bake 12 to 15 minutes or until light brown. Cool completely on cooling rack, about 45 minutes.

2 Spread 2 cups of the ice cream in cooled baked crust. Cover; freeze 1 hour or until firm.

3 Spread hot fudge topping over ice cream. Carefully spread remaining 2 cups ice cream over topping. Cover pie tightly. Freeze at least 2 hours until firm but no longer than 2 weeks.

4 Remove pie from freezer about 10 minutes before cutting. Garnish with candies.

1 Serving: Calories 410; Total Fat 22g (Saturated Fat 12g, Trans Fat 1g); Cholesterol 65mg; Sodium 230mg; Total Carbohydrate 47g (Dietary Fiber 2g); Protein 6g **Exchanges:** 2 Starch, 1 Other Carbohydrate, 4 Fat **Carbohydrate Choices:** 3

"Jamocha" Ice Cream Pie

Bourbon-Chocolate-Pecan Mini Pies

Bourbon-Chocolate-Pecan Mini Pies

12 mini pies | Prep Time: 45 Minutes | Start to Finish: 1 Hour 40 Minutes

• • •

CRUST

- 1⅓ cups all-purpose flour
- ¼ cup unsweetened baking cocoa
- 2 tablespoons granulated sugar
- ¾ teaspoon salt
- ½ cup shortening
- ¼ cup ice-cold water

FILLING

- ¾ cup whole pecan halves, toasted*
- 4 oz bittersweet baking chocolate, coarsely chopped
- 1 egg
- ¼ cup packed dark brown sugar
- 2 tablespoons unsalted butter, melted
- 2 tablespoons light or dark corn syrup
- 2 tablespoons real maple syrup
- 1 tablespoon bourbon
- ½ teaspoon vanilla

TOPPING

- ¾ cup whipping cream
- 2 tablespoons granulated sugar or powdered sugar
- 2 tablespoons shaved bittersweet chocolate

*To toast pecans, sprinkle in ungreased skillet. Cook over medium heat 5 to 7 minutes, stirring frequently, until nuts begin to brown, then stirring constantly until nuts are light brown.

1 Heat oven to 375°F. In food processor, place flour, cocoa, 2 tablespoons granulated sugar and the salt. Cover; process, using quick on-and-off motions, until blended. Add shortening. Cover; process, using quick on-and-off motions, until particles are size of small peas. With food processor running, pour water all at once through feed tube just until dough leaves side of bowl. Gather dough into a ball.

2 Divide dough evenly among 12 ungreased regular-size muffin cups, pressing dough in bottoms and up sides of cups. Sprinkle pecan halves and chopped chocolate into crust-lined cups. In medium bowl, beat egg, brown sugar, melted butter, corn syrup, maple syrup, bourbon and vanilla with whisk. Spoon mixture evenly into muffin cups, about 4 teaspoons per cup.

3 Bake 20 to 25 minutes or until filling is golden and slightly puffed in center. Cool 30 minutes; remove from pan to cooling rack. Cool completely.

4 To freeze, wrap pies tightly. Freeze up to 1 month. Thaw at room temperature. To serve warm, reheat pies in the oven, if desired.

5 In chilled small bowl, beat whipping cream and 2 tablespoons sugar with electric mixer on high speed until soft peaks form. To serve, spoon about 2 tablespoons whipped cream onto each mini pie. Sprinkle with shaved chocolate.

1 Mini Pie: Calories 430; Total Fat 27g (Saturated Fat 11g, Trans Fat 0g); Cholesterol 40mg; Sodium 170mg; Total Carbohydrate 43g (Dietary Fiber 3g); Protein 4g **Exchanges:** 1½ Starch, 1½ Other Carbohydrate, 5 Fat **Carbohydrate Choices:** 3

Fresh Idea To make shaved chocolate, let a wrapped large bar of chocolate (any type) stand in a warm place (80°F to 85°F) until slightly softened, about 10 minutes. Scrape a vegetable peeler against the chocolate, using short quick strokes.

Strawberry-Rhubarb Pie Pops

8 pie pops | Prep Time: 30 Minutes | Start to Finish: 1 Hour 30 Minutes

• • •

¾ cup frozen strawberries, thawed, chopped, drained and juice reserved

⅓ cup granulated sugar

2 teaspoons cornstarch

1 cup frozen chopped rhubarb, thawed

1 box refrigerated pie crusts, softened as directed on box

8 craft sticks (flat wooden sticks with round ends)

1 egg white, beaten

1 teaspoon granulated sugar

⅓ cup powdered sugar, if desired

2 to 3 teaspoons milk, if desired

1. In medium bowl, place reserved strawberry juice. In small bowl, mix ⅓ cup granulated sugar and the cornstarch. Add to strawberry juice, beating with whisk. Stir in strawberries and rhubarb.

2. Unroll pie crusts on work surface. Using 3½-inch round cutter, cut 8 rounds from each crust. Spoon fruit mixture onto 8 of the rounds to within ½ inch of edge. Place 1 craft stick in filling on each round.

3. Flatten remaining 8 rounds to 4-inch diameter. Brush underside of rounds with egg white; place over fruit. Press edges together; seal with fork. Cut small slit in tops of pies.

4. Wrap pie pops tightly. Freeze up to 3 months.

5. Heat oven to 450°F. Place frozen pie pops on ungreased cookie sheet. Brush tops with egg white; sprinkle evenly with 1 teaspoon granulated sugar.

6. Bake 15 to 20 minutes or until golden brown. Remove from cookie sheet to cooling rack; cool 10 minutes.

7. In small bowl, mix powdered sugar and enough milk until glaze is smooth and thin enough to drizzle. Drizzle glaze over pie pops; let stand until set, about 30 minutes.

1 Pie Pop: Calories 310; Total Fat 12g (Saturated Fat 5g, Trans Fat 0g); Cholesterol 5mg; Sodium 270mg; Total Carbohydrate 49g (Dietary Fiber 1g); Protein 2g **Exchanges:** ½ Starch, 1½ Fruit, 1 Other Carbohydrate, 2½ Fat **Carbohydrate Choices:** 3

Fresh Idea Change up the flavors in the pie pops by substituting 1 cup of your favorite canned pie filling for the strawberry-rhubarb filling.

Caramel Apple Mug Cakes

20 servings | Prep Time: 30 Minutes | Start to Finish: 30 Minutes

- - -

CAKE

- 1 box (15.25 oz) butter recipe yellow cake mix
- 1 cup water
- ½ cup butter, softened
- 3 eggs
- ¼ teaspoon ground cinnamon
- 2 large baking apples, peeled, cut into ¼-inch pieces (about 2 cups)
- 1 tablespoon lemon juice

TOPPING

- ¾ cup caramel topping
- ½ cup chopped toasted pecans*, if desired

1 Place paper baking cup in each of 20 regular-size muffin cups; spray paper cups with cooking spray. In large bowl, beat cake mix, water, butter and eggs with electric mixer on low speed until moistened, then on medium speed 2 minutes, scraping bowl occasionally.

2 Remove 1 cup of the batter to small bowl. Add cinnamon to batter in small bowl; stir until well blended. In medium bowl, toss apples with lemon juice. Fold apples into remaining batter in large bowl.

3 Spoon apple batter evenly into muffin cups. Spoon about 2 teaspoons cinnamon batter onto top of each. Using toothpick, swirl batters gently but do not mix completely.

4 Place muffin pans in freezer until completely frozen. Remove cakes from muffin cups; wrap individually or place in freezer container. Freeze up to 3 months.

5 To make 1 mug cake, spray microwavable mug (about 12 oz) with cooking spray. Spoon 1 tablespoon caramel topping and 1 teaspoon pecans into bottom of mug. Peel paper cup off frozen cake; place in mug. Microwave uncovered on High about 1 minute or until cake is set on top. (Do not overcook, or cake will be dry.) Let stand 1 minute. Turn upside down onto serving plate or eat out of mug.

*To toast pecans, sprinkle in ungreased skillet. Cook over medium heat 5 to 7 minutes, stirring frequently, until nuts begin to brown, then stirring constantly until nuts are light brown.

1 Serving: Calories 380; Total Fat 19g (Saturated Fat 8g, Trans Fat 1g); Cholesterol 65mg; Sodium 280mg; Total Carbohydrate 49g (Dietary Fiber 1g); Protein 2g **Exchanges:** ½ Starch, 3 Other Carbohydrate, 3½ Fat **Carbohydrate Choices:** 3

Fresh Idea **Single serve was never more easy or more delicious! For a change of pace, try using chocolate syrup in the topping.**

Caramel-Fudge Cheesecake

12 servings | Prep Time: 30 Minutes | Start to Finish: 4 Hours 20 Minutes

• • •

1½ cups finely crushed vanilla wafer cookies (about 40 cookies)

¼ cup butter, melted

2 packages (8 oz each) cream cheese, softened

½ cup sugar

2 teaspoons vanilla

2 eggs

¼ cup hot fudge topping

1 cup caramel topping

½ cup coarsely chopped pecans, toasted*

1 Heat oven to 350°F. In medium bowl, mix cookie crumbs and butter. Press crumb mixture firmly against bottom and side of ungreased 9-inch glass pie plate.

2 In large bowl, beat cream cheese, sugar, vanilla and eggs with electric mixer on low speed until smooth. Pour half of mixture into pie plate.

3 Add hot fudge topping to remaining cream cheese mixture in bowl; beat on low speed until smooth. Spoon over vanilla mixture in pie plate. Swirl mixtures slightly with tip of knife.

4 Bake 40 to 50 minutes cr until center is set. Cool on cooling rack 1 hour. Refrigerate at least 2 hours until chilled. Store covered in refrigerator. Garnish with caramel topping and pecans just before serving.

5 To freeze, wrap whole cheesecake, or leave whole but cut into wedges and gently separate, placing pieces of waxed paper between slices for easy removal. Or wrap individual slices. Freeze up to 3 months. Thaw in refrigerator.

*To toast pecans, sprinkle in ungreased skillet. Cook over medium heat 5 to 7 minutes, stirring frequently, until nuts begin to brown, then stirring constantly until nuts are light brown.

1 Serving: Calories 390; Total Fat 24g (Saturated Fat 12g, Trans Fat 1g); Cholesterol 85mg; Sodium 310mg; Total Carbohydrate 39g (Dietary Fiber 1g); Protein 6g **Exchanges:** 1½ Starch, 1 Other Carbohydrate, 4½ Fat **Carbohydrate Choices:** 2½

Pumpkin Cheesecake

16 servings | Prep Time: 25 Minutes | Start to Finish: 9 Hours 10 Minutes

. . .

CRUST

1¾	cups graham cracker crumbs (about 24 squares)
2	tablespoons granulated sugar
½	cup butter, melted

FILLING

¼	cup all-purpose flour
2	teaspoons pumpkin pie spice
2	tablespoons brandy, if desired
1	can (15 oz) pumpkin (not pumpkin pie mix)
4	packages (8 oz each) cream cheese, softened
1	cup packed brown sugar
⅔	cup granulated sugar
5	eggs

1 Serving: Calories 430; Total Fat 29g (Saturated Fat 16g, Trans Fat 1g); Cholesterol 145mg; Sodium 290mg; Total Carbohydrate 36g (Dietary Fiber 1g); Protein 7g **Exchanges:** 2½ Starch, 5½ Fat **Carbohydrate Choices:** 2½

Fresh Idea Garnish individual slices with whipped cream sprinkled with pumpkin pie spice.

1 Heat oven to 325°F. Grease bottom and side of 9-inch springform pan with shortening. Wrap outside bottom and side of pan with foil to prevent leaking.

2 In small bowl, mix cracker crumbs, 2 tablespoons granulated sugar and the melted butter. Press crumb mixture in bottom of pan. Bake 8 to 10 minutes or until set. Cool 5 minutes. Refrigerate about 5 minutes or until completely cooled.

3 Meanwhile, in another small bowl, mix flour, pumpkin pie spice, brandy and pumpkin with whisk until well blended; set aside. In large bowl, beat cream cheese with electric mixer on medium speed until smooth and creamy. Gradually beat in brown sugar and ⅔ cup granulated sugar until smooth. On low speed, beat in eggs, one at a time, just until blended. Gradually beat in pumpkin mixture until smooth.

4 Pour filling over crust. Bake 1 hour 15 minutes to 1 hour 25 minutes or until set at least 2 inches from edge of pan but center of cheesecake still jiggles slightly when moved. Turn oven off; open oven door at least 4 inches. Let cheesecake remain in oven 30 minutes.

5 Run knife around edge of pan to loosen cheesecake. Cool on cooling rack 30 minutes. Refrigerate at least 6 hours or overnight. To serve, run knife around edge of pan to loosen cheesecake. Carefully remove side of pan before cutting cheesecake. Store covered in refrigerator.

6 To freeze, wrap whole cheesecake, or leave whole but cut into wedges and gently separate, placing pieces of waxed paper between slices for easy removal. Or wrap individual slices. Freeze up to 3 months. Thaw in refrigerator.

Cookie Ice Cream Sandwiches

12 ice cream sandwiches | Prep Time: 30 Minutes | Start to Finish: 1 Hour

• • •

1 pouch (1 lb 1.5 oz) chocolate chip cookie mix

Butter and egg called for on cookie mix pouch

1 quart (4 cups) ice cream, frozen yogurt, sherbet or sorbet

Candy sprinkles or miniature chocolate chips, if desired

1 Heat oven to 375°F. Make cookies as directed on pouch, using butter and egg—except drop dough by rounded tablespoonfuls 2 inches apart onto ungreased cookie sheet.

2 Bake 11 to 13 minutes or until edges are light golden brown. Cool 1 minute before removing from cookie sheet to cooling rack. Cool completely, about 30 minutes.

3 For each ice cream sandwich, place 1 scoop of ice cream (about ⅓ cup) on bottom of one cookie; top with second cookie, bottom side down. Gently press cookies together (ice cream should spread to edge of cookies). Roll ice cream edges in sprinkles.

4 Wrap sandwiches individually in plastic wrap. Place in resealable freezer plastic bag; seal bag. Freeze up to 3 months.

1 Ice Cream Sandwich: Calories 350; Total Fat 18g (Saturated Fat 11g, Trans Fat 0.5g); Cholesterol 60mg; Sodium 220mg; Total Carbohydrate 43g (Dietary Fiber 0g); Protein 4g **Exchanges:** 2½ Other Carbohydrate, ½ Low-Fat Milk, 3 Fat **Carbohydrate Choices:** 3

Fresh Idea Try any flavor of cookie mix you please—you don't have to limit the cookies to chocolate chip. For a more indulgent treat, drizzle a little ice cream topping (such as chocolate or caramel) between the cookies and ice cream.

Brownie Ice Cream Sandwiches

12 ice cream sandwiches | Prep Time: 15 Minutes | Start to Finish: 2 Hours 45 Minutes

• • •

1 box (1 lb 6.5 oz) supreme brownie mix with pouch of chocolate flavor syrup

Water, vegetable oil and eggs called for on brownie mix box

1 quart (4 cups) vanilla ice cream, slightly softened

Candy sprinkles or miniature chocolate chips, if desired

1. Heat oven to 350°F (325°F for dark or nonstick pan). Line 13x9-inch pan with foil so foil extends about 2 inches over sides of pan; spray foil with cooking spray.

2. Make and bake brownies as directed on box for 13x9-inch pan, using water, oil and eggs. Cool completely in pan on cooling rack, about 1 hour.

3. Place pan in freezer 30 minutes. Remove brownies from pan by lifting foil; peel foil from sides of brownies. Cut into 6 rows by 4 rows; peel remaining foil.

4. For each sandwich, spoon ¼ cup ice cream on bottom of 1 brownie square. Top with second brownie square, bottom side down; gently press together. Roll ice cream edges in sprinkles; place in shallow pan. Freeze until firm, about 30 minutes.

5. Wrap sandwiches individually in plastic wrap. Place in resealable freezer plastic bag; seal bag. Freeze up to 3 months.

1 Ice Cream Sandwich: Calories 310; Total Fat 12g (Saturated Fat 4.5g, Trans Fat 0g); Cholesterol 35mg; Sodium 180mg; Total Carbohydrate 46g (Dietary Fiber 1g); Protein 3g
Exchanges: 1 Starch, 2 Other Carbohydrate, 2½ Fat **Carbohydrate Choices:** 3

Fresh Idea Who knew brownies made such great ice cream sandwiches!? While vanilla ice cream is a classic, you can use any flavor of ice cream here.

Brown Sugar Refrigerator Cookies

6 dozen cookies | Prep Time: 1 Hour | Start to Finish: 3 Hours 10 Minutes

• • •

1 cup packed brown sugar
1 cup butter, softened
1 teaspoon vanilla
1 egg
3 cups all-purpose flour
1½ teaspoons ground cinnamon
½ teaspoon baking soda
½ teaspoon salt
⅓ cup finely chopped nuts

1 In large bowl, beat brown sugar, butter, vanilla and egg with electric mixer on medium speed, or mix with spoon. Stir in flour, cinnamon, baking soda and salt. Stir in nuts.

2 On plastic wrap, shape dough into 10x3-inch rectangle. Wrap tightly; refrigerate about 2 hours or until firm but no longer than 24 hours. Or freeze up to 2 months.

3 Heat oven to 375°F. Unwrap dough; cut into ⅛-inch slices. On ungreased cookie sheets, place slices 2 inches apart.

4 Bake 6 to 8 minutes or until light brown. (If dough is frozen, add 1 to 2 minutes to the bake time.) Cool 1 to 2 minutes; remove from cookie sheets to cooling racks.

1 Cookie: Calories 60; Total Fat 3g (Saturated Fat 1.5g, Trans Fat 0g); Cholesterol 10mg; Sodium 50mg; Total Carbohydrate 7g (Dietary Fiber 0g); Protein 0g **Exchanges:** ½ Other Carbohydrate, ½ Fat **Carbohydrate Choices:** ½

Citrus–Brown Sugar Refrigerator Cookies
Add 1 tablespoon grated lemon or orange peel with the flour. Frost cookies with Vanilla Glaze. For the glaze, in medium bowl, mix 2 cups powdered sugar, ⅓ cup butter, melted, and 1 teaspoon vanilla. Stir in 2 to 4 tablespoons hot water, 1 tablespoon at a time, until glaze is smooth and has the consistency of thick syrup. Drizzle over cookies; sprinkle with grated lemon or orange peel.

Maple–Brown Sugar Refrigerator Cookies
Substitute 2 teaspoons maple flavor for the vanilla.

Toasted Coconut–Brown Sugar Refrigerator Cookies
Add 1 cup toasted coconut with the flour. Frost cookies with Vanilla Glaze (see above) and sprinkle with additional toasted coconut instead of lemon peel.

Dulce de Leche–Stuffed Chocolate Chip Cookies

3 dozen cookies | Prep Time: 1 Hour | Start to Finish: 2 Hours 45 Minutes

• • •

1 can (13.4 oz) dulce de leche (caramelized sweetened condensed milk)

1½ cups butter, softened

1¼ cups granulated sugar

1¼ cups packed brown sugar

1 tablespoon vanilla

2 eggs

4 cups all-purpose flour

2 teaspoons baking soda

1 teaspoon salt

4 cups semisweet chocolate chips (about 24 oz)

1 cup chopped pecans, toasted*

*To toast pecans, sprinkle in ungreased skillet. Cook over medium heat 5 to 7 minutes, stirring frequently, until nuts begin to brown, then stirring constantly until nuts are light brown.

1 Cookie: Calories 340; Total Fat 17g (Saturated Fat 9g, Trans Fat 0g); Cholesterol 35mg; Sodium 220mg; Total Carbohydrate 43g (Dietary Fiber 2g); Protein 3g **Exchanges:** 1 Starch, 2 Other Carbohydrate, 3½ Fat **Carbohydrate Choices:** 3

1 Line cookie sheet with waxed paper or foil. Spoon 42 slightly-less-than-level measuring teaspoonfuls dulce de leche onto cookie sheet. Freeze 1 hour or until slightly firm (dollops will not freeze solid).

2 In large bowl, mix butter, granulated sugar, brown sugar, vanilla and eggs with heavy-duty spoon until well blended. Stir in flour, baking soda and salt. Stir in chocolate chips and pecans (dough will be stiff and chunky; you may need to use your hands).

3 Drop dough by ¼ cupfuls about 3 inches apart onto cookie sheets lined with parchment paper. Press thumb into center of each cookie to make deep indentation, but do not press all the way to cookie sheet. Place 1 dulce de leche dollop into center of each cookie, forming dough around dollop to enclose. Return dulce de leche dollops to freezer if they become too warm to work with.

4 To freeze for future baking, freeze 1 hour or until firm. Place frozen cookie dough balls in resealable freezer plastic bag; seal bag. Freeze up to 3 months.

5 Heat oven to 350°F. Line cookie sheets with cooking parchment paper. Place cookies on cookie sheets. Bake 12 to 15 minutes or until light brown (centers will be soft). Cool 1 to 2 minutes; remove from cookie sheets to cooling racks.

Fresh Idea Dulce de leche is similar to sweetened condensed milk, but it has been caramelized and is much thicker and is caramel in color. It can be found near the regular sweetened condensed milk or in the Hispanic section of the grocery store. If you can't find it, substitute 42 round chewy caramels in milk chocolate (from 12-ounce bag), unwrapped. No need to freeze these; just unwrap from the gold foil and insert in the indentation as directed in Step 3. Continue as directed.

Strawberry-Peach Pops

10 pops | Prep Time: 10 Minutes | Start to Finish: 2 Hours 25 Minutes

● ● ◑

1 cup fat-free (skim) milk

1 cup frozen unsweetened whole strawberries

1 container (6 oz) harvest peach yogurt

1 tablespoon sugar, if desired

10 paper cups (3 oz)

10 craft sticks (flat wooden sticks with round ends)

1 In blender, place milk, strawberries, yogurt and sugar. Cover; blend on high speed about 1 minute or until smooth.

2 Fill each cup with about ¼ cup yogurt mixture. Freeze about 45 minutes or until partially frozen.

3 Cover cups with foil; insert craft stick into center of each pop. Freeze about 1 hour 30 minutes longer or until firm.

4 Store in freezer up to 2 months. To serve, remove foil and peel off paper cups.

1 Pop: Calories 50; Total Fat 0.5g (Saturated Fat 0g, Trans Fat 0g); Cholesterol 0mg; Sodium 20mg; Total Carbohydrate 9g (Dietary Fiber 0g); Protein 1g **Exchanges:** ½ Starch **Carbohydrate Choices:** ½

Fresh Idea Branch out into other yogurt flavors—strawberry for a double dose of that great flavor, or whatever combo speaks to you.

Watermelon Mojito Cocktail Pops

5 pops | Prep Time: 10 Minutes | Start to Finish: 8 Hours 10 Minutes

• • •

2 cups chopped seedless or seeded watermelon

3 tablespoons sugar

3 tablespoons light rum

3 tablespoons fresh lime juice

3 tablespoons water

4 small fresh mint leaves

5 paper cups (5 oz)

5 craft sticks (flat wooden sticks with round ends)

   Lime slices, if desired

1 In blender, place watermelon, sugar, rum, lime juice, water and mint. Cover; blend until smooth.

2 Divide mixture evenly among paper cups. Cover cups with foil; insert craft stick into center of each pop. Freeze about 8 hours or until frozen.

3 Store in freezer up to 2 months. To serve, remove foil; peel off paper cups. Garnish pops with lime slices.

1 Pop: Calories 70; Total Fat 0g (Saturated Fat 0g, Trans Fat 0g); Cholesterol 0mg; Sodium 0mg; Total Carbohydrate 13g (Dietary Fiber 0g); Protein 0g **Carbohydrate Choices:** 1

Fresh Idea This is one pop not meant for the kids! For a kid-friendly version, increase watermelon to 2¼ cups and omit the rum.

Fresh Fruit Frozen Yogurt Pops

6 pops | Prep Time: 10 Minutes | Start to Finish: 6 Hours 10 Minutes

· · ·

2 containers (6 oz each) French vanilla low-fat yogurt

2 cups fresh fruit (blueberries, raspberries, sliced bananas, halved cherries or grapes, or cut-up papaya, peaches or oranges)

1 tablespoon honey

6 paper cups (5 oz) and craft sticks (flat wooden sticks with round ends), or frozen ice-pop molds

1 In blender, place yogurt, fruit and honey. Cover; blend until smooth. Divide mixture evenly among paper cups.

2 Cover cups with foil; insert craft stick into center of each pop. (Or fill ice-pop molds according to manufacturer's directions.) Freeze about 6 hours or until frozen.

3 Store in freezer up to 2 months. To serve, remove foil and peel off paper cups, or remove pops from molds.

1 Pop: Calories 110; Total Fat 1g (Saturated Fat 0g, Trans Fat 0g); Cholesterol 0mg; Sodium 35mg; Total Carbohydrate 22g (Dietary Fiber 1g); Protein 3g **Exchanges:** 1 Starch, ½ Fruit **Carbohydrate Choices:** 1½

Fresh Idea The fruit possibilities are endless! Try strawberries, grapefruit, plums, mango or pineapple for great flavor, too. Save time and make a few batches of different flavors while you have the blender out.

Dulce de Leche Cheesecake Pops

8 pops | Prep Time: 25 Minutes | Start to Finish: 6 Hours 25 Minutes

• • • •

1 package (8 oz) cream cheese, softened

½ cup sugar

½ cup sour cream

1 cup half-and-half

8 paper cups (5 oz)

8 craft sticks (flat wooden sticks with round ends)

⅔ cup dulce de leche (caramelized sweetened condensed milk), from 13.4-oz can

2 tablespoons milk

½ cup Cinnamon Toast Crunch™ cereal, coarsely crushed

1 In medium bowl, beat cream cheese and sugar with electric mixer on medium speed until smooth. Beat in sour cream and half-and-half. Spoon ¼ cup mixture into each paper cup. Cover cups with foil; insert craft stick into center of each pop. Freeze about 2 hours or until frozen. Cover and refrigerate remaining cream cheese mixture.

2 In small bowl, mix dulce de leche and milk. Place ⅓ cup dulce de leche mixture in small resealable food-storage plastic bag; cover and refrigerate remaining mixture. Cut off small corner of bag; squeeze small amounts over frozen cream cheese layer in each cup. Pour remaining cream cheese mixture over dulce de leche layer in cups. Return foil to pops to support sticks. Freeze until firm, at least 4 hours or up to 3 days.

3 About 30 minutes before serving, remove reserved dulce de leche mixture from refrigerator; let stand at room temperature to soften. Remove paper cups from pops. Dip top of each pop into reserved dulce de leche mixture; dip into crushed cereal.

1 Pop: Calories 310; Total Fat 18g (Saturated Fat 11g, Trans Fat 0.5g); Cholesterol 60mg; Sodium 170mg; Total Carbohydrate 32g (Dietary Fiber 0g); Protein 5g **Exchanges:** ½ Starch, 1 Other Carbohydrate, ½ Skim Milk, 3½ Fat **Carbohydrate Choices:** 2

Caramel Ice Cream

1 quart | Prep Time: 15 Minutes | Start to Finish: 2 Hours 45 Minutes

• • •

½ cup sugar
2 cups whipping cream
1 cup milk
3 egg yolks, slightly beaten
¼ teaspoon salt
2 teaspoons vanilla

1 In 2-quart saucepan, heat sugar over medium heat until sugar begins to melt. Stir until sugar is completely dissolved and becomes deep golden brown to amber in color. Remove from heat; carefully and gradually stir in 1 cup of the whipping cream (mixture will boil and splatter at first). Heat over low heat, stirring frequently, until any hardened sugar bits dissolve; remove from heat.

2 With whisk, stir in remaining 1 cup whipping cream, the milk, egg yolks, salt and vanilla until well mixed. Heat just to boiling over medium heat, stirring constantly (do not allow mixture to continue to boil or it will curdle). Immediately remove from heat.

3 Pour milk mixture into chilled bowl. Refrigerate uncovered 2 to 3 hours, stirring occasionally, until room temperature. At this point, mixture can be refrigerated up to 24 hours before completing recipe if desired.

4 Pour mixture into 1-quart ice-cream freezer and freeze according to manufacturer's directions.

1 Serving: Calories 300 (Calories from Fat 220); Total Fat 25g (Saturated Fat 15g, Trans Fat 1g); Cholesterol 160mg; Sodium 110mg; Total Carbohydrate 16g (Dietary Fiber 0g); Sugars 16g; Protein 3g **Exchanges:** 1 Other Carbohydrate, 4½ Fat **Carbohydrate Choices:** 1

Cantaloupe Granita

5 cups | Prep Time: 15 Minutes | Start to Finish: 3 Hours 15 Minutes

- - -

2 cups cubed ripe cantaloupe or honeydew melon

2 cups soymilk or milk

3 tablespoons honey

¾ teaspoon ground ginger

1 Place all ingredients in blender or food processor. Cover; blend on high speed about 30 seconds or until smooth. Pour into 8- or 9-inch square (2-quart) glass baking dish.

2 Freeze uncovered 30 minutes. When ice crystals begin to form at edges of dish, stir mixture with fork. Freeze 2 hours 30 minutes to 3 hours longer, stirring every 30 minutes, until firm. Granita can be frozen covered up to 3 months.

½ **Cup:** Calories 50; Total Fat 0.5g (Saturated Fat 0g, Trans Fat 0g); Cholesterol 0mg; Sodium 35mg; Total Carbohydrate 10g (Dietary Fiber 0g); Protein 2g **Exchanges:** 1 Other Carbohydrate **Carbohydrate Choices:** ½

Granita Slush Make recipe as directed; spoon into 10 serving glasses. Gently stir ¼ cup sparkling mineral water or ginger ale into each glass.

Chocolate-and-Berries Yogurt Dessert

8 servings | Prep Time: 40 Minutes | Start to Finish: 4 Hours 40 Minutes

• • •

1 pouch (1 lb 1.5 oz) double chocolate chip cookie mix

¼ cup vegetable oil

2 tablespoons water

1 egg

1½ cups fresh raspberries

4 containers (4 oz each) whipped mousse-style raspberry mist yogurt

1 cup whipping cream, whipped

2 tablespoons hot fudge topping

1 cup fresh blueberries

1 Heat oven to 350°F. Spray cookie sheet with cooking spray. In large bowl, stir cookie mix, oil, water and egg until soft dough forms.

2 Onto cookie sheet, drop dough by tablespoonfuls to make 6 cookies. Bake 8 to 11 minutes or until set. Cool 2 minutes; remove from cookie sheet to cooling rack.

3 Meanwhile, press remaining dough in bottom and 1 inch up side of springform pan. Bake 8 to 10 minutes or until set. Cool completely, about 30 minutes.

4 In medium bowl, fold ½ cup of the raspberries into yogurt; spread evenly over crust. Crumble cookies; sprinkle over yogurt mixture. Carefully spread whipped cream evenly over cookie crumbs. Cover pan tightly. Freeze until firm, at least 4 hours or up to 2 weeks.

5 To serve, remove side of pan. (If frozen longer than 4 hours, let stand at room temperature 15 minutes before cutting.) Drizzle 1 tablespoon fudge topping over dessert. Top with blueberries and remaining raspberries. Drizzle with remaining fudge topping.

1 Serving: Calories 530; Total Fat 24g (Saturated Fat 11g, Trans Fat 0g); Cholesterol 65mg; Sodium 330mg; Total Carbohydrate 72g (Dietary Fiber 2g); Protein 6g **Exchanges:** 2 Starch, ½ Fruit, 2½ Other Carbohydrate, 4½ Fat **Carbohydrate Choices:** 5

Frozen Chocolate-Granola Cream Cake

8 servings | Prep Time: 20 Minutes | Start to Finish: 4 Hours 20 Minutes

• • •

2 **cups whipping cream**

¼ **cup sugar**

1 **teaspoon vanilla**

1 **box (6 oz) dark chocolate thin granola bars, unwrapped**

1 **cup Cocoa Puffs™ cereal**

1 Line 8x4-inch loaf pan with foil. In large bowl, beat whipping cream, sugar and vanilla with electric mixer on high speed until stiff peaks form.

2 Spread ¾ cup of the whipped cream evenly in bottom of pan. Place 3 granola bars, chocolate side up, on top of cream. Top with ¾ cup whipped cream. Sprinkle ½ cup of the cereal evenly over top. Spread ¾ cup whipped cream over cereal.

3 Repeat layering with 3 granola bars and ¾ cup whipped cream. Top with remaining ½ cup cereal, ¾ cup whipped cream and 3 granola bars. Cover loosely with plastic wrap. Freeze until firm, at least 4 hours or up to 2 days.

4 To serve, let cake stand at room temperature 5 minutes. Remove plastic wrap. Place serving plate upside down over pan; turn plate and pan over. Remove pan and foil. Break remaining granola bar into pieces; sprinkle over top. With sharp knife, cut crosswise into 1-inch-thick slices.

1 Serving: Calories 350; Total Fat 26g (Saturated Fat 15g, Trans Fat 1g); Cholesterol 80mg; Sodium 120mg; Total Carbohydrate 26g (Dietary Fiber 2g); Protein 3g **Exchanges:** 1 Starch, ½ Other Carbohydrate, 5 Fat **Carbohydrate Choices:** 2

Mud Slide Ice Cream Cake

15 servings | Prep Time: 30 Minutes | Start to Finish: 6 Hours

• • •

1 box (15.25 oz) chocolate
  fudge cake mix with pudding

½ cup butter, softened

1 egg

2 tablespoons milk

2 tablespoons coffee-flavored
  liqueur or cold strong
  brewed coffee

1 quart (4 cups) vanilla
  ice cream

1 container (12 oz) chocolate
  whipped ready-to-
  spread frosting

2 tablespoons coffee-flavored
  liqueur, if desired

1 Heat oven to 350°F (325°F for dark or nonstick pan).
Grease bottom only of 13x9-inch pan with shortening or cooking
spray. In large bowl, beat cake mix, butter, egg and milk with spoon
or electric mixer on low speed until well blended. Spread batter
in pan.

2 Bake 16 to 18 minutes or until center is set (top may appear dry and
cracked). Cool completely on cooling rack, about 1 hour.

3 Brush 2 tablespoons liqueur over cake. Let ice cream stand about
15 minutes at room temperature to soften. Spread ice cream over
cake. Freeze about 3 hours or until firm.

4 In medium bowl, mix frosting and 2 tablespoons liqueur; spread
over ice cream. Freeze at least 1 hour. Store covered in freezer up
to 3 months.

1 Serving: Calories 340; Total Fat 16g (Saturated Fat 8g, Trans Fat 1.5g); Cholesterol 45mg;
Sodium 390mg; Total Carbohydrate 46g (Dietary Fiber 1g); Protein 3g **Exchanges:** 1 Starch,
2 Other Carbohydrate, 3 Fat **Carbohydrate Choices:** 3

Fresh Idea **Coffee lovers, substitute coffee-flavored ice cream for the
vanilla!**

Rainbow Sherbet Roll

12 servings | Prep Time: 20 Minutes | Start to Finish: 8 Hours 15 Minutes

* * *

1 box (16 oz) white angel food cake mix

1¼ cups cold water

Powdered sugar

1½ cups raspberry sherbet, softened

1½ cups orange sherbet, softened

1½ cups lime sherbet, softened

1 Heat oven to 350°F. Line 15x10x1-inch pan with waxed paper.

2 In extra-large glass or metal bowl, beat cake mix and cold water with electric mixer on low speed 30 seconds; beat on medium speed 1 minute. Spread half of the batter in pan. Spread remaining batter in ungreased 9x5-inch loaf pan.

3 Bake 15x10 pan 20 to 25 minutes, loaf pan 35 to 45 minutes, or until top springs back when touched lightly in center. Cool 10 minutes; remove cake from loaf pan and reserve for another use. Loosen cake from edges of 15x10 pan; turn upside down onto towel sprinkled with powdered sugar. Carefully remove waxed paper. Trim off stiff edges of cake if necessary. Carefully roll hot cake and towel from narrow end. Cool completely on cooling rack, about 1 hour.

4 Unroll cake; remove towel. Beginning at a narrow end, spread raspberry sherbet on one-third of cake, orange sherbet on next third of cake and lime sherbet on remaining cake. Roll up carefully. Place roll, seam side down, on 18x12-inch piece of foil; wrap in foil.

5 Freeze at least 6 hours or until firm. Remove from freezer 15 minutes before serving. Cut roll into ¾-inch slices. Store tightly wrapped in freezer up to 3 months.

1 Serving: Calories 220; Total Fat 1g (Saturated Fat 0.5g, Trans Fat 0g); Cholesterol 0mg; Sodium 350mg; Total Carbohydrate 50g (Dietary Fiber 0g); Protein 3g **Exchanges:** 1 Starch, 2½ Other Carbohydrate **Carbohydrate Choices:** 3

Fudge Brownie Ice Cream Dessert

20 servings | Prep Time: 15 Minutes | Start to Finish: 4 Hours 20 Minutes

• • •

BROWNIES

- 1 box (1 lb 2.3 oz) fudge brownie mix

  Water, vegetable oil and eggs called for on brownie mix box

- ½ cup chopped pecans

TOPPING

- 2 quarts (8 cups) dulce de leche ice cream, slightly softened
- ½ cup hot fudge topping, heated until warm
- ½ cup chopped pecans
- 1 cup frozen (thawed) whipped topping, if desired

1 Heat oven to 350°F. Spray bottom of 15x10x1-inch pan with cooking spray. In large bowl, stir brownie mix, water, oil and eggs until well blended. Stir in ½ cup pecans; spread in pan.

2 Bake 15 to 17 minutes or until center is set. DO NOT OVERBAKE. Cool completely on cooling rack, about 45 minutes.

3 Spoon ice cream evenly over brownies; smooth with back of spoon or rubber spatula. Freeze uncovered until firm, about 3 hours. Or cover and freeze up to 2 months.

4 To serve, drizzle hot fudge topping over dessert with fork using quick strokes. Sprinkle with ½ cup pecans. Let stand at room temperature about 5 minutes before cutting. Top with whipped topping.

1 Serving: Calories 350; Total Fat 19g (Saturated Fat 6g, Trans Fat 0g); Cholesterol 45mg; Sodium 160mg; Total Carbohydrate 41g (Dietary Fiber 1g); Protein 3g **Exchanges:** 1 Starch, 1½ Other Carbohydrate, 3½ Fat **Carbohydrate Choices:** 3

Fresh Idea Vanilla ice cream can be used in place of the dulce de leche ice cream, and you can use caramel topping instead of hot fudge—or both!

Metric Conversion Guide

VOLUME

U.S. Units	Canadian Metric	Australian Metric
¼ teaspoon	1 mL	1 ml
½ teaspoon	2 mL	2 ml
1 teaspoon	5 mL	5 ml
1 tablespoon	15 mL	20 ml
¼ cup	50 mL	60 ml
⅓ cup	75 mL	80 ml
½ cup	125 mL	125 ml
⅔ cup	150 mL	170 ml
¾ cup	175 mL	190 ml
1 cup	250 mL	250 ml
1 quart	1 liter	1 liter
1½ quarts	1.5 liters	1.5 liters
2 quarts	2 liters	2 liters
2½ quarts	2.5 liters	2.5 liters
3 quarts	3 liters	3 liters
4 quarts	4 liters	4 liters

WEIGHT

U.S. Units	Canadian Metric	Australian Metric
1 ounce	30 grams	30 grams
2 ounces	55 grams	60 grams
3 ounces	85 grams	90 grams
4 ounces (¼ pound)	115 grams	125 grams
8 ounces (½ pound)	225 grams	225 grams
16 ounces (1 pound)	455 grams	500 grams
1 pound	455 grams	0.5 kilogram

MEASUREMENTS

Inches	Centimeters
1	2.5
2	5.0
3	7.5
4	10.0
5	12.5
6	15.0
7	17.5
8	20.5
9	23.0
10	25.5
11	28.0
12	30.5
13	33.0

TEMPERATURES

Fahrenheit	Celsius
32°	0°
212°	100°
250°	120°
275°	140°
300°	150°
325°	160°
350°	180°
375°	190°
400°	200°
425°	220°
450°	230°
475°	240°
500°	260°

Note: The recipes in this cookbook have not been developed or tested using metric measures. When converting recipes to metric, some variations in quality may be noted.

Index

Page numbers in *italics* indicate illustrations

A

Almond Oatmeal, 31
American cheese: Cheeseburger
　　Lasagna, 72, *73*
Anaheim chiles: Slow-Cooker Smoky
　　Chipotle Soft Tacos, 198, *199*
Apple(s)
　　Caramel, Mug Cakes, *260*, 261
　　-Cinnamon–Butternut Squash Soup,
　　　222, 223
　　Classic, Pie, *246*, 247
　　Crisp Refrigerator Oatmeal, 28, *29*
　　French, Pie, 247
Apricot-Stuffed French Toast, 22, *23*
Artichoke-Spinach Lasagna, *236*, 237
Arugula: Creamy Pulled Pork Pasta,
　　84, *85*
Avocado
　　Easy Shrimp Tacos, 184, *185*
　　Turkey Meatball Tacos, 150, *151*

B

Bacon
　　and Hash Brown Egg Bake, *44*, 45
　　Chicken Salad Club Sandwich
　　　Stackers, *112*, 113
　　Corn and Shrimp Chowder, 188, *189*
　　New England Clam Chowder, *190*, 191
　　-Pepper Mac and Cheese, *100*, 101
　　quick freezer ideas for, 216
　　Slow-Cooker Wild Rice and
　　　Rosemary Chicken, 122, *123*
Baked Sausage and Penne, *104*, 105
Baked Tofu and Veggies in Peanut
　　Sauce, 242, *243*
Banana(s)
　　Fruity Green Smoothies, *50*, 51
　　Oatmeal, 31
　　Upside-Down Banana-Walnut
　　　French Toast, *20*, 21
　　Spinach-Pesto Egg Bakes, *34*, 35
Bean and Barley Chili with Cilantro
　　Sour Cream, 224, *225*
Bean and Vegetable Stew with Polenta,
　　228
Beef. *See also* Ground beef
　　Beer-Roasted Rib-Eye, *78*, 79

Pan-Fried Spicy Korean, *74*, 75
Slow-Cooker Asian Beef Short Ribs,
　　80, *81*
Slow-Cooker, Stew Adobo, 76, *77*
Spicy Korean, Kabobs, 75
Beef broth
　　Beer-Roasted Rib-Eye, *78*, 79
　　Slow-Cooker Beef Stew Adobo, 76,
　　　77
Beef Enchiladas, *64*, 65
Beer
　　-Cheese Mac and Sausages, *96*, 97
　　-Roasted Rib-Eye, *78*, 79
Bell peppers
　　Bacon and Hash Brown Egg Bake,
　　　44, 45
　　Bacon-Pepper Mac and Cheese,
　　　100, 101
　　Baked Tofu and Veggies in Peanut
　　　Sauce, 242, *243*
　　Bean and Vegetable Stew with
　　　Polenta, 228
　　Bell Pepper–Mac and Cheese with
　　　Fondue Cheese Sauce, 230, *231*
　　Cheese Enchiladas, *200*, 201
　　Chicken Fajita Strata, 46, *47*
　　Egg and Sausage Breakfast Ring,
　　　41, *41*
　　Meatball Provolone Burgers with
　　　Garlic-Parmesan Aioli, 71, *71*
　　Roasted-Vegetable Lasagna with
　　　Goat Cheese, 234, *235*
　　Shrimp Creole, *186*, 187
　　Slow-Cooker Chicken Paprikash,
　　　138, *139*
　　Spicy Chorizo-Stuffed Peppers, 106,
　　　107
　　Veggie and Bean Burgers, 210, *211*
　　Veggie Burritos, 202, *203*
　　Veggie-Fried Grains, 214, *215*
Berry Ice Cream Pie, *254*, 255
Biscuit Tuna Melts, 178, *179*
Bisquick mix
　　Cheesy Sausage and Egg Bake, 32,
　　　33
　　Impossibly Easy Mini Breakfast
　　　Sausage Pies, 36, *37*
　　Impossibly Easy Tuna, Tomato and
　　　Cheddar Pie, *180*, 181
　　Mexican Chicken Casserole, *120*, 121
　　Sausage-Wrapped Stuffed Chiles,
　　　40, *40*
　　Tuna Burgers, 182, *182*
　　The Ultimate Pancakes, 18, *19*
Black beans
　　Bean and Barley Chili with Cilantro
　　　Sour Cream, 224, *225*
　　Mexican Chicken Casserole, *120*, 121

RECIPE TESTING AND CALCULATING NUTRITION INFORMATION

RECIPE TESTING:

- Large eggs and 2% milk were used unless otherwise indicated.

- Fat-free, low-fat, low-sodium or lite products were not used unless indicated.

- No nonstick cookware and bakeware were used unless otherwise indicated. No dark-colored, black or insulated bakeware was used.

- When a pan is specified, a metal pan was used; a baking dish or pie plate means ovenproof glass was used.

- An electric hand mixer was used for mixing only when mixer speeds are specified.

CALCULATING NUTRITION:

- The first ingredient was used wherever a choice is given, such as ⅓ cup sour cream or plain yogurt.

- The first amount was used wherever a range is given, such as 3- to 3½-pound whole chicken.

- The first serving number was used wherever a range is given, such as 4 to 6 servings.

- "If desired" ingredients were not included.

- Only the amount of a marinade or frying oil that is absorbed was included.

Slow-Cooker Turkey Mole Chili, 154, *155*

Spicy Chorizo-Stuffed Peppers, 106, *107*

Tamale Pies, 62, *63*

Blackberry Oatmeal, 31

Black-eyed peas: Bean and Vegetable Stew with Polenta, 228

Blueberries
Chocolate-and-Berries Yogurt Dessert, 286, *287*

Frozen, Breakfast Bars, 26, *27*

Oatmeal, 31

Blue cheese
Buffalo–, Chicken Burgers, *144*, 145

Cheese-Stuffed Buffalo Chicken Rolls, *116*, 117

Bourbon-Chocolate-Pecan Mini Pies, 257

Breakfast & Brunch
Apple Crisp Refrigerator Oatmeal, 28, *29*

Apricot-Stuffed French Toast, 22, *23*

Bacon and Hash Brown Egg Bake, *44*, 45

Caramel Sticky Rolls, 24–25, *25*

Cheesy Sausage and Egg Bake, 32, *33*

Chicken Fajita Strata, 46, *47*

Chocolate-Cherry Bread, *12*, 13

Cinnamon Rolls, 25

Egg and Sausage Breakfast Ring, 41, *41*

Five-Grain Buttermilk-Cranberry Bread, *16*, 17

Frozen Blueberry Breakfast Bars, 26, *27*

Fruity Green Smoothies, *50*, 51

Ham and Swiss Breakfast Hand Pies, *38*, 39

Impossibly Easy Mini Breakfast Sausage Pies, 36, *37*

Make-Ahead Frozen Yogurt Mini Bites, 48, *48–49*

Make-It-Your-Own Oatmeal, *30*, 31

Mix-and-Match Frozen Yogurt Bark, 48, *48–49*

Monkey Bread, 14–15, *15*

quick freezer ideas for, 216

Sausage-Wrapped Stuffed Chiles, 40, *40*

Skinny Tropical Smoothies, 52

Smoked Sausage Spinach Pie, 42, *43*

Spinach-Pesto Egg Bakes, *34*, 35

The Ultimate Pancakes, 18, *19*

Upside-Down Banana-Walnut French Toast, *20*, 21

Broccoli
Cheesy, and Brown Rice Patties, *204*, 205

Creamy Meatballs and Potatoes, *152*, 153

Fish Sticks Marinara, 166, *167*

Veggie and Bean Burgers, 210, *211*

Veggie-Fried Grains, 214, *215*

Broth. *See* Beef broth; Chicken broth; Vegetable broth

Brownie Ice Cream Sandwiches, *268*, 269

Buffalo–Blue Cheese Chicken Burgers, *144*, 145

Bulgur Pilaf, *218*, 219

Burgers. *See also* Sandwiches
Buffalo–Blue Cheese Chicken, *144*, 145

Cheesy Grilled Turkey, 156, *157*

Crab Cake, 182

Meatball Provolone, with Garlic-Parmesan Aioli, 71, *71*

Salmon Patties with Sour Cream–Dill Sauce, *172*, 173

Spicy Chili Bean, *212*, 213

Tuna, 182, *182*

Veggie and Bean, 210, *211*

Burritos, Veggie, 202, *203*

Butter beans: White Chicken Chili, 132, *133*

Butternut squash
Apple-Cinnamon–, Soup, *222*, 223

Moroccan Garbanzo Beans with Raisins, 220, *221*

C

Cabbage: Easy Shrimp Tacos, 184, *185*

Cantaloupe Granita, *284*, 285

Caramel Apple Mug Cakes, *260*, 261

Caramel-Fudge Cheesecake, 262, *263*

Caramel Sticky Rolls, 24–25, *25*

Cauliflower: Veggie-Fried Grains, 214, *215*

Cheddar cheese
Bacon and Hash Brown Egg Bake, *44*, 45

Bacon-Pepper Mac and Cheese, *100*, 101

Biscuit Tuna Melts, 178, *179*

Cheeseburger Lasagna, 72, *73*

Cheese Enchiladas, *200*, 201

Cheese-Stuffed Buffalo Chicken Rolls, *116*, 117

Cheesy Barbecue Chicken Lasagna Roll-Ups, *126*, 127

Chicken Enchilada Lasagna Roll-Ups, 128, *129*

Chicken Fajita Strata, 46, *47*

Egg and Sausage Breakfast Ring, 41, *41*

Impossibly Easy Mini Breakfast Sausage Pies, 36, *37*

Impossibly Easy Tuna, Tomato and Cheddar Pie, *180*, 181

Sausage-Wrapped Stuffed Chiles, 40, *40*

Slow-Cooker Smoky Chipotle Soft Tacos, 198, *199*

Smoked Sausage Spinach Pie, 42, *43*

Tamale Pies, 62, *63*

Veggie Burritos, 202, *203*

Cheese. *See also specific cheeses*
freezing and thawing, 8

Cheeseburger Lasagna, 72, *73*

Cheese Enchiladas, *200*, 201

Cheese-Stuffed Buffalo Chicken Rolls, *116*, 117

Cheesy Barbecue Chicken Lasagna Roll-Ups, *126*, 127

Cheesy Grilled Turkey Burgers, 156, *157*

Cheesy Sausage and Egg Bake, 32, *33*

Cheesy Turkey-Spinach Lasagna Roll-Ups, *160*, 161

Cherries, Chocolate-, Bread, *12*, 13

Cheesy Broccoli and Brown Rice Patties, *204*, 205

Chicken
and Spinach Stuffed Shells, *130*, 131

Biscuit Pot Pie, 124, *124*

Buffalo–Blue Cheese, Burgers, *144*, 145

Cheese-Stuffed Buffalo, Rolls, *116*, 117

Cheesy Barbecue, Lasagna Roll-Ups, *126*, 127

Coconut-Curry, 142, *143*

Enchilada Lasagna Roll-Ups, 128, *129*

Fajita Strata, 46, *47*

Make-Ahead Shredded, Breast, 110, *111*

Mexican, Casserole, *120*, 121

Oven, Cordon Bleu, 118, *119*

Salad Club Sandwich Stackers, *112*, 113

Slow-Cooker Asian Peach, Thighs, *140*, 141

Slow-Cooker, Paprikash, 138, *139*

Slow-Cooker Rotisserie Spiced,
136, 137
Slow-Cooker Wild Rice and
Rosemary, 122, *123*
Super-Easy, Manicotti, 125, *125*
Taco-Spiced, 114, *115*
White, Chili, 132, *133*
Chicken broth
Apple-Cinnamon–Butternut
Squash Soup, *222, 223*
Bulgur Pilaf, *218*, 219
Corn and Shrimp Chowder, 188, *189*
Creamy Seafood Lasagna, *176*, 177
Easy Caprese Soup, *196*, 197
Slow-Cooker Turkey Mole Chili, 154,
155
Slow-Cooker Wild Rice and
Rosemary Chicken, 122, *123*
White Chicken Chili, 132, *133*
Chile peppers. *See* Anaheim chiles;
Green chiles; Jalapeño chiles
Chili
Bean and Barley, with Cilantro Sour
Cream, 224, *225*
Blanco, *226*, 227
Slow-Cooker Turkey Mole, *54, 155*
White Chicken, 132, *133*
Chipotle chiles in adobo sauce
Pulled Pork Tomato Mole
Enchiladas, 88, *89*
Slow-Cooker Smoky Chipotle Soft
Tacos, 198, *199*
Chocolate
-and-Berries Yogurt Dessert, 286,
287
Bourbon, Pecan Mini Pies, 257
-Cherry Bread, *12*, 13
Dulce de Leche–Stuffed Chocolate
Chip Cookies, *272*, 273
Frozen Chocolate-Granola Cream
Cake, *288*, 289
Cinnamon Rolls, 25
Citrus-Brown Sugar Refrigerator
Cookies, 270
Clams, New England, Chowder, *190*, 191
Classic Apple Pie, *246*, 247
Classic Crab Cakes, 183, *183*
Cocoa: Pulled Pork Tomato Mole
Enchiladas, 88, *89*
Coconut
-Curry Chicken, 142, *143*
Toasted, –Brown Sugar Refrigerator
Cookies, 270
Colby cheese
Beer-Cheese Mac and Sausages,
96, 97

Veggie Burritos, 202, *203*
Cookie Ice Cream Sandwiches, 266,
267
Corn
Chili Blanco, *226*, 227
Corn and Shrimp Chowder, 188, *189*
Texas Tater Casserole, *240*, 241
White Chicken Chili, 132, *133*
Crabmeat
Crab Cake Burgers, 182
Creamy Seafood Lasagna, *176*, 177
Cranberries, Five-Grain Buttermilk-,
Bread, *16*, 17
Creamy Meatballs and Potatoes, *152*,
153
Creamy Pulled Pork Pasta, 84, *85*
Creamy Seafood Lasagna, *176*, 177
Cucumbers
Fresh Flounder Rolls, *164*, 165
Slow-Cooker Asian Beef Short Ribs,
80, *81*

D

Desserts
Berry Ice Cream Pie, *254*, 255
Bourbon-Chocolate-Pecan Mini
Pies, 257
Brownie Ice Cream Sandwiches,
268, 269
Brown Sugar Refrigerator Cookies,
270, *271*
Cantaloupe Granita, *284*, 285
Caramel Apple Mug Cakes, *260*,
261
Caramel-Fudge Cheesecake, 262,
263
Chocolate-and-Berries Yogurt
Dessert, 286, *287*
Citrus–Brown Sugar Refrigerator
Cookies, 270
Classic Apple Pie, *246*, 247
Cookie Ice Cream Sandwiches,
266, *267*
Dulce de Leche Cheesecake Pops,
280, 281
Dulce de Leche–Stuffed Chocolate
Chip Cookies, *272*, 273
freezing and thawing, 8
French Apple Pie, 247
Fresh Fruit Frozen Yogurt Pops,
278, *279*
Frozen Chocolate-Granola Cream
Cake, *288*, 289
Fudge Brownie Ice Cream Dessert,
294, *295*
Golden Pecan Pie, *250*, 251

Granita Slush, 285
"Jamocha" Ice Cream Pie, 256, *256*
Maple–Brown Sugar Refrigerator
Cookies, 270
Mini Peach Pies, 252, *253*
Mud Slide Ice Cream Cake, 290, *291*
Orange Pecan Pie, 251
Pumpkin Cheesecake, *264*, 265
Rainbow Sherbet Roll, *292*, 293
Spiced Gingered Pear Pie, 248, *249*
Strawberry-Peach Pops, 274, *275*
Strawberry-Rhubarb Pie Pops, 258,
259
Toasted Coconut–Brown Sugar
Refrigerator Cookies, 270
Vanilla Ice Cream, 282, *283*
Watermelon Mojito Cocktail Pops,
276, 277
Dulce de leche
–Cheesecake Pops, *280*, 281
–Stuffed Chocolate Chip Cookies,
272, 273
Fudge Brownie Ice Cream Dessert,
294, *295*

E

Easy Caprese Soup, *196*, 197
Easy Shrimp Tacos, 184, *185*
Easy Taco Melts, 68, 69
Eggs
and Sausage Breakfast Ring, 41, *41*
Bacon and Hash Brown, Bake, *44*,
45
Cheesy Sausage and, Bake, 32, *33*
Impossibly Easy Mini Breakfast
Sausage Pies, 36, *37*
Smoked Sausage Spinach Pie, 42,
43
Spinach-Pesto, Bakes, *34*, 35
Upside-Down Banana-Walnut
French Toast, *20*, 21
Enchiladas
Beef, *64*, 65
Cheese, *200*, 201
Chicken, Lasagna Roll-Ups, 128, *129*

F

Falafel, 206, *207*
Feta cheese: Artichoke-Spinach
Lasagna, *236*, 237
Fire-roasted tomatoes
Pepperoni Pizza Pasta Bake, 102,
103
Slow-Cooker Chicken Paprikash,
138, *139*

Spicy Chorizo-Stuffed Peppers, 106, *107*

Fish Sandwiches with Lemon-Basil Mayo, 170, *171*

Fish Sticks Marinara, 166, *167*

Five-Grain Buttermilk-Cranberry Bread, *16*, 17

Flounder, Fresh, Rolls, *164*, 165

Freezer bags, slow-cooker-ready, 92

Freezer burn, preventing, 6

Freezer foods, 6, 8, 9
  hosting party, 134
  quick ideas for, 216
  Freezer-Friendly Turkey Meatballs, 146, *147*
  Creamy Meatballs and Potatoes, *152*, 153
  Mediterranean Turkey Meatball Taco Boats, *148*, 149
  Turkey Meatball Tacos, 150, *151*

French Apple Pie, 247

Fresh Flounder Rolls, *164*, 165

Fresh Fruit Frozen Yogurt Pops, 278, *279*

Frozen Blueberry Breakfast Bars, *26*, 27

Frozen Chocolate-Granola Cream Cake, *288*, 289

Fruits, 8. *See also specific by name*
  Fresh, Frozen Yogurt Pops, 278, *279*

Fruity Green Smoothies, *50*, 51

Fudge Brownie Ice Cream Dessert, 294, *295*

G

Garbanzo beans
  Falafel, 206, *207*
  Moroccan Garbanzo Beans with Raisins, 220, *221*
  Veggie and Bean Burgers, 210, *211*

Goat Cheese, Roasted-Vegetable Lasagna with, 234, *235*

Gochujang, 74
  Pan-Fried Spicy Korean Beef, *74*, 75

Golden Pecan Pie, *250*, 251

Granita Slush, 285

Great northern beans
  Chili Blanco, *226*, 227
  White Chicken Chili, 132, *133*

Greek yogurt. *See also* Yogurt
  Apple-Cinnamon–Butternut Squash Soup, *222*, 223

Green beans
  Bean and Vegetable Stew with Polenta, 228

Slow-Cooker Wild Rice and Rosemary Chicken, 122, *123*

Green chiles
  Cheese Enchiladas, *200*, 201
  Chicken Enchilada Lasagna Roll-Ups, 128, *129*
  Chili Blanco, *226*, 227
  Tamale Pies, 62, *63*

Ground beef
  Beef Enchiladas, *64*, 65
  Cheeseburger Lasagna, 72, *73*
  Easy Taco Melts, *68*, 69
  Horseradish Meat Loaf, 70
  Make-Ahead, *56*, 57
  Make-Ahead Mexican, 60, *61*
  Meatball Provolone Burgers with Garlic-Parmesan Aioli, 71, *71*
  Meat Loaf, 70
  Mexican Meat Loaf, 70
  Mini Meat Loaves, 70
  Sassy Sloppy Joes, 58, *59*
  Slow-Cooker Taco, 66, *67*
  Tamale Casserole, 62
  Tamale Pies, 62, *63*

Gruyère cheese
  Bacon-Pepper Mac and Cheese, *100*, 101
  Bell Pepper–Mac and Cheese with Fondue Cheese Sauce, 230, *231*

H

Ham. *See also* Prosciutto
  and Swiss Breakfast Hand Pies, *38*, 39
  Oven Chicken Cordon Bleu, 118, *119*

Honey Oatmeal, 31

Horseradish Meat Loaf, 70

I

Ice cream
  Berry, Pie, *254*, 255
  Fudge Brownie, Dessert, 294, *295*
  "Jamocha," Pie, 256, *256*
  Mud Slide, Cake, 290, *291*
  Vanilla, 282, *283*

Ice cream sandwiches
  Brownie, *268*, 269
  Cookie, 266, *267*

Ice pops
  Dulce de Leche Cheesecake, *280*, 281
  Fresh Fruit Frozen Yogurt, 278, *279*
  Strawberry-Peach, 274, *275*
  Strawberry-Rhubarb Pie, 258, *259*

Watermelon Mojito Cocktail, *276*, 277

Impossibly Easy Mini Breakfast Sausage Pies, 36, *37*

Impossibly Easy Tuna, Tomato and Cheddar Pie, *180*, 181

Italian cheese blend
  Baked Sausage and Penne, *104*, 105
  Chicken and Spinach Stuffed Shells, *130*, 131
  Roasted-Vegetable Lasagna with Goat Cheese, 234, *235*
  Spinach-Stuffed Manicotti with Vodka Blush Sauce, 238, *239*
  White Lasagna Roll-Ups with Turkey and Prosciutto, 158, *159*

J

Jalapeño chiles
  Cheesy Grilled Turkey Burgers, *156*, 157
  Chicken Fajita Strata, 46, *47*
  Jamaican Loaded Baked Sweet Potatoes, *86*, 87
  Sausage-Wrapped Stuffed Chiles, 40, *40*
  Turkey Meatball Tacos, 150, *151*
  Veggie Burritos, 202, *203*

Jamaican Loaded Baked Sweet Potatoes, *86*, 87

"Jamocha" Ice Cream Pie, 256, *256*

K

Kidney beans
  Bean and Barley Chili with Cilantro Sour Cream, 224, *225*
  Bean and Vegetable Stew with Polenta, 228

L

Lasagna
  Artichoke-Spinach, *236*, 237
  Cheeseburger, 72, *73*
  Cheesy Turkey-Spinach, Roll-Ups, *160*, 161
  Cheesy Barbecue Chicken, Roll-Ups, *126*, 127
  Chicken Enchilada, Roll-Ups, 128, *129*
  Creamy Seafood, *176*, 177
  Italian Sausage, 98, *99*
  Roasted-Vegetable, with Goat Cheese, 234, *235*

White, Roll-Ups with Turkey and
Prosciutto, 158, *159*
Lasagna Cupcakes, *232*, 233
Lemon-Herb Salmon, 174, *175*

M

Make-Ahead Frozen Yogurt Mini Bites,
48, *48–49*
Make-Ahead Ground Beef, *56*, 57
Sassy Sloppy Joes, 58, *59*
Make-Ahead Mexican Ground Beef,
60, *61*
Easy Taco Melts, *68*, 69
Tamale Casserole, 62
Tamale Pies, 62, *63*
Make-Ahead Oven-Roasted Pulled
Pork, *82*, 83
Creamy Pulled Pork Pasta, 84, *85*
Jamaican Loaded Baked Sweet
Potatoes, *86*, 87
Make-Ahead Roasted Roma Tomato
Sauce, 194, *195*
Easy Caprese Soup, *196*, 197
Fish Sticks Marinara, 166, *167*
Pulled Pork Tomato Mole
Enchiladas, 88, *89*
Spaghetti and Spicy Rice Balls,
229, *229*
Super-Easy Chicken Manicotti, 125,
125
Veggie and Bean Burgers, 210, *211*
Make-Ahead Shredded Chicken
Breast, 110, *111*
Chicken Salad Club Sandwich
Stackers, *112*, 113
Mexican Chicken Casserole, *120*, 121
White Chicken Chili, 132, *133*
Make-It-Your-Own Oatmeal, *30*, 31
Mango: Jamaican Loaded Baked
Sweet Potatoes, *86*, 87
Maple–Brown Sugar Refrigerator
Cookies, 270
Maple-Dijon Pork Chops, 94, *95*
Marinara sauce. *See also* Tomato sauce
Baked Sausage and Penne, *104*, 105
Cheesy Broccoli and Brown Rice
Patties, *204*, 205
Meatballs
Creamy Meatballs and Potatoes,
152, 153
Freezer-Friendly Turkey Meatballs,
146, *147*
Meatball Provolone Burgers with
Garlic-Parmesan Aioli, 71, *71*
Mediterranean Turkey Meatball
Taco Boats, *148*, 149

Turkey, Tacos, 150, *151*
Veggie and Bean, 210, *211*
Meatless
Apple-Cinnamon–Butternut
Squash Soup, *222*, 223
Artichoke-Spinach Lasagna, *236*,
237
Baked Tofu and Veggies in Peanut
Sauce, 242, *243*
Bean and Barley Chili with Cilantro
Sour Cream, 224, *225*
Bean and Vegetable Stew with
Polenta, 228
Bell Pepper–Mac and Cheese with
Fondue Cheese Sauce, 230, *231*
Bulgur Pilaf, *218*, 219
Cheese Enchiladas, *200*, 201
Cheesy Broccoli and Brown Rice
Patties, *204*, 205
Chili Blanco, *226*, 227
Easy Caprese Soup, *196*, 197
Falafel, 206, *207*
Lasagna Cupcakes, *232*, 233
Make-Ahead Roasted Roma
Tomato Sauce, 194, *195*
Moroccan Garbanzo Beans with
Raisins, 220, *221*
Roasted-Vegetable Lasagna with
Goat Cheese, 234, *235*
Slow-Cooker Smoky Chipotle Soft
Tacos, 198, *199*
Slow-Cooker Veggie Joes, *208*,
209
Spaghetti and Spicy Rice Balls,
229, *229*
Spicy Chili Bean Burgers, *212*, 213
Spinach-Stuffed Manicotti with
Vodka Blush Sauce, 238, *239*
Veggie and Bean Burgers, 210, *211*
Veggie Burritos, 202, *203*
Veggie-Fried Grains, 214, *215*
Meat Loaf, 70, *70*
Mediterranean Turkey Meatball Taco
Boats, *148*, 149
Metric Conversion Guide, 296
Mexican cheese blend
Beef Enchiladas, *64*, 65
Easy Taco Melts, *68*, 69
Slow-Cooker Taco Ground Beef,
66, *67*
Slow-Cooker Turkey Mole Chili,
154, *155*
Spicy Chorizo-Stuffed Peppers,
106, *107*
Mexican Chicken Casserole, *120*, 121
Mexican Meat Loaf, 70

Mini Meat Loaves, 70
Mini Peach Pies, 252, *253*
Mix-and-Match Frozen Yogurt Bark,
48, *48–49*
Mole, 154
Slow-Cooker Smoky Chipotle Soft
Tacos, 198, *199*
Slow-Cooker Turkey, Chili, 154, *155*
Monkey Bread, 14–15, *15*
Monterey Jack cheese
Beer-Cheese Mac and Sausages,
96, 97
Cheese Enchiladas, *200*, 201
Chili Blanco, *226*, 227
Easy Shrimp Tacos, 184, *185*
Easy Taco Melts, *68*, 69
Egg and Sausage Breakfast Ring,
41, *41*
Sausage-Wrapped Stuffed Chiles,
40, *40*
Spinach-Pesto Egg Bakes, *34*, 35
Veggie Burritos, 202, *203*
Moroccan Garbanzo Beans with
Raisins, 220, *221*
Mozzarella cheese
Artichoke-Spinach Lasagna, *236*,
237
Cheesy Sausage and Egg Bake,
32, *33*
Cheesy Turkey-Spinach Lasagna
Roll-Ups, *160*, 161
Creamy Seafood Lasagna, 176, *177*
Easy Caprese Soup, *196*, 197
Fish Sticks Marinara, 166, *167*
Italian Sausage Lasagna, 98, *99*
Lasagna Cupcakes, *232*, 233
Pepperoni Pizza Pasta Bake, 102,
103
Super-Easy Chicken Manicotti, 125,
125
Mud Slide Ice Cream Cake, 290, *291*
Muenster cheese: Bacon-Pepper Mac
and Cheese, *100*, 101
Mushrooms
Bacon and Hash Brown Egg Bake,
44, 45
Cheesy Sausage and Egg Bake,
32, *33*
Creamy Pulled Pork Pasta, 84, *85*
Impossibly Easy Mini Breakfast
Sausage Pies, 36, *37*
Roasted-Vegetable Lasagna with
Goat Cheese, 234, *235*
Veggie and Bean Burgers, 210, *211*
White Lasagna Roll-Ups with
Turkey and Prosciutto, 158, *159*

N

New England Clam Chowder, *190*, 191

O

Oats
  Apple Crisp Refrigerator Oatmeal,
    28, *29*
  Five-Grain Buttermilk-Cranberry
    Bread, *16*, 17
  Make-It-Your-Own Oatmeal, *30*, 31
  Spaghetti and Spicy Rice Balls,
    229, *229*
  Spicy Chili Bean Burgers, *212*, 213
Orange Pecan Pie, 251
Oven Chicken Cordon Bleu, 118, *119*

P

Pan-Fried Spicy Korean Beef, *74*, 75
Papaya: Skinny Tropical Smoothies, 52
Pasta
  Artichoke-Spinach Lasagna, *236*,
    237
  Bacon-Pepper Mac and Cheese,
    100, 101
  Baked Sausage and Penne, *104*,
    105
  Beer-Cheese Mac and Sausages,
    96, 97
  Bell Pepper–Mac and Cheese with
    Fondue Cheese Sauce, 230, *231*
  Cheeseburger Lasagna, 72, *73*
  Cheesy Turkey-Spinach Lasagna
    Roll-Ups, *160*, 161
  Cheesy Barbecue Chicken Lasagna
    Roll-Ups, *126*, 127
  Chicken and Spinach Stuffed
    Shells, *130*, 131
  Chicken Enchilada Lasagna Roll-
    Ups, 128, *129*
  Creamy Pulled Pork Pasta, 84, *85*
  Creamy Seafood Lasagna, *176*, 177
  freezing and thawing, 8
  Italian Sausage Lasagna, 98, *99*
  Pepperoni Pizza Pasta Bake, 102,
    103
  Roasted-Vegetable Lasagna with
    Goat Cheese, 234, *235*
  Spaghetti and Spicy Rice Balls,
    229, *229*
  Spinach-Stuffed Manicotti with
    Vodka Blush Sauce, 238, *239*
  Super-Easy Chicken Manicotti, 125,
    125

White Lasagna Roll-Ups with
    Turkey and Prosciutto, 158, *159*
Peaches
  Mini, Pies, 252, *253*
  Slow-Cooker Asian Peach Chicken
    Thighs, *140*, 141
Peanut butter: Baked Tofu and
    Veggies in Peanut Sauce, 242,
    243
Pears, Spiced Gingered, Pie, 248, *249*
Peas. *See also* Black-eyed peas; Sugar
    snap peas
  Coconut-Curry Chicken, 142, *143*
Pecans
  Bourbon-Chocolate-, Mini Pies, 257
  Caramel Apple Mug Cakes, *260*,
    261
  Caramel-Fudge Cheesecake, 262,
    263
  Caramel Sticky Rolls, 24–25, *25*
  -Crusted Fish Fillets, *168*, 169
  Dulce de Leche–Stuffed Chocolate
    Chip Cookies, *272*, 273
  Fudge Brownie Ice Cream Dessert,
    294, *295*
  Golden, Pie, *250*, 251
  Orange, Pie, 251
Pepper Jack cheese
  Cheesy Grilled Turkey Burgers,
    156, 157
  Chicken Enchilada Lasagna Roll-
    Ups, 128, *129*
Pepperoni Pizza Pasta Bake, 102, *103*
Pinto beans
  Mexican Chicken Casserole, *120*, 121
  Tamale Pies, 62, *63*
Pizza: Pepperoni, Pasta Bake, 102, *103*
Plum tomatoes
  Easy Caprese Soup, *196*, 197
  Make-Ahead Roasted Roma
    Tomato Sauce, 194, *195*
  Mexican Chicken Casserole, *120*, 121
  Pulled Pork Tomato Mole
    Enchiladas, 88, *89*
Polenta, Bean and Vegetable Stew
    with, 228
Pomegranate Oatmeal, 31
Popcorn: Beer-Cheese Mac and
    Sausages, *96*, 97
Pork. *See also* Bacon; Ham; Prosciutto
  Creamy Pulled Pork Pasta, 84, *85*
  Jamaican Loaded Baked Sweet
    Potatoes, *86*, 87
  Make-Ahead Oven-Roasted Pulled
    Pork, *82*, 83
  Maple-Dijon Pork Chops, 94, *95*

Pulled Pork Tomato Mole
    Enchiladas, 88, *89*
  Slow-Cooker Herbed Pork and Red
    Potatoes, *90*, 91
Pork sausage
  Baked Sausage and Penne, *104*, 105
  Cheesy Sausage and Egg Bake,
    32, *33*
  Egg and Sausage Breakfast Ring,
    41, *41*
  Impossibly Easy Mini Breakfast
    Sausage Pies, 36, *37*
  Italian Sausage Lasagna, 98, *99*
  Sausage-Wrapped Stuffed Chiles,
    40, *40*
Potatoes
  Bacon and Hash Brown Egg Bake,
    44, 45
  Corn and Shrimp Chowder, 188, *189*
  Creamy Meatballs and Potatoes,
    152, 153
  New England Clam Chowder, *190*,
    191
  Slow-Cooker Beef Stew Adobo,
    76, *77*
  Slow-Cooker Herbed Pork and Red
    Potatoes, *90*, 91
  Texas Tater Casserole, *240*, 241
Pot pie: Chicken Biscuit, 124, *124*
Prosciutto, White Lasagna Roll-Ups
    with Turkey and, 158, *159*
Provolone cheese: Meatball Provolone
    Burgers with Garlic-Parmesan
    Aioli, 71, *71*
Pulled Pork Tomato Mole Enchiladas,
    88, *89*
Pumpkin Cheesecake, *264*, 265

Q

Queso fresco cheese
  Jamaican Loaded Baked Sweet
    Potatoes, *86*, 87
  Pulled Pork Tomato Mole
    Enchiladas, 88, *89*
  Turkey Meatball Tacos, 150, *151*

R

Rainbow Sherbet Roll, *292*, 293
Raspberries
  Berry Ice Cream Pie, *254*, 255
  Chocolate-and-Berries Yogurt
    Dessert, 286, *287*
Refried beans
  Slow-Cooker Taco Ground Beef,
    66, *67*

Veggie Burritos, 202, *203*
Rhubarb, Strawberry-, Pie Pops, 258, *259*
Rice
    Cheesy Broccoli and Brown Rice Patties, *204*, 205
    Coconut-Curry Chicken, 142, *143*
    Shrimp Creole, *186*, 187
    Slow-Cooker Asian Beef Short Ribs, 80, *81*
    Slow-Cooker Asian Peach Chicken Thighs, *140*, 141
    Slow-Cooker Chicken Paprikash, 138, *139*
    Slow-Cooker Wild Rice and Rosemary Chicken, 122, *123*
    Spaghetti and Spicy Rice Balls, 229, *229*
    Spicy Chorizo-Stuffed Peppers, 106, *107*
    Veggie and Bean Burgers, 210, *211*
Ricotta cheese
    Baked Sausage and Penne, *104*, 105
    Cheeseburger Lasagna, 72, *73*
    Cheesy Turkey-Spinach Lasagna Roll-Ups, *160*, 161
    Chicken and Spinach Stuffed Shells, *130*, 131
    Italian Sausage Lasagna, 98, *99*
    Lasagna Cupcakes, *232*, 233
    Spinach-Stuffed Manicotti with Vodka Blush Sauce, 238, *239*
    White Lasagna Roll-Ups with Turkey and Prosciutto, 158, *159*
Roasted-Vegetable Lasagna with Goat Cheese, 234, *235*
Rosemary, Slow-Cooker Wild Rice and, Chicken, 122, *123*

S

Salmon
    Cakes, 183
        Lemon-Herb, 174, *175*
    Patties with Sour Cream–Dill Sauce, *172*, 173
Salsa
    Bean and Barley Chili with Cilantro Sour Cream, 224, *225*
    Beef Enchiladas, *64*, 65
    Easy Taco Melts, *68*, 69
    Mexican Chicken Casserole, *120*, 121
    Slow-Cooker Taco Ground Beef, 66, *67*
    Texas Tater Casserole, *240*, 241
    Turkey Meatball Tacos, 150, *151*

Veggie Burritos, 202, *203*
Sandwiches. *See also* Burgers
    Biscuit Tuna Melts, 178, *179*
    Chicken Salad Club Sandwich Stackers, *112*, 113
    Fish Sandwiches with Lemon-Basil Mayo, 170, *171*
    Fresh Flounder Rolls, *164*, 165
    Make-Ahead Oven-Roasted Pulled Pork, *82*, 83
    Sassy Sloppy Joes, 58, *59*
    Slow-Cooker Veggie Joes, *208*, 209
    Taco-Spiced Chicken, 114, *115*
Sausage-Wrapped Stuffed Chiles, 40, *40*
Seafood
    Biscuit Tuna Melts, 178, *179*
    Classic Crab Cakes, 183, *183*
    Corn and Shrimp Chowder, 188, *189*
    Crab Cake Burgers, 182
    Creamy Seafood Lasagna, *176*, 177
    Easy Shrimp Tacos, 184, *185*
    Fish Sandwiches with Lemon-Basil Mayo, 170, *171*
    Fish Sticks Marinara, 166, *167*
    freezing and thawing, 8
    Fresh Flounder Rolls, *164*, 165
    Impossibly Easy Tuna, Tomato and Cheddar Pie, *180*, 181
    Lemon-Herb Salmon, 174, *175*
    New England Clam Chowder, *190*, 191
    Pecan-Crusted Fish Fillets, *168*, 169
    Salmon Cakes, 183, *183*
    Salmon Patties with Sour Cream–Dill Sauce, *172*, 173
    Shrimp Creole, *186*, 187
    Tuna Burgers, 182, *182*
Shrimp
    Corn and, Chowder, 188, *189*
    Creamy Seafood Lasagna, *176*, 177
    Creole, *186*, 187
    Easy, Tacos, 184, *185*
Skinny Tropical Smoothies, 52
    Slow-Cooker Asian Beef Short Ribs, 80, *81*
    Slow-Cooker Asian Peach Chicken Thighs, *140*, 141
    Slow-Cooker Beef Stew Adobo, 76, *77*
    Slow-Cooker Chicken Paprikash, 138, *139*
    Slow-Cooker Herbed Pork and Red Potatoes, *90*, 91
    Slow-Cooker Ready Freezer Bags, 92

Slow-Cooker Rotisserie Spiced Chicken, *136*, 137
Slow-Cooker Smoky Chipotle Soft Tacos, 198, *199*
Slow-Cooker Taco Ground Beef, 66, *67*
Slow-Cooker Turkey Mole Chili, 154, *155*
Slow-Cooker Veggie Joes, *208*, 209
Slow-Cooker Wild Rice and Rosemary Chicken, 122, *123*
Smoked link sausages, Beer-Cheese Mac and, *96*, 97
Smoked Sausage Spinach Pie, 42, *43*
Smoothies
    Fruity Green, *50*, 51
    Skinny Tropical, 52
Soups. *See also* Chili
    Apple-Cinnamon–Butternut Squash, *222–223*
    Corn and Shrimp Chowder, 188, *189*
    Easy Caprese, *196*, 197
    freezing and thawing, 8
    New England Clam Chowder, *190*, 191
    quick freezer ideas for, 216
Soy-protein crumbles
    Lasagna Cupcakes, *232*, 233
    Slow-Cooker Smoky Chipotle Soft Tacos, 198, *199*
    Slow-Cooker Veggie Joes, *208*, 209
    Texas Tater Casserole, *240*, 241
Spaghetti and Spicy Rice Balls, 229, *229*
Spiced Gingered Pear Pie, 248, *249*
Spicy Chili Bean Burgers, *212*, 213
Spicy Korean Beef Kabobs, 75
Spinach
    Artichoke-, Lasagna, *236*, 237
    Cheesy Turkey-, Lasagna Roll-Ups, *160*, 161
    Chicken and, Stuffed Shells, *130*, 131
    Fruity Green Smoothies, *50*, 51
    Ham and Swiss Breakfast Hand Pies, 39
    -Pesto Egg Bakes, *34*, 35
    Smoked Sausage, Pie, 42, *43*
    Spicy Chili Bean Burgers, *212*, 213
    -Stuffed Manicotti with Vodka Blush Sauce, 238, *239*
    White Lasagna Roll-Ups with Turkey and Prosciutto, 158, *159*
Stew
    Bean and Vegetable, with Polenta, 228

Slow-Cooker Beef, Adobo, 76, *77*
Strawberries
    -Peach Pops, 274, *275*
    -Rhubarb Pie Pops, 258, *259*
    Skinny Tropical Smoothies, 52
Sugar snap peas
    Baked Tofu and Veggies in Peanut
        Sauce, 242, *243*
    Veggie-Fried Grains, 214, *215*
Sun-dried tomatoes: Spinach-Stuffed
        Manicotti with Vodka Blush
        Sauce, 238, *239*
Super-Easy Chicken Manicotti, 125, *125*
Sweet potatoes
    Jamaican Loaded Baked, *86*, 87
    Slow-Cooker Beef Stew Adobo,
        76, *77*
Swiss cheese
    Ham and Swiss Breakfast Hand
        Pies, *38*, 39
    Oven Chicken Cordon Bleu, 118, *119*

T

Tacos
    Easy Shrimp, 184, *185*
    Slow-Cooker Smoky Chipotle Soft,
        198, *199*
    Turkey Meatball, 150, *151*
Tamale Casserole, 62
Tamale Pies, 62, *63*
Toasted Coconut–Brown Sugar
        Refrigerator Cookies, 270
Tofu, Baked, and Veggies in Peanut
        Sauce, 242, *243*
Tomatoes. *See also* Fire-roasted
        tomatoes; Plum tomatoes; Sun-
        dried tomatoes
    Bean and Barley Chili with Cilantro
        Sour Cream, 224, *225*
    Bean and Vegetable Stew with
        Polenta, 228
    Cheeseburger Lasagna, 72, *73*
    Cheesy Grilled Turkey Burgers,
        156, 157
    Cheesy Sausage and Egg Bake,
        32, *33*
    Chicken Enchilada Lasagna Roll-
        Ups, 128, *129*
    Chicken Fajita Strata, 46, *47*
    Chicken Salad Club Sandwich
        Stackers, *112*, 113
    Fish Sandwiches with Lemon-Basil
        Mayo, 170, *171*
    Impossibly Easy Tuna, Tomato and
        Cheddar Pie, *180*, 181
    Italian Sausage Lasagna, 98, *99*

Slow-Cooker Smoky Chipotle Soft
        Tacos, 198, *199*
    Slow-Cooker Turkey Mole Chili,
        154, *155*
    Spicy Chili Bean Burgers, 212, 213
    Spinach-Pesto Egg Bakes, *34*, 35
    Tamale Pies, 62, *63*
Tomato sauce. *See also* Marinara sauce
    Cheese Enchiladas, *200*, 201
    Cheesy Turkey-Spinach Lasagna
        Roll-Ups, *160*, 161
    Chicken and Spinach Stuffed
        Shells, *130*, 131
    Lasagna Cupcakes, *232*, 233
    Roasted-Vegetable Lasagna with
        Goat Cheese, 234, *235*
    Shrimp Creole, *186*, 187
    Spinach-Stuffed Manicotti with
        Vodka Blush Sauce, 238, *239*
    Super-Easy Chicken Manicotti, 125,
        125
Tortillas
    Beef Enchiladas, *64*, 65
    Cheese Enchiladas, *200*, 201
    Easy Shrimp Tacos, 184, *185*
    Mediterranean Turkey Meatball
        Taco Boats, *148*, 149
    Pulled Pork Tomato Mole
        Enchiladas, 88, *89*
    Slow-Cooker Smoky Chipotle Soft
        Tacos, 198, *199*
    Veggie Burritos, 202, *203*
Tuna
    Biscuit, Melts, 178, *179*
    Burgers, 182, *182*
    Impossibly Easy, Tomato and
        Cheddar Pie, *180*, 181
Turkey
    Cheesy Grilled, Burgers, *156*, 157
    Cheesy, -Spinach Lasagna Roll-
        Ups, *160*, 161
    Creamy Meatballs and Potatoes,
        152, 153
    Freezer-Friendly, Meatballs, 146,
        147
    Meatball Tacos, 150, *151*
    Mediterranean, Meatball Taco
        Boats, *148*, 149
    Slow-Cooker, Mole Chili, 154, *155*
    White Lasagna Roll-Ups with, and
        Prosciutto, 158, *159*

U

The Ultimate Pancakes, 18, *19*
Upside-Down Banana-Walnut French
        Toast, 20, 21

V

Vanilla Ice Cream, 282, *283*
    Vegetable broth
    Apple-Cinnamon–Butternut
        Squash Soup, *222*, 223
    Artichoke-Spinach Lasagna, *236*,
        237
    Moroccan Garbanzo Beans with
        Raisins, 220, *221*
Vegetarian bouillon cube: Chili Blanco,
        226, 227

W

Walnuts, Upside-Down Banana-,
        French Toast, *20*, 21
Watermelon Mojito Cocktail Pops, *276*,
        277
White Chicken Chili, 132, *133*
White Lasagna Roll-Ups with Turkey
        and Prosciutto, 158, *159*

Y

Yogurt. *See also* Greek yogurt
    Apple Crisp Refrigerator Oatmeal,
        28, *29*
    Chocolate-and-Berries, Dessert,
        286, *287*
    Cookie Ice Cream Sandwiches,
        266, *267*
    Fresh Flounder Rolls, *164*, 165
    Fresh Fruit Frozen, Pops, 278, *279*
    Frozen Blueberry Breakfast Bars,
        26, 27
    Make-Ahead Frozen, Mini Bites, 48,
        48–49
    Make-It-Your-Own Oatmeal, 30, 31
    Mix-and-Match Frozen, Bark, 48,
        48–49
    Skinny Tropical Smoothies, 52
    Strawberry-Peach Pops, 274, *275*

Z

Zucchini: Roasted-Vegetable Lasagna
        with Goat Cheese, 234, *235*